- 2

THAT'S WHY I'M A JOURNALIST

THAT'S WHY I'M A JOURNALIST

*Top Canadian Reporters Tell Their
Most Unforgettable Stories*

by MARK BULGUTCH

Douglas & McIntyre

Douglas and McIntyre (2013) Ltd.
P.O. Box 219, Madeira Park, BC, V0N 2H0
www.douglas-mcintyre.com

Except where otherwise noted, photos © Canadian Broadcasting
   Corporation. All rights reserved.
Edited by Cheryl Cohen
Indexed by Nicola Goshulak
Dust jacket design by Anna Comfort O'Keeffe
Text design by Roger Handling
Printed and bound in Canada
Text paper is FSC-certified

Douglas and McIntyre (2013) Ltd. acknowledges the support of the Canada Council for the Arts, which last year invested $157 million to bring the arts to Canadians throughout the country. We also gratefully acknowledge financial support from the Government of Canada through the Canada Book Fund and from the Province of British Columbia through the BC Arts Council and the Book Publishing Tax Credit.

Cataloguing data available from Library and Archives Canada
ISBN 978-1-77162-083-3 (cloth)
ISBN 978-1-77162-084-0 (ebook)

CONTENTS

Introduction

ASK A CHILD TODAY WHERE MILK COMES FROM and the answer might be, "From the supermarket." But if you had asked me when I was a kid, I'd have said, "From the milkman."

I loved watching that guy at work. I loved that he drove around in a truck. I loved that he could probably drink all the chocolate milk that he wanted. I loved that he arranged bottles of milk in a carrier that became so heavy that he would have to counterbalance the load by leaning far to the other side. I loved that everyone in the neighbourhood looked forward to his arrival.

There's no doubt about it. When I was five or six years old I knew that I wanted to be a milkman when I grew up.

But just a few years later I was even more certain that I wanted to be a journalist.

When I look back at how I came to that conclusion, I can't put my finger on one pivotal moment. I think a few things just fell into place.

First, I saw my father bring home the newspaper every night. He would pick up the *Montreal Star* on his way from work. If the picture in your mind is of a man wearing a nice suit, carrying a briefcase and stopping at a newsstand after a day at the office, wipe that away. My father worked in a factory. He lugged heavy bags of sugar up and down the Redpath Sugar Refinery eight hours a day, five days a week, for more than thirty-five years. He left school in Grade 3. He could barely read. I'm sure he never read a novel. But he bought a newspaper every day. And after dinner he would sit down and read it. My mother read it too. And she wasn't much more literate than my father.

I thought there must be something quite magical in that newspaper. So I started reading it too. And it was magical. The entire world was suddenly in my hands. In *my* hands—a boy who had never left Montreal from the day I was born, except for a short trip to New York City by train to see some relatives who lived there. In fact, I now realize I hadn't even seen all of Montreal. I had never been east of St. Lawrence Blvd., the legendary "Main" that pretty much divides the city in half.

I couldn't wait for my father to come home with the paper every night. Then I discovered there was a way to get it even before he came home. There was a kid in my class who delivered the newspaper after school, with his older brothers. Right on my street. He could put it right at the door of our apartment.

I talked my parents into signing up. After that, when I got home after school I would listen for the *thump* of the paper's arrival, run to open the door and settle down on the floor of the living room to begin inhaling information. I didn't read the business section, I'll admit, but everything else was fantastic. Nothing about the newspaper struck me as routine or ordinary.

A couple of years later, my friend and his brothers decided to give up their paper route and they agreed to recommend me to the lady who organized about a dozen routes from her garage.

If there has ever been a paper boy who took his work more seriously, I'm sure he's still in therapy. The *Star* used to impress upon its carriers that we were the last link between reporters, photographers, editors, printers, drivers—all the people whose labour produced the paper—and the reader at home. I bought that without a second's hesitation. Without me, people on my street wouldn't know the news. It wasn't a paper route, it was a sacred duty. I was a soldier in the service of a free press, a pillar of democracy.

I delivered in pouring rain, snow up to my hips, blazing heat and freeze-your-face-in-one-minute cold. And I didn't toss the paper from far off and hope for the best. I treated my newspapers as precious cargo. Their safe and dry arrival was a standard I would not compromise.

My only flaw as a delivery boy was a lack of urgency. I didn't run down the street. I didn't take stairs two at a time as I made my way through apartment buildings. No, I walked. Slowly. How else could I read the paper as I delivered it?

The money I made from my paper route opened another window on journalism for me. We couldn't afford cable TV at my house. My father's hard work and my mother's ability to stretch every dollar meant my two sisters and I never worried about having a roof over our heads or food on the table. But cable TV was a luxury for other people, not us. We had a television, of course. Black and white. And we could see American channels from Burlington, Vermont and Plattsburgh, New York, with the help of the rabbit ears on the TV set. But the picture was fuzzy and snowy—on a good day.

I longed to see Walter Cronkite more clearly. So I used my paper route money to pay for cable TV. Now my future literally came into focus. I could watch ABC News with Howard K. Smith at 6 PM. Chet Huntley and David Brinkley were on NBC at 6:30. And then Cronkite's *CBS Evening News* was at 7:00. There has never been a richer trifecta.

Lest you think I ignored Canadian news, fear not. *The National* was on my agenda too. But it came on at 11 PM in those days. My mother didn't like me staying up so late. And to tell you the truth, on some days I couldn't keep my eyes open even as I fought with her to let me watch.

I didn't just read the newspaper and watch TV newscasts. I got my hands on every journalist's biography, memoir and autobiography that I could. I lapped up tales of beating the opposition to stories, racing to deadlines, travelling the world to cover historic events. "Sign me up!" I thought.

Like most kids, I read *Superman* comics. But I wasn't attracted by the man's strength or X-ray vision. I was more impressed that he worked at the *Daily Planet*.

In high school I worked on the newspaper, but it came out something like twice a year. Not much to that. So, just for fun, after watching hockey games on TV, I would write up reports. No one ever read them, but I really liked doing it. I was eager to go to university and enter a journalism program.

I had no idea how rare a journalism program was at a Canadian university in 1969. When I went to see my guidance counsellor in my last year of high school, I assumed I would be going to a university in Montreal. I was incredulous when he told me the closest school of journalism was at Carleton, in Ottawa.

I know, I know. Ottawa isn't exactly in another galaxy. But I had never been away from home. I was sixteen years old. I had never been to summer camp. I had visited Quebec City once for a day because I won a carrier contest at the *Star*, and I had gone to Ottawa for a day with my Grade 7 class. But that was the extent of my travels outside Montreal without my family. And neither of those trips involved a sleepover.

My guidance counsellor, trying to be helpful, told me I really didn't have to go to university to be a journalist. He pointed out that the reporter at the *Star* covering high school sports had never gone to university. I thought to myself, "I don't want to cover high school sports. I want to cover big stuff."

So Ottawa it was. I missed my mother's cooking so much that I lost 25 pounds during my first year at Carleton. That's in spite of the fact that every day I was entitled to three all-you-can-eat meals in the cafeteria.

I enjoyed Carleton immensely. And in my last year there, CBC News came to campus looking to hire students for a new internship program. Eight students would be hired from universities across Canada to work at CBC locations for the summer. I did one interview and made it to the short list. The CBC people would return for a second interview, but it turned out they were coming on a day when I would be on a class trip to New York. We were going to see journalists at work at the United Nations. And our professor had arranged a tour of the *New York Times*.

I'm not sure why, but I decided to go to New York and abandon all hope of landing the CBC job.

As we were touring the *Times* a few days later, Hollywood took over my life. Over the loudspeaker in the newsroom I heard, "Could Mark Bulgutch please go to a telephone and call reception." I was being paged at the *New York Times*! Who even knew I was there?

I bit the inside of my cheek a few times. Then I picked up a phone and called reception. The person there told me to call a number in Toronto. So I did. It was the CBC. "Sorry we missed you in Ottawa. We'd like you to come to Toronto to be interviewed."

I had never been to Toronto, but that didn't seem impossible. So I went, was hired for the internship program, was sent to Montreal for the summer, was hired permanently after that and stayed at CBC News for forty years.

I'm sure a lot of people are gung-ho about a career when they're young. And then when they get there, they're disappointed by the reality of it. Not me. Journalism really was my calling. I would have been miserable doing anything else. And I probably would have been incompetent too. My wife thinks I'm a savant. She thinks it's a good thing I'm good at journalism because I'm no good at anything else. She's wrong, of course. I can take out the garbage, change a light bulb and shovel snow. Not a long list of talents, I concede, but a list nonetheless.

In all seriousness, journalism has been wonderful to me. I've seen things and done things that even my boyhood imagination could not have dreamed up. I spent only two years as a reporter. I covered the burning of Montreal during a firefighters' strike, was yelled at on camera by the mayor of Montreal for presuming that I had the right to ask him questions and reported on the 1976 Olympics. I'll never forget the thrill of seeing my first story on *The National*.

But I was soon guided to the desk. My two guardian angel

mentors—Andy Little, a crafty and wise man who later taught me as much about life as journalism, and Elly Alboim, a stirring intellectual force of nature—said I'd be a better editor than a reporter. At first I saw it as a demotion, but I soon realized it was so right for me. I could now control not just two minutes of a newscast with my one story but the entire newscast and every story. Well, maybe not control the whole shooting match, but at least have a hand in everything.

I was the lineup editor in Montreal for seven years. I decided which stories would go to air, and in what order. I read and edited every script by every reporter. I wrote some of the program. And then I went into the control room and made sure the newscast ended right on time. Then I moved to Toronto as a writer on *The National*. After a little while I became the weekend lineup editor, and then the weekday lineup editor. I was on the program for thirteen years. There is still a place in my heart reserved for it. My attachment is incurable.

I then became the senior producer of CBC News specials—elections, major events—and eventually the senior executive producer of CBC TV News, responsible for all live coverage of news.

How many times did I stop to look at my surroundings and wonder how I'd got there? To stand in the control room and call the shots on a federal election night is quite overwhelming. Just sitting in a newsroom is special. It thrums with energy.

I've met prime ministers, governors general, a pope. I've been to every province and territory in our beautiful country. I've travelled extensively overseas as well. To call me lucky is like calling Santa Claus jolly.

The people I have worked with are heroes to me. They really are. Camera operators, audio recorders, editors, writers, anchors, researchers, set designers, graphic artists, producers, directors, studio crews, even some managers. Dedicated, hard-working, smart, creative people who gave and gave and gave.

I put reporters in a special category. For they are what journalism is all about. The rest of us are important, but they are the essence, the lifeblood, the irreplaceable building blocks. I was talking one day with the director I worked with most closely in my career, the brilliant Fred Parker. We agreed that our jobs in the control room were clear. "Reporters go through a lot of muck to get their stories to us. The least we can do is put them on air without mistakes."

Without front-line reporters, journalism is nothing. That's why it is their stories that fill this book.

As I get older I am wary of believing that everything was better in the past. That's simply not true. Computers are better than typewriters. Digital cameras are better than film cameras. Live pictures from just about everywhere are better than packing rolls of film onto airplanes and flying them around the world to be seen days after they were shot.

But there's no doubt we're losing some of the best of what we used to do in journalism. I'm not a fan of incessant opinion chatter on twenty-four-hour news networks. I'm not a fan of cluttering the TV screen with BREAKING NEWS banners even hours after the news is broken. I'm not a fan of turning any snowfall into the end of civilization as we know it.

More important than all of that, though, is how we've changed the definition of reporting. I think it's pretty simple. Reporters should go to where something is happening, they should see what is happening and then they should tell us what they saw. But that basic practice is becoming rarer. Today's television reporters may be sent to a news event to stand in front of a camera all day long and talk for a few minutes every hour. They're expected to tweet as well. And maybe send something along for radio, and maybe for the web too.

When are they supposed to see what is going on? When are they supposed to talk to some of the people involved in the event? When are they supposed to be witnesses? When do they have a quiet moment to think?

We are also plagued by news items voiced by reporters who don't even pretend to have been at the scene. We ask reporters in London to write stories about events in Belgium or Iraq. We ask reporters in Washington to write stories about events in Oklahoma City or Costa Rica. That isn't reporting. It's narrating. It's broadcasting. It is not reporting.

The stories in this book reflect real reporting. Forty-four reporters, who collectively have 1,588 years of experience, each told me about one story that was especially satisfying to them, or that made them proud to be a journalist. Not necessarily the first story in their career that made them feel that way, just one story. Each of the forty-four would have had to choose one story from among many. Because when you're as good as this group is, there are a lot of special days on the job.

Of course I asked myself what day I would choose from my career. It wasn't easy, but it came down to those stories that I shared with my family. I took my wife (at my expense of course) to the fiftieth anniversary of D-Day in England and France, and the fiftieth anniversary of VE Day in Holland. I took her and my daughters to the sixtieth anniversary of VE Day. I didn't see much of them because I still worked a lot, but it was nice to be able to show them part of my world.

But if forced to choose just one story, I would pick the coverage of the sixtieth anniversary of the liberation of Auschwitz, the Nazi death camp. It was January of 2005. I came up with the idea of going to Poland only a month before. Money was tight at CBC News, but I found enough for a small team—David Knapp, who managed news specials; Bill Loucks, a cameraman/editor from our Washington bureau; and Alison Smith, who could anchor our live coverage, do daily news reports and work on a documentary. I also brought my two daughters to share a profoundly moving experience.

Before we left Canada I made contact with several survivors of Auschwitz who now lived in Canada. One of them, Nate Leipciger, would also be going to Poland for the anniversary. He was fifteen when he was imprisoned at Auschwitz. He and his father survived. His mother and sisters did not.

We went to Auschwitz with Nate. On a freezing cold morning he took us to the barracks where he had suffered unimaginable treatment. He told us how he would look up through a window near the ceiling and see smoke in the sky, a telltale sign that more Jews had been murdered. Suddenly he climbed into one of the bunks. Then he lay there remembering what it was like sixty years earlier. We could see pain in his face. It left the rest of us speechless. Then he lit a memorial candle for his mother and sisters and recited the Jewish mourning prayer. It was impossibly poignant, impossibly sad.

To tell that story? Yes, that's why I'm a journalist.

With only a couple of exceptions, the journalists in this book are people I have worked with. Without exception, they are deeply committed to doing journalism properly. None of them had to talk to me for this book, yet all of them agreed almost immediately to be interviewed and were then generous with their time and their memories.

The range of stories is wide. Some happened in a day or a week. Some took years of reporting. Some are major stories that history books have recorded in great detail. Some are smaller stories that carry personal significance.

I would invite you to read the short biographies I've provided to note what the journalists have in common. First, they moved around. They gained experience all over the country. Moving from place to place isn't without sacrifice. If you have a family you always have to consider your spouse and children. Even if you're single you'll be leaving behind friends and colleagues.

Second, they worked like dogs. No one steps into a major-league newsroom and leaps to the top of the food chain. No one gets the juiciest assignments before covering two-alarm fires, Kiwanis club lunches and protests over water taxes. Success in journalism doesn't just happen: it's earned.

Journalism is undergoing existential threats. Buying a newspaper and watching a TV newscast at a set time of the day both seem like prehistoric rituals. News has never been more accessible, yet paradoxically important news has become harder to find, often buried by pseudo-news of celebrity, lifestyle tips and the latest viral video of a water-skiing squirrel. The inconsequential competes with the meaningless for your attention, and you lose either way.

I've taught journalism part-time for almost thirty years at Ryerson University. I've yet to meet a student who wants to be a journalist so that he or she can report on trivia. There's plenty of optimism, energy, enthusiasm and high-mindedness still in the pool. Tomorrow's reporters are going to have to paddle hard, though, to fight the current pushing them toward insignificance. Perhaps the stories in this book can serve as reminders that the battle is worth continuing. The power of journalism is a wonder to behold.

The internet has led far too many people to conclude that news can be had at no cost. We forget or ignore the fact that news aggregators don't actually gather news from the field but simply collate other people's work. What if there were no "other people"? Journalism without reporters is like an election without voters. Some countries have tried that. Want to live in any of those places?

Ask a child today where news comes from and the answer might be, "From the internet." Be afraid. Be very afraid. Replacing the milkman was easy. Replacing real reporters is impossible.

David Common:
Earthquake in
Haiti

Photo courtesy CBC

DAVID COMMON IS ONE OF THOSE GUYS who look too young to have done everything they've done. He has explored the world and anchored major newscasts. He has also interviewed Elmo from *Sesame Street*, which to his daughters is probably the most impressive event in his career.

He began as an intern with the CBC London bureau in 1998. Since then he has been in perpetual motion. He's lived in Toronto, Fredericton, Winnipeg, Regina (though he seemed to live in Afghanistan during most of those years), Toronto again, Paris, New York, and now in Toronto again. He has reported from more than sixty countries, including Haiti.

If misery were a mountain, Everest would be in Haiti.

The country simply forgot to get in line when the good things in life were being distributed across the Americas. It is by far the poorest country in the hemisphere: 78 percent of Haitians live on less than $2 a day, and 54 percent on less than $1 a day. Unemployment runs at about 66 percent. Half the children in the country are malnourished.

It may have seemed impossible for things to get worse, but on January 12, 2010, they did. For a few terrifying seconds late that afternoon, the earth shook and shook, and just about everything in Haiti came tumbling down. At least 230,000 people were killed. More than 300,000 were injured. A million and a half people lost their homes.

David Common, based in New York for CBC News, was among the first Canadian reporters to reach the disaster zone.

I was fixing a videotape machine and had both my arms inside it when the phone rang. I answered with my nose. An assignment editor from Toronto was on the other end and there was urgency in his voice: "Get to Haiti. Get to Haiti."

It was about thirty minutes after the earthquake.

It was too late to go anywhere that night, but the next day I flew to the Dominican Republic, rented a car and drove to the border with Haiti. But by then it was dark. I slept in some building—it wasn't a hotel, more like a closet. The next day at 5 AM the sun came up and the border opened on the Dominican side. On the Haitian side there was nobody. I had a car, a rental car that I was not allowed to take out of the Dominican Republic. So I promptly took it outside the Dominican Republic.

I drove in with some Japanese journalists, and at first we saw no damage. Everything was fine until we got to within about forty-five minutes of Port-au-Prince. Now we could see bodies and body parts, flattened by crushed buildings, all over the place. Hundreds and hundreds of bodies and body parts.

I separated from the Japanese crew and headed for the airport. I figured I could find someone there who would let me use their satellite phone. And I did find someone. I called the assignment desk in Toronto. The last time I had checked in was when I had woken up. And at that point Toronto was telling me to stay put on the Dominican side of the border until they could send me some support. "Do not go into Haiti," they told me. "Do not go into Haiti." And I had said, "Listen, I am going in. We're not going to debate this. Goodbye."

Now it was three hours later, and the message from the desk was very different. It wasn't, "We told you to stay put. How dare you disobey?" It was, "We're putting you on the air immediately."

Shortly after that a Canadian military plane landed. It had a few relief supplies, but it also had the CBC satellite uplink. The military moved everything to the Canadian Embassy, so that's where we put the uplink—on the embassy's back lawn. Now we could feed our pictures to Canada. And we could do live reports all day and all night.

Over the next few days, CBC sent in other reporters, and cameramen and technical support. The appetite for material was never-ending. I was on the air just about every hour. When I wasn't on the air, I often went out with a camera to gather elements that I could piece together later for a story.

On one of those excursions, I ran into a woman who had just arrived from Montreal—a Haitian Canadian. She had come because she couldn't reach her mother or sister, who still lived in Haiti, by phone. She had heard that the neighbourhood she had grown up in had been hit hard. I had a car, and she knew the way to go, so I drove her.

When we got to the area, the woman from Montreal got

out of the car and people in the neighbourhood recognized her right away. And they started telling her, "Your mother's over there." She was just elated that her mother was alive. And grateful. But then she saw her mother's face, and she went from that emotional high to deep despair. She could see in her mother's face that her sister was dead.

The woman from Montreal walked around to the back of the house. I followed her with my cameraman. But then we smelled the smell. This was a few days in, so bodies were rotting in the intense heat. I stopped the cameraman.

"This is as far as we have to go."

We heard a scream. And wailing and crying. And the woman took the time she needed to take, looking at the crushed body of her sister. Then she went back to her mother.

When we did the story we showed pictures of the sister's arm. There was a lot more to see, but that is what we showed. Some would say even that was too much. But people needed to recognize the gravity of it. Sometimes you need those punch-in-the-face emotional moments to remind people why it's important. You're connecting human to human. You forget about race or country, or whatever the things are that separate us. This was a woman who happened to live in Canada. This was a woman who came back to her home to see her sister not just dead but having died terribly. Her entire neighbourhood, her whole existence as a child, had been erased from the earth.

By that point we were talking about a quarter of a million people dead. It's a huge figure. And people back in Canada were probably saying, "Wow, a quarter of a million people." It's much easier to understand the experience through that one person.

There was another incident around this time that hit me hard. About a week and a half after the earthquake I was still sleeping outdoors and it was quite comfortable. But one person in our crew had a room in a hotel. And the room had a shower. So the rest of us, about twelve of us, would all use that one shower. One day I had to kill time while someone else was having a shower. So I went for a walk.

I walked to one of the big city squares. They had all become refugee camps. People couldn't stay in their homes because they were gone or because they weren't safe. So they went into the city squares. It was very crowded, but civil in its way. Space was carved up: families would have a small rectangle of space that was theirs.

I began walking through all this, everyone trying to cope, and I saw one particularly small bit of space with two people in it. There was just enough room for those two people. One was a girl, six years old. The other was a baby, maybe one year old. There was no adult. It struck me because I have two daughters. At the time my older one wasn't as old as this six-year-old. I asked the woman in the space next to the kids, "What's the story here?"

She said, "Well that's it."

"What do you mean, 'That's it'?"

"That's all that's left of the family. The mother is dead. The father is dead. Sisters are dead, brother is dead. It's that girl and the baby. That's it."

That was the moment for me that crystallized things. I realized there were bodies burning in the streets. There were body parts still stinking and falling out of the rubble of buildings. But you can't think about the dead. Nothing can be done for them. Think about the living, and hope something can be done for them. Who knows what happened to that six-year-old girl? Her prospects weren't particularly good. So that was a defining moment. It really told me what it was all about. Don't focus on the dead.

What you're ultimately trying to do is bring people to the

place where you are standing. Show them why they should care. The lesson for me was that, after I'd repeatedly said "a quarter million," "a quarter million," "a quarter million," I realized the number wasn't everything. It wasn't as important as that little girl, or the woman who came from Montreal. The survivors.

My job was to tell their stories. I think there is value in that job. What you are doing helps in some way, and it is important.

Adrienne Arsenault: Moshe and Munir

Photo courtesy CBC

ADRIENNE ARSENAULT HAS WORKED FOR CBC NEWS HER ENTIRE CAREER, making her way up from editorial assistant to senior foreign correspondent. She has been based in Toronto, Vancouver, Toronto again, Washington, Jerusalem, London, and yes, Toronto again.

Earthquake in Iran, assassination in Pakistan, revolution in Libya, Ebola epidemic in Liberia, death of a pope, wars in the Middle East—she has pursued the biggest news stories around the world with relentless energy. And she has seen enough tragedy to test the limits of the human spirit.

In 2007, Adrienne reported a particularly bittersweet story.

There's a phrase that has been on the front burner of the world news agenda for more than half a century without ever coming to a boil: *peace in the Middle East*. Every once in a while something positive happens. Israel has peace treaties with Egypt and Jordan, for example. But mostly it's been war, conflict, terror, incursion, occupation, uprising, bloodshed and hatred.

At the centre of all this is the relationship between Israel and the Palestinians, who have no state to call their own but who live adjacent to Israel. Some Israelis live in settlements on land the Palestinians say is theirs. At the worst of times, the two sides engage in short and destructive wars. Even at the best of times there is simmering hostility. So a meeting between a Palestinian and an Israeli after a gap of more than fifteen years was remarkable.

It was 2004. The second intifada, or Palestinian uprising against Israeli occupation, was still going on, and this was also a period in which there had been some violence from Israeli settlers. In fact, a settler had recently shot a man near Nablus, and that's when someone told us about Munir Darwish. He was apparently very upset about the shooting. The victim was his friend. And we knew he spoke a little bit of English. We were trying to find a way to explain the tensions between settlers and Palestinians so we thought we would just pop down there, have a little poke around and see what Munir had to say.

Munir took us right to the spot of the shooting. He was determined to tell us his story, but it was hard to follow his narrative. Then it got even harder because he seemed to be trying to tell us something else. He got down on his knees and made a motion as if he were hugging somebody. So I kept saying,

"Sorry, what you trying to say? Forgive me, I don't speak enough Arabic to understand." It was a bit daunting.

He was struggling to articulate that he didn't think all Israelis were his enemies. He wanted us to know that what had happened to his friend was absolutely terrible. He said the settlers were racist killers. "But," he said, "I don't see the settlers as Israelis. I don't see them as the Israelis that I know and the Israelis that I have loved." That's not a distinction that Palestinians rushed to make. It was an unusual thing to hear someone like him say, which immediately made him a fascinating man.

He invited us back to his house, where his wife brought us water and food. While we enjoyed her generosity, Munir disappeared for about fifteen minutes. When he came back, he had photos, some old snapshots. They were of a time when he'd worked in Israel for a man who built swimming pools. One picture was particularly important to Munir. It showed him with a little boy named Gidon, who was the son of his Israeli boss. The boss was named Moshe Shinaar. That he would keep these pictures after everything he'd been through was another reason to think Munir was special.

It was one of those moments when you feel a certain something go up your back and you think, "There's only one thing that I should be doing right now and that's finding Moshe."

Israel isn't a big country, so tracking down a man named Moshe Shinaar who builds swimming pools wasn't all that hard. Within a couple of days we had phone numbers for him. Within about another week or two we had made contact. But it took another month to get him to agree to meet with us. We represented the foreign media to him, at a time when a lot of Israelis didn't particularly like the idea of foreign media. The notion of talking about the old days with Palestinians and being on camera was completely unappealing to Moshe and his family.

Our producer, Ian Kalushner, gets all the credit for changing their minds. He went out to shoot some swimming-pool con-struction, and he slowly built up some rapport and established a relationship. He kept working them on the phone. Eventually we just said, "Look, we have this special piece of tape that we have to show you." I think that's what finally did it.

We went to the house one night and met Moshe and his wife, Candy. They were very friendly. They were sitting around the kitchen table. Their son, Gidon, was there—the one Munir remembered. He still had a key chain Munir had made for him years before. There was also a younger daughter in the family, but she had no sense at all that Palestinians and Israelis could be friends. The thing that was always interesting about the story was that as the generations evolved there were fewer Israelis who had connections or relationships with Palestin-ians. Moshe and Munir had had a business relationship, but at the same time they formed a bit of a bond. Gidon remembered it a little bit. But the daughter had no clue.

We did a short interview with Moshe and Candy, which relaxed everyone. Then we brought out the tape player. We put the tape in of Munir at his home in Nablus and played it for them. Candy was the first to get emotional. Then Moshe started shaking his head. And I immediately thought of what a Sabra was. It's what people born in Israel call themselves. But it's also a desert fruit. It's prickly and thorny, hard on the outside but mushballs on the inside. And I thought, "Wow, I'm looking at a Sabra."

All the tension went out of the room. They realized we were sincere about having this special piece of tape that meant something to them personally. We talked a little bit but then came frustration again. Moshe said, "Munir and I will never see each other again. That's it. I'm not going there and he can't come here. And that's the end of that." That's how he felt but that's not what we wanted to hear.

Still, we had avoided the worst-case scenario, which would

have been Moshe looking at the tape and saying, "That's very nice. Thanks for coming. Goodbye." We were thrilled we had made a connection and thought we were onto something. But honestly we didn't know what to do next. We just kept going back to Moshe. "What if we took you to his house? What if we could bring Munir here?" And he kept saying, "No, no, no, no. Not going to happen." He was scared. He thought an Israeli going into Nablus would get caught up in trouble. And getting Munir to Tel Aviv, where Moshe was, would have been very difficult.

So it was a bit depressing. We had arrived at the intersection where either we were going to become forcefully involved in the story or we were going to drop it. Were we going to stop observing the story and cross the line to become participants? It was a difficult decision. Would a strong story at the other end justify the journalistic leap? We thought about it for so long that my time in Jerusalem came to an end. I was posted to London.

Before I left, though, I hid the tapes of Munir and Moshe. The producer was staying, so he knew where they were. And we told each other we weren't done with this story. We thought one day there would be a way to tell it. It felt ever more urgent to tell it because there was so much anger between Israelis and Palestinians. People were hardening in their attitudes. Our editor at the time was an Israeli Arab and our cameraman was Palestinian. They were invested too. None of us wanted to let go.

In the summer of 2007 I was asked if I could go back to Jerusalem just for a month to fill in for our regular correspondent who was going on vacation. I didn't need to be asked twice. I was on the plane lickety-split. There was plenty of news to cover but the first thing I said to our producer was, "This is it. This is our last opportunity for Munir and Moshe. Let's hope they're both okay and let's see what we can do." And he said, "Yup."

So he called the Israeli military and he laid it out for them. He said, "Here's what we want to do. It's not a negative story.

We want permission for Munir to pass through a checkpoint to go to the outskirts of an Israeli settlement. We're not talking about going to Tel Aviv or to Jerusalem. Just to a settlement not far from where he lives. So please." And finally the military said, "All right."

Then we had to convince Moshe, and that wasn't easy. "I'm a busy man. I'm recovering from heart surgery. I really don't want to go into the occupied territory." He was pretty clear. I then said to him, "Please. Munir really wants to see you. He's had a very bad time looking after his sister who had cancer and now she's died. His mother has just died as well."

I think Moshe began to think that he would do it for Munir. He still didn't want to do it, but he would do it for Munir.

The plan was for Ian and a cameraman to go get Munir at his house. I would go with another cameraman to get Moshe and Gidon. And we would meet at the Israeli settlement.

I showed up at Moshe's house and Gidon wasn't there. Moshe made an excuse, and I was sad that Munir wouldn't be seeing the little boy he remembered, the little boy who was now a man. I confess I was emotionally all in on this story.

But Moshe was there. So we got in the car and drove. We arrived at the appointed time and it was exceptionally hot. I was talking by cellphone to our producer coming with Munir, and there was a holdup of some kind. Munir was in the car. He had brought olive oil, treats and food from his wife. He was saying this was the best day of his life. But getting past the checkpoint wasn't going smoothly.

We waited for more than an hour past the appointed time. And I started to think, "This is not going to happen." I thought, "My God, what have we done to these two men?" Because we had done this. We had made this happen. And I thought, "Moshe is going to bolt. I'm going to lose him. He's just going to go because it's hot and he's stressed out and he's just had heart problems."

And then Ian called and said, "Start rolling." Our camera-man did just that. The car with Munir pulled up. It took every-thing I had to keep my mouth shut and just watch.

You talk about a moment! Standing there when those men hugged. I will never forget that. It was silent, but in my head it was noisy. It went on and on and on. I was thinking, "They're still holding onto each other. I can't believe this." And it made me think we had been right from the beginning. There was something to this. This lost relationship was so real, so raw. These two men were the story of this land.

Eventually they stopped hugging and we all relaxed a little bit. They went to sit at a table. Two old guys holding hands and showing photos. We took our pictures for a few min-utes and then we let them be. Our cameras were off for about forty-five minutes and they continued their conversation. When they left, their cars went in totally different directions. And that was pretty symbolic.

Another big story broke that day and we had to race to cover it.

It was only the next day when we sat down to look at our tape. Then I wanted to write the story so badly the words were bursting out of my fingers. We started to edit, but before we finished I had to go back to London.

But about a month later Ian ended up in London on another assignment and he brought all the tape with him. Three years after we started the story, it was finally finished.

A lot of people who saw the piece told me they felt con-nected to Munir and Moshe.

I always thought it was a sad story. I'm sad for both of them. Sad for that land and all the lost relationships. I'm sad that their children will probably never understand what it was that made those men hug each other. Those two guys broke my heart.

Diana Swain:

Boy Scout

Scandal

THE EDITOR OF THE *CHILLI-WACK PROGRESS* IN 1983 must have had an eye for talent: that's when Diana Swain showed up looking for work. She said she was ready. After all, she had already finished high school. And that's how she began her career—as a part-time writer for her hometown newspaper. She stayed in British Columbia for a few years, going to school and working in Burnaby, then Kamloops and Prince George. She moved to the bright lights of Winnipeg and became part of something you

Photo courtesy CBC

don't see on television often—a father–daughter anchor team. That was with Brian Swain at the independent CKND.

Her CBC days began in 1990, first in Winnipeg, then in Toronto. She's become one of Canada's best anchors and reporters, especially sharp at politics and investigations.

One of her major stories centred on Scouts Canada, an organization that isn't reluctant to boast about its accomplishments. Its website says, "For more than 100 years, we have brought a world of adventure, outdoor experience and friendship to 17 million Canadian youth." That's true, no doubt. But there was a dark side as well. And no one wanted to acknowledge that dark side for a long time.

Over the years, some Scouts had been sexually abused by Scout leaders. From time to time, the organization made financial settlements with those who complained about abuse, but the settlements assured that the details never became public. We might still know nothing today, except for the work that a team from *the fifth estate* did in 2011—and the reporting of Diana Swain.

Harvey Cashore, one of our producers, was reading a newspaper when he came across a story, just a small story, about a legal case in the United States. A grown man was suing a guy who had been a Scout leader. In the course of the suit it had been revealed that Boy Scouts of America kept something called perversion files. Sometimes they were called confidential files. Someone whose name was in the files would be removed from Scouts, but the police were never called in. Which meant the abusers were free to keep abusing elsewhere. That is how they had dealt with rumours and innuendo and allegations of abuse.

They had been keeping these files for decades. And when

the files were released they showed just how horribly the Scouts had handled things. In fact the Scouts had been a most attractive place for pedophiles. And if the Scouts had read their own documents, they would have known this.

So the simple question was: How had this been dealt with in Canada?

We thought we would call the Scouts and ask. I thought we would ask them, "Do you have confidential files?" And they would say, "Yes, of course. If people made allegations or raised concerns, we wrote it down and we kept it somewhere." That seemed to me to be completely logical. If they had a list we might have concluded that there was no story. But they insisted they had nothing. It was that need to deny—to deny even the logical stuff—that kept us going.

It was a ridiculous answer. If what they said had been true it would have raised the worst scenario imaginable. They were telling us that when someone came forward to say, "I've been abused," or, "I think someone is abusing a child," they didn't write it down. They didn't do anything.

And that became the pattern for every question we asked. Every time they could have given us a simple answer, they would give us an answer that would dig their hole even deeper. I lost track of the number of times we got off a phone call with our heads shaking. We thought they must be lying. But what could we do about it? How could we possibly prove they had files that they denied having?

I went down to California to work on another story, and we decided that since I was there we would connect with the guy at the centre of the American lawsuit. The man in that first newspaper story we had read. We'd do an interview with him just in case this Scouts thing ever went somewhere.

That was a gut-wrenching interview, incredibly raw as he described his experiences. It was at that moment when we decided we couldn't just drop the story. It didn't matter that this man was on the other side of the border. If the Boy Scouts of America had messed up this badly, Canadians would be interested. So initially our story was going to be driven by the US experience.

We sat down to interview the man's lawyer in Los Angeles. I've never made a lawyer cry before so it was stunning to have him start to cry. He thought the victims had been belittled and ignored for so long. He'd worked so hard on the case because he couldn't be the next person to turn away from them. So here was somebody who got it as I got it: what happened was so wrong.

Then we started looking into the case of Richard Turley, a Canadian who was a Scout leader in California in the 1970s. And his story was extraordinary. He had kidnapped a Scout and sexually assaulted him. This was front-page news at the time in California. He was convicted and sent to a mental institution. After eighteen months he was released. Incredibly, he went right back to the Scouts and assaulted three more boys. The Scouts covered it all up and told Turley, "Just get out of this country. Go back to Canada."

So Turley went to British Columbia and, you guessed it, he became a Scout leader again. And he assaulted three more boys. And even though other Scout leaders had voiced their suspicions about Turley, the organization did nothing.

We found more victims of abuse. Every single one of them was broken in some way. One man told me that as an adult he had bowel trouble because of the number of times he had been raped. I wanted to cry but I couldn't. He was holding it together, and he was the person who had gone through it, so how dare I fall apart just listening? All the victims had so much wrapped up in their heads and in their hearts, and talking to me was their chance to get it all out. They had been profoundly affected by what had happened to them.

I would get angrier and angrier, thinking, "How could all those adults know, and nobody did the right thing? One after the other no one did the right thing. How is that possible? How is it that everyone wanted to look the other way?"

At a certain point the Scouts conceded in letters they wrote to us that they did have some files. They had gone from saying, "We have no files" to "We have some files, but not that many." It was like playing Whac-A-Mole. We couldn't nail things down. They wouldn't tell us, for example, how many files they had.

We tried to get an interview with the head of Scouts Canada, but she wouldn't agree to sit down with me. We would rather not ambush people—just show up with a camera. I would never go to someone's home. You have the right not to have someone ask you hard questions in front of your kids. But you don't have a right to just say no and that's it. I'm just asking you a question—if you're telling me the truth, it's easy to answer.

We waited for her outside the Scouts office. She was walking out of the building with two colleagues. I started walking toward her. She saw me, stopped, spun on her heels and started walking the other way. So I started chasing her through the parking lot. I actually wanted to say to her, "Just turn around. For the love of God, turn around." By the time she got to the door I think she'd had enough time to conclude that no matter what she said, it wouldn't be as bad as running away from a camera.

She engaged in some wordplay. "They are not confidential files. They are not perversion files. They are not pink files. We don't call them that."

I didn't really care what they called them. I cared about what was in them, and what happened to the information in them. My question was, "Did you tell the police?" That really was the bottom line. I didn't care if they kept these things on Post-it Notes or posters. I didn't care if they wrote things down using calligraphy. The bottom line was, "Did you do what you were supposed to do? Someone came to you with a very serious allegation. Did you take down the information? Did you call the police?"

If she could have answered that the Scouts had done the right thing, she would have been anxious to tell me. But there was no straight answer. When people choose their words so carefully when faced with a simple question it tells me I'm on the right track.

They said their policy was to share every allegation with the police. But we knew about Turley so what they were telling us was just not possible. There were two choices: either Scouts Canada had had one awful lapse of policy, or maybe they were being less than truthful. They kept saying, "Of course we did the right thing." But the reality was that they hadn't done the right thing.

Eventually we discovered that Richard Turley was living in Alberta, managing a small motel. So we went there one cold morning, while it was still dark, and waited for him. I have different layers of preparation for these kinds of confrontations. I'm five foot four and in the neighbourhood of 115 pounds. He was much bigger than me. In the back of my head I was wondering what to do if he took a swing at me.

But I also prepare in terms of journalism. I knew that our entire meeting might last just four seconds. I'd ask one question and he'd turn around and walk inside the motel. So if the only moment was four seconds long, then my question had to get right to the heart of the matter. Because you get one shot.

So I told Turley who I was and he knew immediately why I was there. And I thought about his victims. I thought it was my chance to stand up for them. I owed it to them to have a conversation with Turley. It wasn't my job to beat him up, to stand there and shake my finger at him for being a pedophile. I asked him to help me understand how we could prevent future cases of abuse. He kept saying how his criminal behaviour was behind him now. He said he was so much better. So I challenged him to prove it. "What do organizations need to do to put someone like you down and out? How do parents detect someone like you coming their way?"

He went inside to think things over, and to his credit he came back out and agreed to do an interview, but not in front of the camera. So we talked for an hour. He couldn't emphasize enough how easy it had been for him to be a serial abuser. He said adults were so afraid to suggest this horrible thing was going on. And so many people just didn't want to get involved. That was the most maddening thing for me. That was much more infuriating to me than just about anything else.

[Two months after The Fifth Estate *story went to air, the Scouts came out with an apology. And they hired a forensic auditing team to go through their records to expose the truth about the confidential files. It turned out that there were at least sixty-five cases where the Scouts did not go to the police about someone who had been accused of inappropriate behaviour with children. By then Scouts Canada had a new chief commissioner, Steve Kent. He agreed to sit down for an interview with Diana.]*

Steve Kent was willing to talk to me for hours about what Scouts meant to him and how it had framed who he was as a man. All the good things he experienced. But that was never the point. I think the Scouts first took the position that the media was coming in and dredging up things that had happened fifty years ago. That kind of dismissive, condescending tone you encounter all the time in this business. But at a certain point Kent got it. I think he felt sick that an organization he cared so much about had allowed this to happen. He wanted to be part of the process that would fix it somehow. He understood why this was important. And he understood that the Scouts had been wilfully obstructing the sharing of information that was going to help people. It wasn't about airing the Scouts' dirty laundry.

For the victims we had spoken to, the apology fell far short of what they all wanted. It's a bit quaint to just say, "I want someone to say they're sorry." They wanted a lot more at that point. They wanted something bigger than that. Maybe not money. I'm not sure they could articulate what they wanted. But I think for them at that point "sorry" seemed like such a small concession for the Scouts to have made. The victims were aware what we were being told throughout the eighteen months we worked on this story. If we were frustrated, imagine what they went through. They kept saying, "That's just wrong. That's just not right." In a way the Scouts had victimized them again. It was making them out to be liars again.

As a journalist you can do a lot of stories where you know you are not making any difference. You're broadcasting information that people may or may not process and that may or may not affect decisions they make. But this story was different. We took one of the oldest, most highly regarded organizations in the country and forced it to be honest. We sided with people who had been horribly treated and gave them a measure of justice, if only emotional justice. They had been seen as troublemakers, problem kids. Now, people in their lives could understand them better, could appreciate what they had survived. That was really meaningful to me. I think if you can do that with your job then you've done something good, something useful.

Journalism is about making things better. A nurse makes things better, but I'd have been a horrible nurse. A firefighter makes things better, but I would have been a lousy firefighter. This is my way of contributing. It's my way of making the world better.

Ian Hanomansing: Riots in Los Angeles

IAN HANOMANSING'S FIRST SCOOP AS A JOURNALIST came when he was working at a radio station in Moncton, New Brunswick. He was the first to report an end to a teachers' strike that had started just one day earlier. The truth can now be told about how he found out before anyone else. His parents were teachers. When they got the call from their union to tell them the strike was over, Ian was the next to know. His scoop earned him "employee of the month" honours.

The Moncton job was Ian's

Photo courtesy CBC

second. He had started at a radio station in Amherst, Nova Scotia. He did summer fill-in work at CBC Radio in Moncton, then with a law degree in hand, he started full-time work at CBC Halifax before moving to CBC Vancouver. His West Coast base put him in perfect position to get a jump on covering the San Francisco earthquake of 1989, the Exxon Valdez spill in Alaska and the handover of Hong Kong to China. He has also covered several Olympic Games, and anchored a boatload of programs and newscasts.

In 1992, Ian was sent to Los Angeles to cover part of the Rodney King story.

King had been driving drunk one night in 1991, and speeding too. When LA police tried to stop him, he stepped on the gas and the chase was on. When he was finally stopped, angry officers pulled him from his car. From across the street a man pointed his camera and started to record the scene. King was tasered and kicked. He was hit more than fifty times by police batons. By the time the beating was over King had eleven fractures and severe cuts and bruises.

In 1991 it was still rare for people on the street to capture dramatic events on video, and the King tape created a sensation. Not long after it was shown on television, four LAPD officers were charged with criminal offences, including assault with a deadly weapon. Thirteen months later, on April 29, 1992, all four were acquitted.

....

I was in the Vancouver newsroom. Late in the afternoon, someone on the national news desk in Toronto called and said, "We need you to go to Los Angeles. Get going as quickly as you can." It was the first time I'd been sent to a story that hadn't happened yet. The story I was sent to cover wasn't the acquittal of the four officers—it was the riots that we expected.

I got into a van with a cameraman and a producer and

headed right to the airport. I confess I found it all very exciting. I'd never done a story out of Los Angeles before and I had always looked forward to this day. We got onto a flight to LA and then we were completely insulated as to what was developing in the story. The rest of the world watched live TV coverage of the start of the rioting, but when we landed we had seen nothing. Everything seemed normal at the airport, and we got into our rental car.

We turned on a radio station at random and they were talking about fires. And they were talking about a firefighter who had been shot. They were talking about mayhem, and we had no idea at that point that anything like that had happened. Every station that we turned to had the same narrative. We drove onto the freeway and fortunately the cameraman knew Los Angeles very well and he knew which off-ramp to take. We came to a DO NOT ENTER barrier and, being good Canadians, we actually stopped for a moment and looked around, but there was nobody there. So we drove around the barrier into the heart of South Central LA.

It didn't take long to get to a spot where we saw a couple of television satellite trucks. We thought that would be a relatively safe place, so we parked. I looked around and there were fires on three corners of the intersection. There was a store on the fourth corner that wasn't on fire. I said to a couple of people who were standing around, "What's going on? How come that store isn't on fire?" They looked at me, puzzled, and they said, "Take a look." So I looked and that's when I saw the sign BLACK OWNED BUSINESS. That's when I realized this was a lot more complicated than just a reaction to the acquittals of the police officers. There were a lot of things going on in this neighbourhood.

A little later I was standing next to an African-American woman and I said to her, "So what is this neighbourhood like?" I was thinking I had some level of connection to her because my skin is brown. But she looked me up and down and she said, "You wouldn't last one minute here." Of course I was still wearing the clothes I had put on in Vancouver that morning. And I thought, "I guess a guy wearing a suit doesn't look like part of this neighbourhood."

We just kept jumping into the car and everywhere we drove there was something going on. We came into the parking lot of what they called a swap meet, what in Canada we might call a flea market. It looked like a big old supermarket that had a bunch of stalls inside where people would sell things. And it was just being looted—not angry looting, but enthusiastic looting. The windows were broken and people were going through them. After about half an hour, four LA police cars with their sirens screaming roared up. The looters scattered, and the police just drove off. We were discovering that the police were obviously overwhelmed.

We came back to that place a couple of hours later and this time police cars were there and police officers were out of the cars. They drew their guns and started walking into the building. The cameraman and I ran right behind them. The glass was crunching beneath their feet. I kept waiting for them to say, "Get the heck out of here. What are you doing?" But they never did. We followed them until they had cleared the building. The night was just filled with incredible moments like that.

Every time we encountered the police, something memorable happened.

It was on this assignment that, for the first time in my career, a gun was pointed at me. We were driving around another swap meet and we startled a couple of officers sitting in their car. They aimed their guns at us, told us to leave. We didn't argue with them.

The next day we approached a police officer sitting in his cruiser. He was watching the looting in broad daylight. We had the camera rolling as I walked up to him and asked why he wasn't doing anything. And he just looked at the looters, then back at us. "What do you want me to do?"

We talked to looters as well. They were ransacking stores nonchalantly. It was like, "Hey, you need an 8½-size sneaker? Let's go see what we have here." People were just so willing to talk. That's a real American trait. I often felt they were going to be disappointed if they realized that the pictures we were taking would be seen only in Canada. I think they assumed it would be seen on one of their local channels.

It was disorder spread over a huge area of the city. I was able to go to places where no other reporters were going, not because I was special, but because the riots were spread over such a wide area. We were doing so much, and running on so much adrenalin, you almost forget about the danger. But in almost every place we were, my cameraman and my producer were the only Caucasians. They were very aware of feeling vulnerable.

We went to another store that was being looted and I was doing part of a report, standing there speaking directly to the camera, and a young guy next to me kept talking while I was talking. I was tired so I turned to him and, perhaps a little sharply, asked him to stop. The cameraman gave me a long, hard look. When I watched the tape later I saw that it looked like the guy was going to punch me for telling him to stop bothering us. One of the things the cameraman said afterwards is that he thought as long as people didn't notice us, didn't focus on us, we would be okay. But he was worried that if a bunch of people started to yell at us, or hit us or steal something from us, then we'd suddenly be in deep trouble. As long as people weren't paying attention to us he felt pretty safe.

I remember talking to a man who ran an optical store. His father had started the business, and he took it over. He was a Caucasian. I asked him, "How afraid were you on the first night?" He said, "I wasn't afraid. I realized what was going on, got into my car and started driving home. I was listening to the radio and took a few turns to avoid the worst of the rioting. But I have a gun in the glove compartment. So I was thinking to myself that if a couple of rioters stop me, there are going to be a couple of dead rioters." He didn't say it with a harsh or loud tone. It was very matter-of-fact.

We stayed in Los Angeles for a week. At the end I would say my biggest impression of being there was not the damage or the riot. My biggest impression was of how bleak South Central LA was. Riot aside, you could just tell by looking. How few stores there were, how many people had nothing to do.

Different reporters get excited by different things. Some reporters do long investigative pieces. I've never been a guy who likes long-term projects. I've always loved spot news stories. I find them thrilling. And LA was a story unfolding so quickly right in front of me.

[In the events following the acquittal of the four LAPD *officers, fifty people were killed, two thousand more were hurt and a thousand buildings were destroyed.]*

John Blackstone:
Meeting Mia

ON THE ONE HAND, JOHN
BLACKSTONE SEEMED DES-
TINED FOR A CAREER in broad-
cast journalism. He was, after all, one
of the founding members of his university's radio station. On the other
hand, he was turned down for an
on-air position just a few years later
at another university radio station.
How that happened is one of life's
mysteries. There's an old joke that
some people have the perfect face
for radio. John has the perfect voice
for TV: you could listen to him all day
and all night.

He reported at the *Ottawa Citizen* for a short time, but it's been

Photo courtesy John Blackstone

television the rest of the way. He's worked for CBC News in Ottawa and Toronto, and also for CBS News, based in London, Paris and San Francisco. He's covered wars in the Middle East and Central America, revolutions in Africa and natural disasters just about everywhere. He's done celebrity profiles and explained a total solar eclipse, and he is among what is likely only a handful of journalists to have reported from both the North and South Poles.

One story that left a lasting mark on him was about a girl named Mia and her foster parents.

Being a foster parent is often difficult. Many children who need fostering have lived through circumstances that no child should experience. They carry scars—sometimes physical, sometimes emotional, sometimes both—that never completely go away. Sharon and Bob Behrens, a couple in California, had looked after several foster children, but never anyone like Mia. What that baby had gone through went far beyond cruel. She had been brutalized to a degree that left you weeping for humanity. It seemed impossible to give her a life anywhere near what most of us would consider normal. But when John Blackstone met Mia, she was eighteen years old and had been transformed.

My producer and I had done a couple of stories about kids who had been abused or kids who had been in trouble in one way or another, and we'd built a relationship with a child psychiatrist in San Francisco. Her name was Lenore Terr. We were talking to her one day and she said, "I've got to tell you about this girl. I can't identify her, but I do have her permission to write a paper about her under a pseudonym." And she began describing a girl she had been working with for more than twelve years. She called the girl Cammie. We found out later that her real name was Mia.

Dr. Terr said Mia's story was more common than one

would expect. She told us there are children who from the earliest age are just terribly sexually abused and are so destroyed that they end up like animals. They don't talk. They're violent. They don't trust anybody. It's hard to work with them in any way. They don't have a life. And they get cast aside, ending up homeless, or institutionalized or imprisoned. They don't have a chance in life because of what happened to them in their very first two or three years. She said this little girl was saved because a foster parent saw something in her eyes one day. The foster mother had looked into this little girl's eyes and said, "There's something in there. There is a child in there."

The mother worked with Mia, and she came to see Dr. Terr once or twice a week for counselling. That was a 250-mile trip each way. Now Mia was close to graduating from high school and the doctor had written an academic paper about her. It was aimed at other professionals. To let them know this story.

Dr. Terr also said that Mia might be willing to go public in some way, perhaps go to a meeting of child psychiatrists to talk about her recovery as a way to help other kids. She also said to Mia, "I've worked with the news media from time to time, especially with a couple of people from CBS News. I've built up a relationship with them. They're very nice guys. Maybe your story could be told to a larger audience, and you won't just reach psychiatrists who might run into these very troubled kids. You might be able to reach families who are dealing with a kid like this—adoptive families and foster families."

The doctor's conversations with Mia went on for several months. Finally she told me, "Mia is ready to meet with you."

So we went to meet her and she was very shy. She was in her senior year of high school, eighteen years old. She seemed like a completely normal eighteen-year-old—very attractive— except she was terrifically shy. It became clear quickly that it was going to take some powerful persuasion to get her to agree to co-operate on a story.

We also met Mia's foster mother, Sharon. In many ways, she had dedicated her life to saving Mia. She told us she had video footage of Mia when she was younger. I think as much as anything she had shot the video trying to document Mia's behaviour to explain why she was going to return her to the foster agency. She had to show them why Mia was just impossible to handle.

When I first saw the video footage it was horrifying. It was very disturbing to watch. It showed exactly what Sharon had told us about Mia. She bit, she scratched. She screamed as much as twelve hours a day. When she wasn't screaming, she growled. We heard what had happened to Mia and it was so bad we couldn't put the details in our story. She had had vaginal and anal reconstruction because of the damage that had been done to her. Apart from the horrible physical injuries, she had severe mental damage. Dr. Terr said, "If you gave her paper and crayons, she drew biting monsters. She drew naked women lying in pools of blood—the most ghastly pictures you can imagine a three-and-a-half-year-old drawing."

One of the reasons Mia was reluctant to appear on television was because she was afraid of her birth father. He was in prison for killing her infant sister and she feared that he would be released on parole. I mean, she was seriously afraid of him. Because he was Hispanic, for a long time Mia had great difficulty going out in public, worried that she would see a Hispanic male—anybody who reminded her of her father—and start to freak out. She couldn't go to the mall with a group of friends because she'd see some guy on the other side of the mall who looked somewhat like her dad and she would lose it.

Finally the parole board decided that the father was going to stay locked up for a very long time. So that removed another of our obstacles.

We had a couple more meetings with Mia and then we said, "How about we come with the camera? We won't do a full story, but let's do an interview with you. We won't put it on the air right now. We won't do the story until you're ready to do the story. But let's do an interview so you can see how it works, see if you're comfortable." She agreed to that. We sat down, did an interview, and after that she was more at ease working with us.

So we were making progress and over the next several months we gathered more of what we needed. We contacted people who had been involved in her story along the way. We met the district attorney who had prosecuted her father, her kindergarten teacher, her school principal—people like that.

We edited everything together and the piece was five minutes long. After commercials, that's about a quarter of the airtime on the evening news. We tried doing the story in two parts, but it just wasn't as strong. And the editors in New York agreed. It's the only five-minute piece I've ever had on the news. That's happened to others from time to time, but it's rare.

After it ran, I got all kinds of notes. People told me they were in tears. People told me how they admired Mia's bravery. Some people wrote to say they knew a kid who might benefit from hearing Mia's story, so we would put those people in touch with her family.

Mia began to get offers to go to major medical conferences to talk to large groups of professionals, and she started to do that. To every conference, she took a starfish. And she told the story of a boy who comes upon a beach covered with thousands of starfish. He's picking them up and throwing them back into the ocean and somebody comes along and says, "Why are you doing this? Look at all the starfish. You can't possibly save them all." And the boy says, "You're right, I can't save them all. But I can save this one." Mia tells that story, looks at the starfish she brought, and says, "There are kids out there you can save."

As a journalist, you think you're going to change people's minds or tell them something they don't know. I've been doing this for many years and what you learn is that people often see what they want to see in a story. They see things that will reconfirm their own biases. You don't change many minds and you rarely change anybody's life. You certainly have stories that may change one or two lives in a small way for a short period of time, but this was my chance to address an issue that people just don't talk about. Even to consider that this kind of child abuse goes on is beyond what most people can imagine. So for us to shine a light on that is very satisfying. And to shine a light on it in a way that gives professionals in the field some reason to carry on with what they're doing is an accomplishment as well.

No matter how important or significant a story is, a journalist inevitably moves on to the next one. But at least this time I knew that the story had an impact. It had an impact on Mia's life. It gave her an opportunity to get out to those conferences and help to change other people's lives. We can take at least indirect credit for that.

Alison Smith:
9/11 Survivor

ALISON SMITH WASTED NO TIME STARTING HER CAREER. The day after writing her last university exam she started on the bottom rung of the ladder at the local CBC Television newsroom in Toronto. Four years later she had experience both on the desk as an editor and in the field as a reporter. The national newsroom gobbled her up and when CBC Newsworld was created in 1989, she added anchoring to her skills. She covered federal elections and federal budgets; the death of Diana, Princess of Wales; the first

Photo courtesy CBC

multiracial election in South Africa; and the fiftieth anniversary of the state of Israel.

She became a CBC Washington correspondent and covered the historic election of Barack Obama. Then she moved back to Toronto, where she ended her CBC career in 2014 as the anchor of *The World at Six*, CBC Radio's flagship news program.

In the frenzied aftermath of the 9/11 attacks, Alison Smith met a man who told her a one-of-a-kind story.

For those of us who live in North America, the really bad news usually happens somewhere else. But on September 11, 2001, the really bad news was here at home. And it was scarcely believable. Four commercial airliners hijacked: one flown into the Pentagon in Washington, DC; one flown into a field in Pennsylvania; two flown into the twin towers of the World Trade Center in New York City.

The New York attack left the deepest scars. It played out before our eyes on morning television. A plane hit the North Tower, then another hit the South Tower. For a time, both Manhattan towers withstood the ferocious violence of the impact. Jet fuel fed intense fires on the upper floors. Faced with the prospect of burning to death, some people chose to jump from a hundred storeys up. Before long, both towers collapsed. A total of 2,573 people were killed. Every one of their stories was achingly sad. But one survivor's story stopped us cold as well. It exposed the fragility of life and the thin line that separates life from death.

That morning I was home in Toronto getting ready to go to work. My husband phoned and asked if I had the TV on. I said, "No." He said, "I think you'd better take a look." So I did. And I said, "Oh my God." I hopped into my car and started to drive to work. But the news desk called and told me to go back home and wait there for a camera crew. Before long they were at my door—a cameraman and two producers—and we started to drive to New York.

When you think about that day and what it was like for most people, it was about having their eyes glued to the television as those towers came down, time and time again. That wasn't my day. My day was spent on the road. We listened to the radio to find out as much as we could, but we saw no television. We were just about the only thing moving on the road, though we did see ambulances from upstate New York and other emergency vehicles headed to New York City.

We made it to New Jersey that evening, just across the Hudson River from Manhattan. I did a live report for *The National* that night from the New Jersey side. The big thing for me was being able to listen to the program. So I heard the interviews they were doing with Canadians who had families in the towers. I knew that chasing down some of those Canadians who had survived would probably be my story the next day.

That night we drove up and down the Jersey side of the river trying to get over to Manhattan. Everything was closed. We finally persuaded the guards on the George Washington Bridge to let us cross. And it was one of the most eerie experiences that I have ever had. It was like something out of a science fiction movie. Normally the George Washington Bridge is like a parking lot, there's so much traffic. But now as we drove across that bridge we were alone. On the other side, the streets were empty. It was bizarre: Manhattan as you've never seen it.

The next day we started scrambling, trying to find Canadians who were involved in some way. By late morning we had a few elements but not enough for a full story. And nothing really stood out. We kept working the phones, and finally we got a lead on one of two Canadians who had apparently escaped from the eighty-fourth floor of the South Tower.

The name we had was Ron DiFrancesco. I talked to his wife on the phone. She was a mess. She said to me, "I haven't been able to speak to my husband. He's in a hospital. I have small children. I'm beside myself. I'm just not in any shape to talk to you." Then she said, "My husband's boss was in the building too."

I asked, "Do you think he might talk to us?"

She said, "He's a Canadian. He might."

She was good enough to call him on our behalf and when he agreed to talk to me, she called me back. She told me his name was Brian Clark and she gave me his phone number.

It was close to two o'clock in the afternoon. I was starting to panic because our deadline was coming fast and this Brian Clark fellow was out in New Jersey. I called him right away and we had a brief conversation. He was so matter-of-fact and calm that I was thinking he wasn't going to be able to convey the horror of what he'd been through. But we were on deadline and there was no Plan B, so we went.

We pulled up near this lovely suburban home. Brian Clark came out. He looked like Everyman. In hindsight, one of the things that appealed about that interview was that he did look so casually normal—he wasn't one of those dusty, fear-stricken people we'd seen the day before. We set up two chairs in his driveway and we sat down.

I often say it was one of the easiest interviews I ever did because all I had to do was let him speak. The only thing I had to ask was, "And then what happened?" There were no complicated questions. The two producers started taking notes as I was talking to him, but at some point I saw that they were so drawn in by his story that they had stopped writing.

He told an incredible story. He was the fire warden on his floor, so when the planes struck it was his job to gather people up. He had a vest. He had a flashlight. And it was his job to escort people out of the building. So that's what he was doing. He went to the nearest stairwell and started to go down. He said the building was in bad shape. There were cables and wires dangling. Drywall was falling around him.

On the eighty-first floor they met a couple of people coming up from lower floors, and those people said, "You shouldn't go down, you should go up. There's fire down there." They were hoping to be rescued by helicopters from the roof. While they were having this conversation Brian heard a noise—knocking or crying—somewhere on that floor. So he went to try to find and help whoever was in there. He found a man named Stanley, and came out with him back to the stairwell. In those few minutes, all the people he had been discussing things with had gone. They had continued to go up, trying to make it to the roof. And he said, "Every fibre in my body, every instinct that I had said go down." So from the eighty-first floor, he and Stanley—just the two of them—started to make their way down.

On their way down they stopped to phone home. Brian actually called his wife and said, "I'm okay. I'm on my way out of the building." And Stanley called his wife. They finally got to the main lobby of the building. Rescue personnel there said, "Run!" And so they ran across the plaza as fast as they could. In a manner of minutes the tower collapsed.

It was only when he got near the end of his story that he began to tear up a bit. He described what happened when he got home. His family was all there because they were all concerned about him. And his wife actually was far more traumatized than he was because she thought he was dead. She had got the phone call from him saying, "I'm on my way out of the building," and then she watched on TV as the building collapsed. It was sometime later before he was able to call her again and apparently she fainted right away. Because she had just assumed that he was dead. Here was this voice from the dead calling her.

So he got emotional at the end, but who wouldn't get emotional? Oftentimes when you come back from doing an interview, people in the newsroom will ask you how it went. And sometimes you say, "It was good—he cried." But if someone had been wailing and crying all through this interview I don't think it would have had the same impact. Brian's control was so much better. He was able to tell the story in enough detail that you felt you were walking down the stairs with him. You were with him. It was a simple story for him to tell. Yet it was an astonishing story. It was astonishing on its face. But what we didn't know at the time we did the interview was that Brian was one of only four people to escape from the South Tower from above the point where the plane crashed into it.

Brian and I have kept in touch over the years. He has family in Canada, so once when he came to visit them, he had dinner at my house. I also invited some of his old friends to come over. So this is a story that has given me a continuing personal connection, and that doesn't happen often.

I've been lucky enough to cover some big days in Canadian and world history. But this one stands out for me because it was one man's story. I wasn't being asked to put the events of September 11 into some big global context. I was really telling one guy's story—a very moving story. It had impact on me and so many others have told me it had impact on them. So I'll never forget it. I'll remember it as much as I remember standing in New York looking down at the wreckage of the World Trade Center, and the smell, and the grit on your skin from the dust in the air. I'll always remember sitting in that driveway listening to Brian Clark tell his story. It will always stay with me.

Brian Stewart:
Famine in
Ethiopia

BRIAN STEWART SAYS HE NEVER DREAMED of being a television reporter. He wanted to work in newspapers. And he did, at first. He started at the *Oshawa Times*. Then he crossed the Atlantic to work in England at the *Richmond and Twick-enham Times*. The managing editor there was David Dimbleby, who went on to become a major anchor at the BBC, but that had nothing to do with Brian's TV conversion. That didn't happen until he returned to Canada, where he worked at first with another newspaper, the *Gazette*, in Montreal. Then he made the switch to television

Photo courtesy Brian Stewart

and stayed at CBC Montreal for a decade, before moving to the network's bureau on Parliament Hill.

In 1982, CBC posted him to London. He spent five years dashing around the world from crisis to crisis before NBC News lured him away to do his dashing for them. But after two years he returned to Canada and the CBC, where he was a senior reporter until his retirement in 2009.

When famine hit Ethiopia in the 1980s, the BBC alerted the world. But it was Brian Stewart's reporting on CBC—vivid, powerful, painful—that truly shocked everyone who saw it, and forced even reluctant foreign governments to try to stop the suffering. We can all trace our history back to Ethiopia, as the 1974 discovery there of the bones of a female who had lived more than three million years ago confirmed. She was the oldest ancestor of human beings ever found.

Yet most of the world used to turn a blind eye to the country even in desperate times. In 1974 no one noticed a major famine in Ethiopia until the BBC aired a documentary it called *The Hidden Famine*. A decade later, when it happened again, another widespread famine almost went unreported.

....

At the CBC bureau in London, we started hearing worried rumours from humanitarian aid workers that something awful was starting to happen in northern Ethiopia. So in February or March of 1984 our producer, Tony Burman, started asking the Ethiopian Embassy for visas. And they said, "No way. No way."

There was an evil history in Ethiopia of governments fearing their own downfall if famine broke out, because famine was a sign that the government was totally incompetent. Ethiopia had a Marxist government at the time and was fighting a civil war in the north. The government was determined to get through the crisis without declaring a disaster and was hoping to manage the story in such a way that it wouldn't appear to be totally dependent on the outside world. The leaders knew that if television reports got out, there would be no way to deny how bad things were.

Tony went to the embassy every two weeks asking for visas until finally, in September, we got them. We knew it was going to be a rough trip. There had been talk of typhoid breaking out. We knew we had to really be ready for this one. We had just come out of a stream of difficult stories: we'd been in Beirut, covering war stories, catastrophe stories. We were already pretty worn down. I remember saying to the crew, "We're really going to have to get fit for this one, live healthy and try to stay healthy, because it's going to be a torturous assignment."

I prepared by reading all I could about famines and what causes them. The regime was still refusing to call it a famine. The outside world hadn't declared it a famine. But in the eyes of the aid agencies it sure as hell was. I spent at least two to three weeks thinking about Ethiopia all the time, worrying about it and fretting that we were going to be too late to make a difference.

The BBC was ahead of us by about a week, but they had only a single-entry visa, good for just a few days. For some unexplained reason we were given multi-entry visas that were good for three months. That's why when the BBC went into the famine zone they were in and out and they weren't allowed back in. Aid agencies told us the famine was getting worse by the day, so I knew there was still a story to tell.

We got on the plane in London with a crew and flew all night. I don't sleep on airplanes so I had been dreaming during the flight of just landing and getting to a hotel for some sleep. But at the airport in Addis Ababa, the capital of Ethiopia, Tony said, "I just managed to arrange a flight on a World Vision plane going to the north. We can get on it."

It was very difficult to get up to the north, so of course we jumped at this opportunity. Instead of getting into the comfortable bed I was dreaming of, we scrambled onto another plane and off we went.

We flew over what looked like an environmental holocaust. I don't use that term lightly, but it was a human catastrophe beyond imagining, just as the Holocaust was a human genocide beyond imagining. I associated the Holocaust with black and white newsreels of concentration camps like Auschwitz. When we flew over northern Ethiopia what struck me was the monotone colour of everything—beige and brown. Everything was beige and brown. It was deforested. There were dust storms. Mini-cyclones. It looked like a moonscape, only beige and brown rather than grey and black. You could see that, Holy God, something had really gone wrong here. I thought I was watching a corner of the end of the world.

It was the first time I had ever seen the consequences of a massive drought. The famine was caused by war and incompetence, but it was also true that drought had seared northern Ethiopia for several years. It looked like a totally blasted country. When the plane started its descent we were flying low enough to see along the roads. I could see long lines of small black dots. These were people. I found out later they'd typically been walking along the roads for two or three days to try to get to a feeding centre. It was a hair-raising thing to see.

When the plane landed we headed for Korem. That's the place—a small town with a feeding centre—that the BBC had called "the worst hell on earth." We got there too late at night to go to the camp right away. We weren't allowed to travel at night for fear of the rebels fighting the government. Several foreigners had already been kidnapped. We didn't fear for our lives. We didn't think the rebels would kill us if they kidnapped us, but we thought they'd like to have a TV crew reporting on the war from their side. So we had no doubt the possibility of being taken was real.

We booked into a hotel where a room cost $1.20 a night. I hadn't slept now for more than a full day, and I got very little sleep that night. I kept hearing weird sounds all night long—like barnyard animals of some kind, but I couldn't distinguish the animals. It was only in the morning, when we were finally let out of our rooms, that I saw the source of the noise. I saw this long line of shapes on the road and realized there was an endless, endless line of people lying or huddling or waiting on the road for some kind of help. They were exhausted, no longer in possession of the ability to walk. They were groaning or calling out. It was an inhuman sound that I will never ever forget.

The feeding centre was about a mile away. We arrived at first light. We looked around and found ourselves alone—just our CBC crew—in the middle of eighty thousand people. There was nobody else. There were no health workers, no aid workers, no police, no guards. The aid workers weren't allowed out of their quarters until well into the morning. They were afraid the rebels could come through at any moment and snatch them away.

So we started to film. We filmed and we filmed and filmed. Thousands of people in bare, thin, beige or grey rags. Gaunt. You might expect eighty thousand people to be very loud, but all I could really hear was coughing. The prevailing sound was coughing. We went into the barracks just as gravediggers started coming around to pick up the dead bodies. Pick one up here. Pick one up there. They were all over.

The gravediggers carried the bodies to a mortuary that was basically a giant green tent. We walked into the tent and there were long lines of bodies being washed and prepared for burial. By that stage a hundred people were dying every day.

You don't associate Ethiopia with cold, but it was so cold, really cold. The wind was howling. I knelt down beside some kids and adults and I looked into the camera and said, "People are not only dying of hunger, but they're freezing during the night. I'm wearing three layers of clothes right now and I'm very cold. But all through the night people have been trying to get through wearing bare rags."

I did another stand-up at the end to get across the thought that as incredibly awful and horrible as these pictures are, this might not be the worst of the famine, only the beginning of it. It seemed clear that the amount of food getting through to the starving wasn't nearly enough to prevent what looked likely to become millions of deaths. That was the message we tacked onto the first item.

Then we left Korem and went to Makelle. It had been the epicentre of the famine when the BBC was there, but now things were worse. Another hundred thousand people had poured in. There were several camps, all of them filled with people. We started filming right away. We got incredible interviews with nuns and nurses saying that people were dying because they were just too tired to go on. These are the kinds of interviews you get only a few times in your career—absolutely appropriate to the moment.

We said to ourselves that we couldn't stay in the field any longer. We had to get the story out. We thought that every day it didn't get to the world was a day lost.

So we raced back to Addis Ababa. I told the news desk in Toronto, "We have material the likes of which you have never seen before in your lives. We have stuff that nobody has ever seen."

I had had only a couple of hours' sleep over the last three nights, but still I could hardly sleep that night. I was driven by the fact that the story couldn't wait. I knew I had to write the story quickly so it could be edited and then taken out of the country to be put on a satellite to Canada.

Tony Burman had arranged for a videotape editor from London to fly in and he was in the hotel when we arrived. He stayed up all night watching every second of footage we had. When I woke up I opened my old portable typewriter. It's the only script I ever wrote that I didn't rewrite, rewrite, rewrite. I'm an obsessive rewriter. But this just completely wrote itself. Everything fell into place. Our cameraman, Philippe Billard, had captured the most vivid images not only of that famine but of any modern famine ever. And the editor, Colin Dean, in an incredibly short space of time picked exactly the right pictures—bang, bang, bang. (Having seen all the terrible images, Colin couldn't sleep for days. He was a wreck.)

Now it was up to Tony. He raced to the airport with the tapes and saw that Ethiopian customs people were very carefully searching the bags of everybody leaving. We had both said this was the biggest story we were ever going to work on, so we had to do whatever we could to get the story out and on air. Lives were literally at stake. So he went to the washroom and taped the cassettes to his back. He smuggled the tapes out of the country by walking right through Ethiopian airport customs security.

When he got to Nairobi, he made the satellite feed, and the story was in Canada. It was November 1, 1984.

None of us ever realized the effect the story would have. It ran for about four minutes at the top of that night's *National*, and it just had an explosive effect, a volcanic effect on Canada.

Our anchor, Peter Mansbridge, called me to tell me that people watching in the studio were in tears. Years later I talked to Brian Mulroney about it. He had been prime minister for less than a month and a half. He told me he'd been sitting with his family at 24 Sussex Drive and every one of them had burst into tears. First thing next morning he called Stephen Lewis, who was heading off to New York to give his maiden speech as our ambassador to the United Nations. Mulroney said, "Did you happen to see *The National* last night?"

Lewis said, "I did, Prime Minister. And I hope you're going to ask me to do what I think you are going to ask me to do."

Mulroney said, "Yes. Go alert the whole world."

Lewis gave a dramatic speech to the General Assembly about what he had seen on Canada's national newscast. And he demanded that the world get involved. Mulroney began to lobby the White House and 10 Downing Street. He said, "I don't care that it's a Marxist regime. I don't give a damn. We've got to get in there."

And in Canada—in communities all over the country— churches, schools, businesses started to raise money.

We just continued to work. We went back to the camps and shot more and more. We stayed for weeks.

We spent some time in a camp that was under siege by hyenas. They had already killed all the animals in the countryside and now they were starving. So they started attacking humans. I saw a woman whose body had been eaten by hyenas. I saw a kid who came in with his hand bitten off by hyenas. I heard the shrieks of people who were trying to run away from hyenas. The nurses were utterly distraught at this sound. That was the kind of horror my brain had not been at all prepared for.

We went to back to Makelle. We had been filming funerals that were going on all over the place. Out of the corner of my eye I saw a father with a young child, a small girl. The girl just slumped over and collapsed beside the building. I shouted out to one of the nuns, "Quick, quick! Someone's collapsed here. We have to help her."

One of the nurses ran over to the girl, picked her up, ran her inside and put her on a table. She was gasping, really gasping horribly. I went in with the cameraman, who started recording.

The nurse said, "She's not going to make it, I'm afraid. She's dying. She's too far gone. She'll die within a few minutes."

I was totally stricken. I said we should at least give her the dignity of some privacy as she died. So we went back outside. I was very shaken. We still had a lot to do elsewhere that day, so Tony and I agreed that we would leave and try to come back later for her funeral. They were preparing her gravesite as we left.

We drove off and all day long we talked about what an awful scene it had been. The face of that girl was really haunting. She looked like the image of an entire nation. A child dying for want of care.

We went back expecting to see a funeral, but instead as we drove in the nuns waved at us, and one of them came toward us with this little bundle in her arms. She said, "Here she is."

I couldn't believe my eyes. Was this the same girl? And of course it was. They had stuck a needle in her, and to everyone's amazement she had rallied and come back. I was looking at the girl whose funeral I had come to cover. How often is that going to happen in a reporter's lifetime? I did that story, the story of Birhan Woldu, and it was run by television networks all around the world.

Two weeks later we went back to the camp just as she was leaving with her father. We got a brief shot of them as they disappeared into a howling dust storm outside.

Four years later I really wanted to find out what had happened to that girl. So we flew to northern Ethiopia in 1988 and we went looking for her. I thought there was little chance of finding her, but in fact we found her in a day and a half. We drove out to where we were told she lived and we did a documentary on her called *Life after Death*, in which I tried to show that she had healed and she was well.

The family had an incredible story. They had been forced down to the south where people had died by the thousands.

Her sister had died there. Her father decided that if his family was going to live they had to escape. So he picked up his two daughters in his arms and walked something like 1,000 kilometres back to the north.

I established a relationship with Birhan and her family. I paid for her education and for her siblings' as well. She's married now, the mother of two children.

When I think back to those weeks in Ethiopia, I remember it as a trip that seemed to go on forever. I had seen pretty awful stuff before, but I always tried to shield myself from psychic scar tissue. I would look away from gruesome sights while the cameraman did his necessary work. In Ethiopia there was no looking away. There was desperation everywhere. It went on day after day. I wasn't prepared.

The Red Cross estimated that there were six or seven million people at risk of dying in the famine. In the end a million died. Still a tragic number, but it means five or six million lives were saved by the prompt action of the world.

It was journalism, reporting, and nothing else that had made the world aware. I knew that our pictures would bring a clarity and immediacy to the story right into living rooms. I've covered other big stories, history-making stories. But there were always other reporters there too. In Ethiopia, I felt the responsibility weighing heavily on my back. I think that's what kept all of us going when we were exhausted beyond endurance, sometimes depressed beyond endurance: that feeling of being at the right place at the right time to handle the biggest story of our careers.

Patrick Brown:
The King is Dead

PATRICK BROWN HAS COV-
ERED MANY MAJOR NEWS
EVENTS in remote corners of the
world, including the invasion of Lebanon in 1982 and the Gulf Wars in
1980, 1990 and 2003. At the CBC,
he was fearless in pursuing the news,
usually on his own, without a producer or camera operator, and was
often one of the first reporters to
arrive on the scene.

His first media job was with *Reader's Digest* in Montreal. He quickly
moved into broadcast media as an
editor with Radio Canada International, and then as a reporter with

Photo courtesy Patrick Brown

CBC Radio. He became a foreign correspondent in 1980, based first in London, then in Beijing, New Delhi, Bangkok and back in Beijing. He reported in English and French for radio and television.

He is a co-founder of Jilu.tv, which produces documentaries in China, and has published a memoir called *Butterfly Mind*. He left CBC News in 2008.

Patrick has covered so many major events over so many years, yet he remembers a story he covered early on. It was in August 1977, when Elvis Presley died of a heart attack.

Elvis Aaron Presley hardly needed his last two names. The King of Rock 'n' Roll was essentially one of the first one-name superstars in modern music. And his music was unlike anything that came before. It was rock 'n' roll. It was country. It was gospel. And it was accompanied by wildly gyrating hips that so alarmed 1950s North America that CBS censors demanded he be shot only from the waist up when he appeared on television. He had eighteen number-one singles, and is still one of the bestselling solo artists in the history of popular music.

By the 1970s he had changed dramatically from the early days. He was drug-addled and bloated, living life behind the gates of a palace called Graceland in Memphis, Tennessee, where he wandered around all night and slept all day. His death at the age of forty-two was related to his overuse of prescription drugs.

....

I was on the Jacques Cartier bridge in Montreal, driving back to the newsroom from a news conference of no consequence, listening I confess to a rival radio station, when I heard the news. Elvis was gone! I nearly drove off the bridge. I wasn't a big Elvis fan, but I had (and have) considerable appreciation for his position in the pantheon of rock 'n' roll. There is no doubt about that, but I wasn't obsessive about it.

I thought it would be great to cover his funeral, but I was just a local reporter at the time so I had to find a local angle if I was going to get there.

I soon discovered a group that called itself the Elvis Presley Appreciation Society of Quebec. And it was chartering an aircraft to go down to Memphis for the funeral. The opportunity was too much to turn down. I booked myself onto the flight. I did that even before any of my bosses approved the assignment. I didn't think they would reject the story. And I expected the flight would be full, so I made my move.

It was my first assignment outside Canada. It was also the first time I was in the middle of something really different and unexpected and something that had everybody's attention. Whether you liked Elvis or not, Elvis dying was a big deal.

On the morning of the funeral I got on the plane with maybe a hundred other people. A full load. It was a cross-section of Quebec society, mostly French Canadians. Some I talked to were going to the United States for the first time, for this slightly kitschy event.

Two passengers in particular grabbed my attention and made good radio. One guy, who was in his seventies, spent the whole time flying down to Memphis singing "I'm All Shook Up" at the top of his voice. The other star was the president of the Elvis Presley Appreciation Society of Quebec. Hard to believe, but he was deaf. I liked him because he was able to appreciate Elvis without the actual musical component. That had a kind of purity about it. He was into Elvis-ness as a whole entity, separate from the actual musical experience. That was kind of fun. I say he was deaf, but he might have been able to hear just a little bit. I managed to do an interview with him as he leaned in very close to me to catch what I was saying.

When we landed in Memphis I was keen to get on the air. My priority was to find a telephone (because we didn't have cellphones back then). Everyone else on the flight piled onto buses to continue on to the funeral but I had to find a phone. So I peeled away, found a phone and did a report. Then I made my way to Graceland.

I was with the crowd as the casket went by. It was easy to find people who had something to say to a reporter. There was a kind of soap opera nature to the Elvis thing. People showed genuine theatrical grief. Men and women from all over went to Memphis to be there for the moment. Somehow celebrities—these great icons—touch people. Those thousands of people didn't know Elvis personally but they had a deep personal connection to him. He meant something to their lives, and their fandom and their love for him was a very big part of what made them who they were. I heard it all the time: "I'm an Elvis fan," "I love Elvis," "I love Elvis more than any other musician," "I love Elvis more than any other star."

I guess I thought there was something amusing or laughable about this—that there was a kind of irrationality about it—especially since Elvis in his later years had become a parody of himself. But that had no place in my reporting. I could not assume that everybody in my audience had the same kind of attitude toward it and we could all have a good laugh together. Lots of people on the other side of the radio saw this as the funeral and the loss of an important figure in their lives. I would have been quite wrong to turn it into a big joke. I don't think we would want to turn anybody's funeral into a commentary on the absurdity of modern life. At the same time I wanted to give a sense of the unusualness of the people who came out of the woodwork to be in Memphis.

When the funeral ended I took a cab back to the airport and rejoined the Quebec group for the flight home. The atmosphere on board was pretty much the same as it was on the way down, amplified by the provision of free drinks on a charter flight. Elvis didn't draw people because of his great contribution to relieving the plight of the poor and downtrodden. He drew people because he was a great star with an oversized personality, unforgettable music and flamboyant dress. It wasn't a silent flight going home, reflecting on the loss to the world of a great man. It was a party atmosphere.

The Elvis story has always stuck in my mind. It was important to me. That's partly because of the spontaneity of everything and everyone. Nobody had been expecting Elvis to die. Therefore it had the same template as a lot of events that I was to cover later in my career, like Tiananmen Square, the fall of the Berlin Wall, everything that happened after 9/11, Afghanistan, and Iraq. Something dramatically new and unexpected happened. It's like the shake of the kaleidoscope. Nobody has a script for what they're going to tell you. Nobody has a spin. Nobody has a prepared position. The spontaneity in the people I was dealing with is what I always treasured. I think of it as being journalism of a pure kind. So much of our work is talking to people who have thought out extremely carefully what they're going to say and it doesn't necessarily reflect what they really feel. Whereas when Elvis died what people presented to me was largely what came into their head at the moment. There wasn't a roadmap for what was going to happen next. That's a dramatic experience for a journalist. For me, anyway.

Anna Maria Tremonti:

Siege in Mostar

Photo courtesy CBC

HENRY KISSINGER WALKED OUT OF AN INTERVIEW with Anna Maria Tremonti one day. Whether that was a highlight of her career or a lowlight is for history to determine. But we don't have to wait for history to declare with certainty that Anna Maria has had an impressively rich career.

It's a career that started at a radio station in New Glasgow, Nova Scotia. Anna Maria stayed in private radio in Ottawa, Fredericton and Halifax. Then she moved to CBC Radio, first in Fredericton and next in Edmonton. She switched to television in 1983 and was based in Edmonton,

Ottawa, Berlin, London, Jerusalem and Washington. She came back to Canada to be a host on *the fifth estate*. In 2002 she returned to her radio roots as the first host of *The Current*.

Soon after Yugoslavia fell apart, Anna Maria Tremonti was assigned to go there.

When Josip Broz Tito, the president-for-life of Yugoslavia, died in 1980, the six republics that made up the country were held together by the flimsiest of ties. By 1991 things couldn't hold together any longer. When Muslims and Croats in Bosnia and Herzegovina decided to hold a referendum on forming their own country, the Serb minority there—which was opposed to any new country—decided to boycott it. Without those No votes, the referendum approved independence by an overwhelming margin, which led in time to war between Serbs and Bosnians.

That war was especially savage. It's unknown how many people were killed, but the best estimate is around 100,000. On top of that the Serbs engaged in ethnic cleansing and mass rapes that led to war crimes trials. And there were two long sieges—civilians helplessly trapped, first in Sarajevo, the capital of Bosnia and Herzegovina, and then in the southern city of Mostar.

....

When I went to Sarajevo in June of 1992, it was all new to me. I had done nothing like this. We landed at the Serb-held airport, and started down a road controlled by Bosnians into the city. It was basically an invitation to get shot at the whole way. We were in a van with six or seven jerry cans of gasoline. Every time we came to a checkpoint we'd lose a can as the price of getting through. Sarajevo was a city under siege. The Serbs were in the hills around it with snipers. There was a lot of mortar fire. Had we been hit by a shell or by gunfire, we would have gone up in flames.

The first night I was there we stayed in what amounted to a garage behind the Sarajevo television communications building. We slept on sleeping bags on the floor as all kinds of stuff flew through the air.

The next day we met a Serbian radio guy and he started working with us. He showed us where the snipers were and to avoid them we drove at lightning speed to the Holiday Inn. It was completely bombed out in the front, but the walls were still standing and I could put my satellite phone out a window and file a story. My hotel room was full of bullet holes. The bed was against the wall. The first night I couldn't sleep because I kept thinking something could easily come through that wall—bullets, grenades, artillery shells—so I decided I would sleep in the hallway. I thought that would be safer. I took my sleeping bag and a pillow and my flak jacket into the hallway. But then I looked around and saw there was glass along the walls and I thought if something hit that I would get sprayed with glass and badly cut. So I decided to sleep in the bathroom, a room with no exterior walls. I thought I would sleep with my head near the toilet, which was on the far wall, but I saw the sink on the other wall and thought if a rocket or a shell hit us, the sink would come flying across and that would get me. So finally I just said, "To hell with it," and went back into the bed. I remember saying to myself, "You asked for this." I was a foreign correspondent and I had seen other foreign correspondents covering wars and I thought it was important to cover this one. I wanted to do it.

I was there for about ten days and after that I lobbied hard to keep going back into the country. Which is why I was in Mostar about a year and a half later. I knew there were stories there. I felt we needed to get in. This was the war in microcosm.

I arranged the trip with a correspondent from ABC Austra-
lia named Max Uechtritz. Our networks would share costs.
So there was a CBC cameraman, Louis DeGuise, and an ABC
soundman.

Mostar was completely surrounded at the time. The Croats
were on one side of the Neretva River and controlled all the
roads into the city. The Bosnian Muslims were on the other
side of the river, completely enclosed. Mostar was even more
cut off than Sarajevo had been.

We started in Medjugorje, a town about 25 kilometres from
Mostar, and tried to figure out how to get in. We thought we
would talk our way past the Croat checkpoints. There were
three checkpoints. The first was run by the United Nations.
And we were immediately turned back. They weren't going to
let us get anywhere near Mostar. So I went to see the UN people
and found a retired British general was in charge, working to
bring in aid.

I said, "Look, we think you're doing worthwhile things in
Mostar. There's a story there to do but if we can't get in, we're
going to leave. So can you help us get in?"

He said, "Yes, I can help you. But you're going to have to
come in my vehicle."

So that's what we did. He had a boxy little minivan that had
no windows and we sat in there with some UN workers. We got
through the first Croat checkpoint and then there was only one
more to go. Just before we got to it the general said, "If there's
shooting, just get out and jump into a ditch by the side of the
road. If there's shooting it's going to get ugly. But just sit there
until it stops."

There was no shooting when we got there, but the guard
opened the door of the vehicle and I thought, "Great. They're
going to tell us to get out. They're not going to let us go through."

Instead the guards started to give us parcels. They were basically care packages for people on the inside. They were labelled with people's names and addresses on them. These Croats were trying to help out people who used to be their neighbours. We put the packages on our laps and on the floor. The guards didn't care that we were journalists. They just let us through as long as we promised to deliver the packages.

When we got to the city, the general introduced us to a woman he said might be able to give us a place to stay. She had a little bit of room in her house, but not much. We all slept in the same room. There was no bathroom. We literally peed in the garden. We worked from there as our base and to get around we either hitched rides or we just walked.

For whatever reason, we hit on a relatively quiet time in Mostar. There was no massive bombardment while we were there. Still, I could hear explosions and some shooting, and people were jittery. We were walking around in our flak jackets and our helmets.

We were trying to be careful. We asked a lot of questions—"Can we go here?" "Can we go there?" "Where's the danger?" We didn't stay anywhere for very long. We'd go out for twenty minutes and then scurry back into a building.

We took pictures everywhere we went and just started talking to people. There was a lot of devastation. There was a lot of rubble. It was grey. It looked ominous. There were places that were bombed out. There were streets that had walls and doors more than they had buildings. We went to a high-rise apartment where everybody was living in the basement because they were so afraid of more bombardment. It just wasn't safe to stay above ground.

They had a bit of light and an electric cord that went to a little TV. So when they had electricity—and that was hit and miss—they watched the news to see what was going on. They were literally living like rats in a cellar because they were afraid to come up. They never knew what was going to happen. If they did come out, they ran. If they needed water, they'd hurry to put water in jugs and get back. They didn't wander. They didn't loiter. They didn't stroll. They knew there were soldiers in the hills who could see them, and soldiers across the river who could see them. And everybody looking at them had guns.

People lived in fear. They ripped up anything they could to get firewood. They were rationing their food. They had nothing. All they could do was wait it out. They were really trapped.

I was trying to put together stories to show what it was like in that place.

We found our way to a medical facility. It was a clinic that had been turned into a hospital. It was really not much more than a room with several beds. It wasn't a proper hospital. The real hospital was on the other side of the river, so they had no access to it.

The doctors had only rudimentary supplies. When we got there a man was lying on a table. His leg had been injured earlier but now it had become infected. The doctors were operating as two nurses held candles to provide light. We had a flashlight so Max ended up holding that, shining it onto the man's leg so the doctors could see what they were doing.

We met a woman at the clinic who told us a terrible story. She had a son, but he could never go outside because it was just too dangerous. But at one point it had been quiet for two days so she let her boy out to play with his cousin. Suddenly a mortar landed, killed the cousin and put shrapnel in her son's brain. He was in the clinic with shrapnel still lodged in his head, and she was there staying with him.

Another time we were walking down a street and we ducked into a little place. It was completely dark. We heard a woman's voice calling to us from the basement. I looked down and the first thing I saw was a hand coming up—a bony little hand. It was an old woman—about eighty years old, I thought, although people aged quickly so she might have been younger. We gave her some candles. She wanted to make us coffee but we wouldn't let her. We figured she had so little of everything we didn't want her to give any of it to us. But it made me think that here was someone being so kind and so generous in such awful circumstances. Even today I still see that hand coming up from the little dark space.

Being in that place at that time I understood the reality of living in a war. The inequality. The instinct of people to survive. The randomness of the whole thing. You're standing in the wrong place and poof! You're gone. Or you have shrapnel in your head. People could have looked at us and said, "What the hell are you doing here?"

But instead they said, "Please come in."

They had nothing, but they offered us everything. It was impossible not to marvel at the kindness and generosity of those people.

These were victims of war. But they weren't one-dimensional victims. I saw them as people caught in a terrible moment in time. I heard about their lives before the war, which of course were so normal. But their world got smaller. There were good days and bad days, good hours and bad hours. I felt I was seeing something that I really had to tell. I needed to show how they lived. I felt really privileged that I got to see it.

I was the kind of correspondent who was interested in political decisions and the effect those decisions had on ordinary people. I don't need pictures on my wall showing me with world leaders. That's not the journalism I want to do. I need to talk to regular people who live through the consequences of what the leaders decide.

Lots of reporters do the stories that go down in history, and I did them too. It's great to be part of the big story. But it's the little stories that other reporters aren't doing that have always mattered more to me. You can find out about the big stories anyway. But the people in Mostar—not a lot of Canadian journalists were telling their story. In fact, at that point I don't think any others were.

Dan Bjarnason:
Under the Sea

DAN BJARNASON TOOK A TRIP TO CUBA IN 1963 when he was still in university. He wrote a photo essay for the now-defunct wire service UPI. That piece caught the attention of the now-defunct *Toronto Telegram* (is there a pattern developing?) and he had himself a job. He worked in Regina for a while, then came back to Toronto for CBC News.

Since then he's been based on Parliament Hill, Winnipeg, London and back in Toronto. He's covered wars from Rhodesia to Lebanon, and his interest in military history has taken him from Little Bighorn, Montana to Batoche, Saskatchewan, and from Vimy Ridge, France, to El Alamein, Egypt. He is the author of a book called *Triumph at Kapyong*, about a major Canadian contribution to the Korean War.

In 2001, he went on an underwater assignment.

Just before the twentieth century became the twenty-first, Canada decided to buy four used submarines from Britain. The price was right—that is to say, low—because the British were going nuclear and had no place for diesel-powered vessels. Several years were spent refitting and upgrading the boats to Canadian specifications. And then, one by one, they made their way under the Atlantic Ocean to Canada. We can now safely say the submarines were no bargain. At one point, all four subs were out of commission at the same time. One ship caught fire on its maiden voyage and a man was killed.

But in October 2001, when HMCS *Windsor* (the British had called it *Unicorn*) started its trip from Barrow-in-Furness, England, to Halifax, optimism was the order of the day. The sub carried its regular crew, plus two civilians: cameraman Brian Kelly and reporter Dan Bjarnason.

....

When I was in high school I was in the air cadets and in what they called the high school militia. When I went to university I went to a program called the COTP—the Canadian Officer Training Plan. But that's as far as my military career went.

Thirty-eight years later, a producer called me and said he had made an arrangement with the navy to get our cameras where no camera had gone before. The navy had agreed to allow a reporter and cameraman aboard a submarine they were bringing over from Britain. He asked if I wanted to go.

I've always been interested in submarines and in military history. But I'm claustrophobic. A submarine didn't sound like the best place for me, but I thought it was a once-in-a-lifetime opportunity.

The navy's idea was to have the submarine leave England. Then when it was about four days out from Halifax they would put me and my cameraman into a helicopter, fly us over the Atlantic, get the submarine to surface, and then lower us onto the deck in a basket or by rope ladder or something. Then we would cover the last four days of the voyage. I thought, "Gee, I don't know. Getting down to a submarine in the middle of the Atlantic as the waves roll it around—there must be a simpler way. Why don't we just go over there and get on the submarine when it sails and do the whole trip from beginning to end?" Happily, the navy agreed.

When we got to the submarine base, they took us onto *Windsor*, where we were introduced to the captain and the executive officer. They were polite. They weren't lovey-dovey, but they were polite. Submariners in the navy call themselves the silent service. They don't like outsiders. And they certainly weren't hot on the idea of journalists. So there was a certain reluctance—not hostility, but reluctance—on the part of the crew to having journalists on a ride-along. The coolness vanished quite quickly, but it was there at the beginning. Once we got rolling, after about two days, it was as if we were part of the crew.

We signed a document that basically said if anything happened to us, our widows couldn't sue the navy. They didn't give us any formal safety training. I just decided I would do whatever they told us to do. They told us about the safety hatches. But the sub would have had to go down in about four feet of water for these escape hatches to have done any good. Everybody was pretty realistic about what would happen if the sub got into trouble. So for me it was pretty much, "Do as you're told. Don't panic. Stand aside."

I was free to ask questions and to talk to anybody. If a crewman wanted to talk he was free to. If he didn't want to talk, I was supposed to leave him alone. And we could take pictures of almost anything we saw. One exception was the code room. That's the most secret part of the boat. Remember, this was right after 9/11 and who knew what the sub could be called upon to do. We weren't allowed to go into the code room and we weren't allowed to talk to the men who worked there about their code-room duties. I found that understandable. The submarine's only real defence is its ability to hide. Giving away codes could help an enemy track the sub's position. So I found the restriction perfectly reasonable. In the end, the navy never asked to see our tape. They took us at our word that we would abide by our agreement.

We were on the surface for the first day and a half. Then it was time to submerge. I had been thinking about this moment for about two or three weeks. "Oh my God, they're actually going to submerge." I wanted to think about anything but my claustrophobia. Before I stepped onto the submarine I told myself that if worse came to worst they would just have to bring that helicopter out to take me off. But there was a medic on board and now I was trying to take comfort in what he had told me at the outset.

I had asked him, "What's the plan if someone goes funny down there?" He said, "Well, there is a plan. We have a restraining board. We strap the man into that. Then we knock him out with an injection." Then came the comforting part. "But don't worry about it," he said. "It won't happen to someone like you. It will probably happen to someone who's been doing this for thirty years. They get up one morning and they decide they just can't do it anymore."

As they took the submarine down, everybody was really quiet. Everybody had to focus. The helmsman was reading out the depth as they went down. "Two hundred metres." The captain acknowledged every report. "Two hundred metres, aye."

"Three hundred metres."

"Three hundred metres, aye."

A short time before this trip a Russian submarine called the *Kursk* exploded under water and lost all its crew—more than a hundred men. That was on everybody's mind as we got deeper and deeper. As we went through the depth where the *Kursk* was lost, we all just looked at one other. There was total silence. In my notepad, I was writing the depth levels we were reaching. I thought if something happened and we all died, they might find my notebook when the submarine was recovered, and my record could be helpful in determining at what point we had run into trouble.

There's a lot going on when a submarine dives. It's a complicated procedure and it's got to be very tightly controlled. The crew has to be unbelievably well trained. Everybody's got to know what everybody else is doing. You can hear water flowing back and forth. There's creaking as the metal is compressing. The ocean is actually squeezing the boat. So there's that outside pressure that compounds the psychological pressure of a dive.

When we finally reached our planned depth every department checked in with a status report. I kept hearing things like, "Engine room: no new leaks. Torpedo bay: no new leaks." And I was thinking, "No *new* leaks?"

I soon discovered that leaks were going to be quite an issue. There was a leak, for example, where the periscope entered the submarine. There was water dripping. So they rigged up a garden hose with duct tape and the garden hose ended up in a bucket. That's how they dealt with things. There was a problem so they fixed it with whatever they had on board.

We had to surface one day because they discovered an emergency signal system had jammed. Nobody knew why. As they stood looking at it, on a rocking submarine in the middle of the

Atlantic Ocean with no land in sight, along came a crewman carrying a hockey stick. He poked around with it and he fixed the jam. We could never figure out why there was a hockey stick on the submarine in the first place. But that was the kind of initiative that was expected.

That was the only time we surfaced in two weeks. The rest of the time we were under water, completely isolated. An astronaut sees more than people in submarines. The sub could receive messages from a naval base somewhere, but for the ordinary crew member there was no outside world. No internet. No telephone. No newspaper. No radio. No television. Nothing. There were no clouds or birds. No sunrise or sunset. There was no point in wearing a watch. If you wanted to, you could keep track of dates and time, but most of the guys thought there was just no point to it. You slept when you were sleepy. You ate when you were hungry. When the trip began I thought, "Two weeks. How will I survive?" But one day just kind of flowed into another. I guess that's how convicts get through long prison sentences: they don't think about what day it is.

There is no such thing as extra room on a submarine. The captain had his own little cabin. It was about the size of a phone booth. The crew slept in bunks that were almost unimaginably small. If you wanted to turn over you had to get out, do your turning while out, and then get back in. If you were lying on your back on the bottom bunk, the guy above you was about three inches from your face.

I didn't sleep in one of those bunks. There were no torpedoes on the sub for this trip, so I slept in one of the bays where a torpedo ordinarily would have sat before it was rolled into a firing tube. The space was extremely cramped. There was no privacy. Everything was a little damp. There was constant gurgling because there was water flowing all through the submarine as they kept it both buoyant and stable. Oddly enough, I didn't sleep badly.

But I did have to play a mind game to relax and to deal with the claustrophobic thoughts that would creep into my head. What I did was make myself believe that if I just walked down the hall and turned left I would be in a Saskatchewan wheat field. There'd be blue skies and white clouds and I could just go down there for a breath of fresh air. It sounds goofy, but it worked.

I think the navy understands that it can't allow the crew to become bored. A bored crew would become lax. And the consequences of that could be fatal. The danger is constant on a submarine—it never goes away. Night or day there is no moment when the ocean stops trying to kill you. And fire is the most terrifying thing that can happen to a submerged submarine, so there were fire drills seemingly all the time.

If you're thinking about the fire drills you went through in school, think again. The drills on the boat were so intense that it was impossible not to think there really was a fire. There was so much noise. Clanging and more clanging. Everybody put on an oxygen mask. It's very hot inside. And they waste not a second. If they don't get on top of a fire in under two minutes it'll start using up all the oxygen on the boat. People need oxygen, of course, but the engines also need oxygen. If you lose your engines you lose your hydraulic system and you lose control of everything. You can't steer, dive, surface. You can't do anything. The smoke would be so thick you couldn't see. And it would be poisonous smoke. So they have got to get on top of a fire right away. And nobody slacked off. It was actually quite frightening to go through a drill.

When we reached Halifax, there was no formal goodbye. Everyone on the crew was happy to be home. I took my tapes and a few weeks later we aired our documentary. The navy brass didn't like it. They thought we showed too many things going wrong. I said, "You guys are nuts. We showed your men as heroes, well trained, extremely professional."

On the other hand, the crew and their families were delighted with it. The guys were especially delighted that their families got to see what they did. They thought that it portrayed the difficulties and the perils they lived with.

It was an unbelievably exciting and unique experience for me. There had never been a Canadian journalist who had done what I did. Journalists had gone on subs in dock or perhaps taken a trip around the harbour, but nothing like this. Even if I joined the navy, the chances of my ending up on a submarine would be small. I can remember almost every moment of that two-week trip. When I'm in my rocking chair at the old folks' home, I'll be thinking about this story.

Joy Malbon:
Fall of the Berlin Wall

Photo courtesy CTV News

DURING THE 2004 FEDERAL ELECTION, Joy Malbon drove back and forth across Canada in a CTV motorhome dubbed The Election Express. It was as if she were retracing the path of her early career. She had worked in a lot of places. After brief stints at *The Globe and Mail* in Toronto and the *Calgary Herald*, she got her first real job at a radio station in Simcoe, Ontario, as a reporter and news reader. From there she moved to another Ontario radio job, in Cambridge.

Her first TV work was in Kitchener, and the next in Sault Ste.

Marie. There were two CBC jobs—in Edmonton, followed by Windsor. Then she worked for Global TV in Toronto. CTV hired her to be its bureau chief in Winnipeg and that network never let her go. She has been based in Halifax, Toronto, London, Ottawa and Washington.

As the Berlin Wall was coming down, Global News sent Joy Malbon to cover the story.

The wall stood for 10,316 days. It was the physical manifestation of the Cold War. Berlin had been divided after World War II, so that the Western half was controlled by the United States, Britain and France, and the Eastern half by the Soviet Union. Between 1949 and 1961 nearly three million people moved from East to West. Many were young and skilled doctors, teachers, engineers, scientists.

In 1961, from June through August 11, a total of 65,000 people moved across the border. On August 12 alone, another 2,400 moved—the largest defection on a single day. The East German government was embarrassed and faced an unsustainable future. That night, the Soviet Union gave the East Germans permission to erect a wall at the border immediately. It was more than 150 kilometres long, and it was ugly. East German soldiers patrolled day and night. Anyone making a dash for it had to deal with trip-wire machine guns, floodlights and vicious dogs.

On November 9, 1989, an East German government official suddenly announced at a news conference that all travel restrictions between East and West were lifted. It appears he didn't really mean to say what he did. But his words touched off a joyous march to the wall by thousands of people who began taking sledgehammers to the barrier.

Like everyone else in Canada, I saw the amazing pictures from Berlin—the people dancing on the wall, hammering away at the wall, drinking champagne on the wall. All very interesting, but I didn't think it had anything to do with my job. I was a kid really, a reporter in Toronto covering local news. I was in the newsroom when my news editor came up to me and said, "Hey, how would you like to go to Germany and cover the fall of the Berlin Wall?" I don't know why he picked me. I had never been overseas on a story before. I'd never done any foreign reporting. But of course I jumped at the chance.

I was teamed up with a cameraman who had been an army brat and had lived in West Germany at some point in his life. He said he knew a bit of the language, but it didn't take long to discover that he couldn't speak much German at all. About all he could do in German was order a Big Mac. I guess it meant we weren't going to starve, but beyond that his language skills weren't very useful.

I felt the butterflies in my stomach. I asked myself, "Can I do this?" But I never said that out loud.

I had no plan when we got off the airplane. Nobody back in Toronto was giving us any direction about where to go or who to talk to. These were the days before the internet, Facebook, Twitter, where you can find people in a flash. I didn't have any local contacts. We were really just two stupid kids, trying to find a story. My orders were to come up with a story every day. No excuse was going to be good enough if I failed to do that.

Our hotel was close to Potsdamer Platz in the centre of Berlin. I heard, maybe from a cab driver, that they were going to take down one of the sections of the wall there. We got up at three o'clock in the morning to check it out. I still remember that I was either so excited or so nervous that I forgot to put socks on. I just had running shoes on and it was cold.

Sure enough, when we got to the wall there were people everywhere. They had champagne and beer and the mood was joyful. On the other side of the wall, a big bulldozer was ready to push down one section at a time. Everyone counted down, "Ten, nine, eight …" and then the bulldozer took a run at the wall. But nothing happened. So it backed up and tried again. "Ten, nine eight …" And again nothing. There was a guy there with a beard who had a bottle of champagne and he would take a sip now and then. He came up to me and with his mangled English explained, "What do you expect from East German machinery?" It went on for hours. But people were just so happy they didn't care. It was like New Year's Eve. "Ten, nine, eight …" over and over again. Finally, a piece of the wall came down to loud cheering.

The big American networks had built big platforms in front of the wall. They had three or four cameras up there and were broadcasting their morning shows and evening newscasts back home live. I skulked around like a little criminal and when their guests came down after appearing on American TV, I would grab some of them. I would just say, "I'm Joy Malbon with Global News in Canada" and they were happy to talk to me.

That's how I found Norbert Shultz. He told his story on American TV and then he started talking to me. As a kid he'd lived in West Berlin, right near the border with the East. So he had lots of friends on the other side. He had watched them build the wall. He told me how he'd been separated from classmates that he never saw again. He was saddened by how families had been separated. But now, as a grown man, he was watching the wall come down. He was so excited. He said, "Come back to my house." So again that's how I stumbled into a story.

He lived literally right beside the wall. He had old photos of classmates. He was going through them, saying, "I never saw him again … I never saw her again … They split us apart …" People were coming across from the East and he was greeting them. "Come in. Come in. You are my family. You are my friends. We haven't seen you in so long." Tears were streaming down his face. He was so expressive. It was impossible not to like him.

So I was finding stories, but then we ran into another

problem. We had an old camera with us. It seemed to weigh about 500 tons. When a sprocket broke we needed to fix it fast. We saw a store that repaired Sony equipment. But they were used to small home-video cameras. They said they could fix our camera but it would take a whole day. So now we had no camera. My mind was racing. "I've got to get a story every day. I cannot fail. I must find a story today."

We walked over to a place where relatives were being reunited from East and West. And there was Tom Brokaw, the anchor of NBC news. Everybody was really happy. It was such an exhilarating atmosphere. Just exuberance. Brokaw and his crew were interviewing East Germans and West Germans, relatives who had never seen each other before. When he finished, I'm not quite sure how but we struck up a conversation. Basically, I poured my little heart out and said, "Our camera broke. We can't do anything." And he said to me, "Use mine then. I'm finished with my camera crew. You use them." I was so grateful and wasted no time. I used the NBC crew, shot some reunions, and there was another story for me.

That wasn't the last favour from NBC. One day I was hanging around their platform at the wall and saw they weren't broadcasting so I hollered up, "Hey, can I use your position to do a stand-up? It'll take maybe five minutes." A cameraman looked at his watch. "Sure," he said. "Our anchor isn't going to be here for a bit. Come on up." I started climbing and I remember thinking that I was afraid I was going to forget what I wanted to say because so many American network cameramen were going to be watching me. But, in fact, I got it right on the first take. And that was the money shot. Right in front of the wall.

When the assignment was finished I'm not sure the magnitude of what I had witnessed sank in right away. I had been so afraid to fail; it was that fear that overwhelmed everything else. But looking back, I realize that's when I caught the bug. I decided right then and there that I wanted to be a foreign correspondent. I was really young. I didn't know what I was doing. I had covered Guelph City Council and things like that, but nothing like this kind of major world event. It taught me that in every story people really matter. The wall physically came down and we saw that, but what stayed with me were the Germans and their happiness.

Paul Hunter:

Boston

Marathon

Bombing

Photo courtesy CBC

IN PAUL HUNTER'S FIRST JOB, IN WINGHAM, ONTARIO, he was a TV reporter, radio reporter, cameraman, tape editor, assignment editor, lineup editor and anchor—once all on the same day. Young journalists today, much more familiar with the concept of multi-tasking, may wonder why he didn't also feed the newsroom cat and scrub the toilets, but he certainly would have had anyone asked. He is very talented.

He took his talents to CBC News in 1985 and has since worked in Saskatoon, Toronto, London, Calgary,

Ottawa and Washington. He covered the Haiti earthquake, Japanese tsunami, Newtown school shootings, war in Gaza and Afghanistan, the Blue Jays' first World Series win, and two American and three Canadian elections.

Paul Hunter was based in Washington at the time of the Boston Marathon bombing. Still, he had to scurry to be in the right country to cover the story.

Running a marathon has become sport since the days in Greek legend when Pheidippides is said to have run from the plains of Marathon to Athens. Pheidippides delivered the news that the Greek army had defeated the Persian army, and then collapsed and died. Occasionally a runner dies in a modern race and that is recorded as tragedy. At the 2013 Boston Marathon, death was recorded as terrorism. Two bombs exploded near the finish line. Three people who had been watching and cheering were killed. Another 260 people were hurt, including sixteen who lost legs.

Nothing even remotely approaching that level of horror had happened in the 116 previous Boston Marathons, dating back to 1897. The attack triggered a massive police response. Within four days, two brothers who had lived in the United States for about ten years were identified as the bombers; one was killed after a shootout with police, the other was wounded and arrested after hiding in a boat in a suburban backyard.

....

When the bombs went off I was in an edit suite in the CBC building in Toronto, editing a documentary about education in the United States. My cellphone was turned down low so I wouldn't be disturbed. I didn't know that the newsroom was looking for me. No one had any idea where I was in the building and they couldn't find me until I left the suite and ran into someone on the way to the bathroom. That's when they said, "Have you heard what's going on in Boston?"

I had the same first reaction as everyone else, which was, "Holy shit!" followed immediately by, "What a drag. I've come up to Toronto to edit a documentary on education and now I'm going to miss this big story." But everyone agreed to let me put the documentary on hold and get down to Boston first thing the next morning.

I got off the plane before breakfast and walked into a city that was in a state of stunned disbelief. The look on every face was as if people had been kicked in the gut. It was as if nobody could accept what had happened, or understand what had happened, or believe what had happened.

By then I'd lived in the United States for six years. Living in Canada, you think you know Americans. You grow up watching them on TV, seeing them in the movies, visiting them. But you don't really know them until you live with them. They are the most outgoing, the friendliest, warmest, most generous people I've ever met. They will talk to you on street corners, in the elevator, in the subway. They will invite you over to dinner having just met you. But when I landed in Boston that day there was none of that. It was people walking around in silence, with their eyes down. The blood had drained from their faces. It was a contradiction of what the marathon is all about—it's about cheering, excitement, happiness, fun. For this attack to happen there was horrific.

My assignment was to find stories beyond the news of the day. We had other reporters who would concentrate on that. I was supposed to find fresh angles away from the big spotlight. The first day I found some Canadians who had been running in the marathon and I talked to them. That worked well. But what happened late the next day said a lot about Boston.

It was two days after the bombing, and there was a hockey game between the Bruins and the Buffalo Sabres in the evening. It was the first major sporting event since the marathon. I went to the TD Garden, where the security was insane. Everybody got patted down on the way in. There was some speculation earlier that day that nobody would show up for the game. After all, if they were going to bomb a marathon who knew what might happen at a hockey rink? Instead it was packed. Everybody came out because it was important for them to say "Boston Strong," the phrase that became ubiquitous that week. So the arena was jammed.

I was standing in the press box as it was almost time for the game to begin, and I was thinking about my deadline approaching. I thought that maybe I should get downstairs to our trailer behind the building and start editing. But I knew that if I waited another eight minutes, which is a precious eight minutes at that time of night, I could see with my own eyes the national anthem being sung. I thought, "It might be something, it might not be something, but I wouldn't mind watching it." So I stuck around for those precious eight minutes. The lights went down and the anthem singer came out and sang the first few words, and as I'm describing this even now I'm getting shivers up and down my back. He stopped singing, held out the microphone to pick up the crowd, and those thousands of people belted out the national anthem. My eyes filled with tears. It was so incredible, so emotional. Boston was saying that it could be knocked down but it would stand up again. We're here and we're not going to let this define us or change our lives. We are here tonight and we're going to be here tomorrow too. That was my story that night.

I was in something of a panic the next day, wondering what story I could put together. I hung out a bit on Boylston Street, where the bombs had exploded, talking to first responders and firefighters at a fire station, but nothing was really jumping out as great television. That was the day the police released pictures of the suspects, though, so there was plenty of news.

When I finished working that night I went back to the hotel and my crew and I were all watching television when we saw the news of the shootout that day. A police officer at the Massachusetts Institute of Technology had run into the suspects and they had killed him. A little later the bombers hijacked a car and led the police on a wild chase, throwing explosives out the window, and eventually stopping to shoot it out on Laurel Street in the suburb of Watertown.

We thought about going out but decided it was pointless because everything was moving so fast and we would never catch up. So we made a decision not to go out, but to set our alarms for very early and see where things stood when we woke up.

We all got up at three in the morning. By now, one of the bomber brothers was dead but the other was still on the loose. Just about every reporter and camera crew in Boston had gone to Watertown, where a media centre had been set up in a shopping mall parking lot. So we thought, "We don't want to go there. Let's go around to the other side of the town." So that's what we did.

As we were driving I noticed that there was nobody else on the streets. It was early in the morning, but it was still striking that nobody was around. Just freaky. We saw a police car, so we decided to follow it, and we found ourselves just two blocks from where the shootout had been. There were only three or four other journalists there. We parked ourselves and kept expecting the police to tell us to get out, but they didn't. In fact, they parked a car a couple of blocks behind us so no one else could get as close. It was 5 AM and I was inside the police lines.

That day I saw more police and tactical units and soldiers and guns than I had seen since Afghanistan. Every available officer in the region had shown up to be part of the manhunt, with their gear and their vehicles. Some of them came by the busload, with big guns and wearing bulletproof vests. There were snipers on the rooftops, helicopters in the air. It was tense, and it was intense. The guys with their guns had a job to do. They were fine with us hanging out there but if you got in their way you kind of knew we didn't really matter that much. At one point an NBC cameraman lifted up the tail door of his van and pulled out a tripod. In my hostile environment training I'd been told that from a distance a tripod can look like a weapon. *[CBC News, like most major networks, sends its people to be taught how to handle themselves when covering wars and disasters. The training is intense and covers things like how to avoid being shot but what to do if you are, how to avoid being kidnapped but what to do if you are, and how to survive if you're separated from your crew and friendly combatants.]* Sure enough, the snipers on the roof of the car dealership 100 metres away started shouting at the cameraman, "Get down on the ground! Drop that!" They trained their rifles on him until they were sure he wasn't a threat. So I knew I always had to be careful. I was in a place where a lot of people had powerful guns and fingers were on triggers.

Another thing we learn at hostile environment training is never to forget that you're not in Kansas anymore. When you're in Afghanistan or in the Gaza Strip, you're in a dangerous place. It's not like anything you've ever done or seen in your life and you shouldn't forget that. You need to think twice before you take a step out onto the street because it might be your last step. In a war zone things are so unfamiliar that it's easy for that kind of advice to stay with you. But you don't expect to be thinking that way in Boston. It looks just like home.

At one point there was a kerfuffle at a car dealership or car repair shop. A Honda was parked there—and one of the cars the brothers had used the night before was a Honda Civic. For some reason word spread that maybe the missing brother was in it. So everybody started running down there. Suddenly there was a mini-panic because people started shouting, "Sniper! Bomb!" Someone actually yelled right at me, "Paul, there's a bomb!" And even though I'd had all that training about how to react to bomb threats, there I was—instead of running away from it, I was running down the road to get a closer look. Good thing it was another false alarm.

Late in the afternoon I had a story to put together, so we came out from our spot inside the police line and joined the media pack at the press centre. When the news went on the air that night, the second brother had been located and while I was doing a live report, he was arrested. Right behind me cheers erupted and cars were going up and down the street with people waving flags and chanting, "USA! USA!"

I had been up since 3 AM and I got to bed that night at about 1 AM, so it had been a long day. But we all got up the next morning pretty early again and started thinking about the next story we could do. We really had no idea what it might be. We had an interview lined up with the Watertown police chief. We drove out there but the chief backed out on us. I said to the producer that I wouldn't mind taking a look at Laurel Street just to see where all the shooting went on when the first brother was killed. I said, "Let's just go have a look before we go back to our hotel and tell the assignment desk in Toronto that we don't have a story." It was the gawker tourist in me.

Laurel Street was perfect American suburbia—white clapboard houses, white picket fences. When we got there everybody was out on their front porches, in their driveways, on the sidewalks, like it was the 4th of July. They were in a picnic and partying festive mood. They all wanted to talk and show me the bullet holes in their fences and cars and tell me what they'd heard and what they'd seen out their windows as they huddled with their babies. This was classic Americana too. Americans love to tell stories. And they are so welcoming to people like me who come to record their stories and tell them to other people.

Nobody turned me away. Everybody told me, "Come on up. Get closer. Let me tell you what it was like. Look at this bullet hole. Look at where the shrapnel hit." It was out of Hollywood. There really had been guys shooting at each other from one end of the street to the other end of the street.

We spent an hour and a half recording nonstop. These were people at the centre of what was at that time the biggest story in the world, yet we were the only television crew there, which was totally surprising. I kept wondering, "Where is everybody else?" I was waiting for CBS and NBC and CNN to show up. But nobody did. They did in subsequent days. But on the day after the shootout, we were it. And we came away with a fantastic story of a crazy night in the life of a city.

It was all very satisfying. One of the reasons I got into journalism is a selfish reason: I thought it would give me the chance to see important events around the world with my own eyes. I thought that would be fascinating and interesting. The other reason I got into this business was to tell stories about the things that I might see, and tell them my way—perhaps without poetry, but also without jargon. I just like to tell stories straight-ahead. Here's what happened; here's why it mattered; here's some context for you. I felt I achieved both my goals that week in Boston.

The magic of TV isn't the same as it may have been in the 1960s. Back then, just being on TV was enough. That isn't enough anymore. Today, everybody's going to hear about a big story on any channel they choose. So you have to find a way to make your version of the story the one that matters. I think I achieved that in Boston.

Hana Gartner:
Solitary
Confinement

Photo courtesy CBC

HOLLYWOOD ACTORS, WE ARE TOLD, LIVE WITH THE FEAR of being typecast. They make such convincing cab drivers or warm-hearted teachers that they worry they will never be given juicier roles as rock stars or evil genius villains. Well, nobody ever typecast Hana Gartner. Throughout her journalism career, she played every role smash-ingly well.

She did radio in Montreal, then TV. When she moved to Toronto she started as the host of a variety/

current affairs program, then became the host of the afternoon talk show *Take 30*. In 1982 she joined CBC's *fifth estate* and for thirty years—with a little time out to co-host a small program called *The National*—she chased prime ministers and contract killers, investigated everything from polygamy to airport security, and became a master at skewering the corrupt and the inept. She retired in 2011.

It was the work of Hana Gartner and her colleagues at *the fifth estate* that in 2010 brought to light the sordid secret of how a nineteen-year-old had ended up dead in a federal penitentiary three years earlier.

We would all like to believe that the story of Ashley Smith comes from a dark age, long past—from a time when a fifteen-year-old girl could commit a minor crime and be thrown into a Kafkaesque nightmare of a justice and penal system from which there would be no waking. But no, the story of Ashley Smith is from our time. To our shame.

In 2013 a coroner's inquest found that Ashley's death was a homicide.

....

Part of the job is constantly trolling for stories, trying to find something that resonates with me and will resonate with the public. I was going through the newspapers one day. I think it was a year after Ashley Smith died. There was a little announcement that Ashley's family was going to sue the government of Canada and the Correctional Service. It was just a paragraph or two. It said a nineteen-year-old girl in solitary confinement had strangled herself while she was on suicide watch—watched by seven guards who were videotaping. I read it three times and thought, "This is very interesting."

We're conditioned to ask ourselves about the other side of the story. But I thought, "What the hell other side can there be?" So I started to look into it. I was so excited I didn't even write up a proposal. I grabbed one of my favourite producers and a researcher, and yammered at them as I do, and dragged them into the executive producer's office. And I sold him on the idea.

We started calling people right away. We got all kinds of information. We were getting confidential documents, anonymous tips, independent reports, but no one wanted to talk to us on camera. There had been plenty of conflict between guards and the Correctional Service—disagreements about how to handle difficult inmates—but every time one of their formal arbitration fights was settled, a gag order was imposed. So no one would talk—not nurses, guards, Correctional Service staff, wardens. There was a total information shutdown. We were blocked.

The only thing that we had in the beginning was exclusive access to Coralee Smith, Ashley's mother. I went to interview her in Moncton, New Brunswick. That was very hard. I was trying to be fair, and trying to be balanced, and trying not to be an advocate. I didn't want to do a bleeding heart piece. But I understood right away that it was a two-pronged story. It was about what happened to a girl who started her road to incarceration at the age of fifteen and was sent to juvenile detention. It was also about a system—and this is what was making me crazy, that this was a government agency supported by tax money, and we were being shut out in the most ham-fisted way.

As I prepared for the interview with Coralee Smith I thought, "Everyone wants to blame the mother." There were signs this was a troubled kid from the time she was thirteen. So my first inclination was, "Yes, all these institutions failed her, but what about her parents? Where were they?" I pushed her a little bit and it was very difficult and painful for her. It was still very raw.

She basically said, and it was very eloquent: "I accept my

part of the blame. What I need is the school psychologist, the justice system, the detention system, the youth detention centre, the psychiatrists who were supposed to see her, the system that was supposed to help her, the system that promised me they would help her, I want to know why they let her down."

In the interview she asked how a nineteen-year-old girl could mature normally when she'd spent her time in isolation from the age of fifteen. She said Ashley may have gone in as a fifteen-year-old who was troubled, but the prison system drove her to mental illness. She wanted to know how a girl dies on a concrete floor, strangling herself, while cameras are capturing it and seven guards come in and go out. She agonized over the fact that the guards spent so much time contemplating what rules they might be breaking if they took the ligature off from around Ashley's neck. Meanwhile Ashley is turning blue. And by the time they finally cut off the ligature it's too late. She's dead.

I don't think I was ever so exhausted as when I was asking such horrible questions of this mother whose child had died in such a tragic, violent, ugly way. We had an instant rapport, and when it was over she said I would be the only reporter she would talk to.

Of course we knew there was a videotape of what had happened to Ashley. We became determined to get it, but it would be a two-year fight with the Correctional Service to make that tape public, to expose the truth. And it was a dirty fight by the other side.

Our argument in court wasn't trail-blazing. We weren't asking for new laws. We were standing up for a principle that needed to be honoured, not just in theory but in practice —the principle of an open court. And finally the court agreed that the media represent the Canadian public and they should have access to whatever exhibits exist. In this case, that was the videotape of Ashley's death.

The first time we watched the tape was the worst time. We just sat there. We sat there in silence. It was just horrible. It's a horrible thing to sit and watch, in real time, somebody die. Of course we didn't watch it just once. Sitting in an edit suite, endlessly watching Ashley Smith over and over and over again, I think it just got to me. I was a mother with children around the same age. It was easy to understand Ashley's death intellectually—yeah, this is terrible. But when you see the tragedy unfold, and you see the guards' response to her, it just takes your breath away. And we could all understand now why the Correctional Service wanted the truth withheld.

That's why getting that videotape was so important. We originally thought Ashley was a kid who fell between the cracks, because that's the line the Correctional Service was giving us. But the tape was a huge indictment of this whole institution. The story was about justice, about the law, the media, about what the public is permitted to know and see.

Most people have a bias about prisoners. The prejudice is that you're in prison only if you did something wrong. They get what they deserve. But here was a girl sentenced to one month in a juvenile facility for throwing crabapples at a letter carrier. Because she was defiant they kept her in seclusion, isolation, without human contact for almost four years. You don't have to be a psychiatrist to know that you keep anybody, even a healthy person, in seclusion and isolation twenty-four hours a day for four years, and they're going to go out of their mind. This was inhumane. It was torture. That's why that videotape was so effective.

We had long discussions about our own ethics. What do we show? How much do we show? How much is beyond what the public should see or needs to see? What about Ashley's dignity?

It was terribly important to me that everything we showed was approved by Coralee Smith. She was determined: "I want the public to see how my daughter died and I want them to ask who gave the order not to go in and save her life. Who gave the order not to go into her cell if she is still breathing?"

The Correctional Service never agreed to answer that question, or to answer any of our questions in an on-camera interview. But a former guard and someone from the guards' union did sit down with me. And I was tough on them. I'm sure they thought I was unfair. But I had to ask, "How do you stand outside a cell watching a nineteen-year-old strangle herself?" Their answers showed that their priority was for their own safety. Perhaps this girl was setting a trap for seven guards. And since they had been ordered not to go into Ashley's cell as long as she was breathing, they feared for their jobs if they went in too soon.

What was also revealing, though, was what they said about the system. They lamented the fact that the psychiatrists would go home at the end of the day and the guards were left with the problem of dealing with these people. They were not psychiatrists or psychologists. So the only thing they could do to secure these people was to confine them, or get someone on the phone to authorize an injection that would immobilize them. They were fairly eloquent in describing their lack of resources trying to deal with somebody like Ashley.

I don't think there has ever been a story that has affected me so profoundly. There was never a story I was more emotionally invested in. I am proud of the work we did and the difficult road we travelled to put it all together. Coralee Smith said, "Hana, there wouldn't have been a coroner's inquest without you. The public wouldn't know about Ashley."

But the inquest made the same kinds of recommendations we've heard before. And I think there's a danger people will just move on, and think of Ashley as yesterday's news.

[The coroner's jury made twenty-eight recommendations, but the government rejected most of them, including the recommendation that indefinite solitary confinement be abolished. The government said the practice could not be abolished "without causing undue risk to the safe management of the federal correctional system."]

Ashley was the victim of a homicide, and where's the accountability? The Correctional Service of Canada broke the law. They failed to do everything they should have. They didn't follow their own rules. They didn't review her placement, which is against the law. They failed to care for her, which is against the law. But they have never been held to account. That's what frustrates me. I wanted them to have to answer for this.

Joe Schlesinger:
Ping-Pong
Diplomacy

SOMETIMES JOURNALISTS GET CARRIED AWAY in describing someone who may be famous or important. It's common to inflate the résumé of the subject of a profile. But that's quite impossible with Joe Schlesinger. He's done it all. Wars, revolutions, natural disasters, politics—the nonstop carousel of news. And he's done it around the world.

His first paying job as a journalist was in Prague in 1948 with the Associated Press news agency. He came to Canada in 1950, where his first jobs were in construction. But before long he was at the University

Photo courtesy CBC

of British Columbia, editing the campus newspaper and working part-time for the *Vancouver Sun*.

He would also work at the *Vancouver Province* and the *Toronto Star*, and in Europe again for United Press International in London and the European edition of the *New York Herald Tribune* in Paris. But his true journalistic home was CBC News. He was the executive producer of *The National* for a time, but when he hit the road, he really made his mark. He was based in Hong Kong, Paris, Berlin and Washington. Then he was the CBC's chief political correspondent in Ottawa. His memoir is called *Time Zones*.

Joe Schlesinger received a surprise phone call in 1971. The reason was probably because Canada was one of the few Western countries that recognized the People's Republic as the legitimate government of China, rather than the regime based on the small island of Taiwan.

At the time, the People's Republic of China was better known in the West as Red China. Red as in communist. More than 800 million people lived there, but they were almost completely cut off from the rest of the world. That's how the Chinese leadership wanted it. It was just about the end of the Cultural Revolution—a time when Mao Zedong (written as Mao Tse-tung back then) purged all of his opposition, real and imagined. Hundreds of thousands of people, perhaps even millions of people, were killed.

....

It was October of 1970 when I arrived in Hong Kong, the new correspondent for the CBC. It was a British Crown colony, and we had a bureau there because there were stories to tell from there. And it was also a place where you had good access to the war in Vietnam.

At that time China was completely closed off. There were a few Western correspondents in Beijing *[called Peking in those days]*, but they couldn't go anywhere or do anything. So we did our best from Hong Kong to decipher what was going on in China. But our best wasn't really very good.

All the foreign correspondents in Hong Kong wanted to go to China. We did all we could do to get there. We sent letters to the foreign ministry in Beijing. And we lobbied the people who worked for Xinhua in Hong Kong. That was the Chinese news agency that also acted as a representative of the Chinese government. We lobbied them by eating with them. We'd go to restaurants and have fine meals, and we'd make our best case for being allowed to go to China and do some reporting. The Chinese would never say no. But they never said yes. I had some wonderful meals, but all the eating never led to a visa. This went on month after month.

Then one day in April of 1971, out of the blue, I got a phone call. The voice on the other end said he was from the official China Travel Agency and he asked, "How would you like to cover a Ping-Pong tournament in Beijing?"

I didn't know anything about a Ping-Pong tournament in Beijing, but I said, "Of course I would like to. Where should I go to apply for a visa?"

"Oh, don't bother with a visa. Just show up at the train station at such-and-such a time, tomorrow morning."

I had no idea what the Chinese were up to. I had *no* idea. I should have had an idea. I should have known something was brewing. But I didn't question it. They offered me a chance to go to China, so I took it.

The next morning I showed up at the train station with my cameraman. There were a few other reporters, but I was the only one from Canadian TV. And off we went. We were going to cover Ping-Pong games between China, the United States, Canada and some European countries. The surprises kept piling up. The Chinese had invited American Ping-Pong players. That took some getting used to. They would be the first Americans invited in since 1949!

We crossed the bridge into China and it was like another world. There were bicycles everywhere. Loudspeakers told the workers of the world to unite. And they played two, only two, patriotic songs. Very loudly. Everybody wore the Mao uniform—tunic and pants. Everyone also had a medal on their chest, a medal with a picture of Mao. And they all carried "The Little Red Book" filled with the thoughts of Chairman Mao. It was just so proletarian. It was a country mobilized in pursuit of the ideals of now. Anything old was useless. Intellectuals had been sent to the countryside to work on farms because all intellectual life was banned. Confucius? To hell with Confucius. To hell with Chinese tradition. Everything was Mao.

The country had virtually no tourism. And that showed in the hotel they put us in—it was very primitive. There wasn't even a flush toilet.

One of the things you noticed immediately at the Ping-Pong tournament was that the Chinese, who were world champions and far superior to the Americans and Canadians they were playing, still managed to lose games. No one could explain it. There was something fishy going on. The answer soon became apparent: the Chinese had been told to lose. It was supposed to be a sign of friendship.

Apparently China had hinted before that it wanted better relations with the United States, but the Americans and Henry Kissinger [President Richard Nixon's national security adviser] had missed the hints. So this time, the Chinese took no chances. No more subtlety.

There was a grand reception for the table-tennis players and we journalists at the Great Hall of the People. Premier Zhou Enlai [Chou En-lai] made small talk for a while. Then he went to a microphone and talked about how the American people and the Chinese people should be friends. He said it was time for the governments of the two countries to warm up to each other. The message was quite clear now.

I realized that I had to get out of the country. I would have liked to do more stories, but I couldn't just sit there. I had to get the story out. The Chinese tried to be helpful because they wanted the story to get out. But they didn't have the facilities. You couldn't send anything out of China. There were certainly no satellites going out. I had to take our film out of China by hand. We got on a flight from Beijing to Guangzhou [Canton] and then took a train to Hong Kong. And when I got to Hong Kong there was a helicopter waiting to take my footage to the lab to process.

I did four pieces. They ran not just on CBC, but also on CBS in the United States. After all, it was the Americans who were supposed to notice. And they did. Kissinger noticed. Nixon noticed. And the next thing you know there's a secret mission by Kissinger to China. And then of course Nixon accepted an invitation to visit China. It all became known as Ping-Pong diplomacy. It changed the history of China and changed the history of the world.

So here was a scoop just handed to me. But at least I knew what to do with it. Look, I covered all sorts of stories in a very long career. But this was so much more than just another story. I was one of the few journalists to take out of China a message that changed the world. To me that is mind-boggling.

Kevin Tibbles:

Swissair Crash

Photo courtesy Kevin Tibbles

KEVIN TIBBLES SHOWED EARLY
ON THAT HE HAS THE DOGGED
DETERMINATION you find in the
best of reporters. After graduating
from university, he auditioned for
a radio job in Toronto. The man
doing the interview concluded the
session by saying, "Well, I won't be
hiring you." Undeterred, he got a job
as a copy clerk at the CBC, running
around the newsroom doing everything that had to be done that was
beneath the dignity of a reporter or
a producer. He also lobbied to write

stories as often as he could and even do some reporting. A higher-up told him, "You'll never be a reporter."

That prediction can be filed right beside the prediction that Babe Ruth would never be a home-run hitter. Kevin was hired as a CBC reporter in Edmonton, then moved to Calgary and later Montreal. NBC came calling, and sent him to London. From there he travelled the world to cover war (Iraq, Bosnia, Kosovo, Afghanistan, Uganda, Rwanda) and peace (Northern Ireland, South Africa).

These days he's based in Chicago, where he has reported on weather, politics and, from time to time, goings-on in Canada. On the night that a Swissair flight started going down off the Maritimes, though, Kevin Tibbles was on the other side of the Atlantic Ocean, in London.

There are few places on the good earth more serene than Peggy's Cove, Nova Scotia. Its permanent population is about sixty, a number that swells every summer with tourists who come to see the picture-postcard lighthouse and the Atlantic crashing against a barrier of rocks. But just after 10 PM on the night of September 2, 1998, the tranquility was shattered. People who lived in the area heard a frightful noise in the dark sky. An airplane was obviously in trouble.

A few moments later there was a terrific thunderclap, unmistakable auditory evidence that the plane had crashed into the ocean. Swissair Flight 111 had taken off from New York, headed for Geneva with 229 people on board. All of them were killed. A painstaking investigation would take four and a half years to conclude that the cause of the crash was faulty wiring, which had started a fire and filled the cabin with smoke.

· ·

My telephone rang before dawn. It was the foreign editor at NBC in New York, who told me that a plane had gone down off the coast of Nova Scotia. He said, "We want you to get to Halifax as soon as possible."

I said, "You must know that Halifax is about an hour from New York and I'm in London." I was kind of scratching my head trying to think what was going on. He said to me, "Well, you're the only Canadian we have so we want you there. You speak their language." I'm almost sure he was speaking metaphorically. I don't think he was under the impression that the people of Nova Scotia spoke Gaelic and were unable to speak English.

I raced to Heathrow airport and caught the Concorde to New York. [*British Airways flew the Concorde, a plane that travelled at twice the speed of sound, from London to New York between 1976 and 2003. It crossed the Atlantic in about three and a half hours, as opposed to about eight hours for a subsonic flight.*] From New York I hopped onto a chartered plane with several other people from NBC and we were in Peggy's Cove just after lunchtime.

I had been to Peggy's Cove as a child. My family drove from Toronto like so many other Canadian families. I was in the back, lying across the back window most of the time. We didn't even think about seat belts back then. When we left on that trip my grandmother gave me a little travel diary in which I was supposed to write down the events of the day —where I stayed, what I did. That was my first introduction to journalism. I wrote religiously in that little diary all the way to Halifax and Peggy's Cove.

Now I was back for a horrible disaster. The circumstances were obviously terrible, but I was glad that I had been asked to cover the story.

NBC had sent satellite trucks from New York and from Boston. We had producers and camera crews on-site. Every television network in North America was there. By the time I arrived we were already setting up shop in a fisherman's hut. We rented one man's fish shack and we set up a little bureau right there on the water near his boat. We set up edit rooms and parked our satellite truck on the hill beside the shack.

It was about six hours from deadline when I got there. NBC had an aviation reporter, Robert Hager, who would do the nuts and bolts of what might have happened to the aircraft. My assignment, which is what I migrate to quite naturally, was to talk to people. I talked to the people who ran the little restaurant that's right on the water. I ended up renting the owner's work shed because he had the only telephone line that I could find. I did interviews with the local United Church minister, and fishing families. Everyone had a story to tell.

The one story that really sticks in my head is from one of the fishermen who lived on St. Margarets Bay. As I poked around Peggy's Cove I learned that a lot of people had gone out onto the water after hearing the plane crash. They went originally hoping to find survivors but soon realized that was a futile effort. I had been given the name of one fellow who, I was told, had found a body in the ocean. The first instinct is of course the newsman's instinct. Here's a guy who went out and found a body and you're driven by the newsier side of that information to go find him.

I didn't want to phone before I met him, so I got into a car with a producer and with the camera crew and just drove until we found where he lived. It was a bit off the road and as we drove down toward the house it was very obvious to anybody inside that strangers were coming to visit. It was a lovely yellow cottage. The fisherman's wife came out and said, "Can I help you?

And I said, "I'm looking for your husband. I heard he went out on his boat after the crash."

She said, "He's out on the water now. Would you like to wait?"

Of course we were offered tea and cookies while we waited. She told me her husband had been quite shaken by the events at sea.

After about forty-five minutes he came back. I didn't know

if he would talk to me because lots of times Canadians like to keep to themselves. But he was willing to talk so we sat down and did an interview—an interview that has stayed with me ever since. It was just one of the most powerful experiences I've ever had. So many people ask me, "Who was the most important person you ever talked to?" They're looking for me to name someone famous, and I could. That's why I don't talk about this interview very often. No one wants to hear this kind of answer.

This Nova Scotia fisherman couldn't have been more salt of the earth. I can still remember him saying to me that he heard the plane coming down. He heard something go over the house. He heard the plane go down. He knew that something really terrible had happened. He spoke to his wife about it and he said he was going to go out in his boat. And his wife said, "Are you sure? It's very dark right now." But he said that St. Margarets Bay was his backyard. He knew it as well as— maybe even better than—anyone else, so he wasn't afraid to go out in the dark.

I asked him why he would go out and he said he felt a duty. He had to go see if he could help anyone. And I said to him, "What do you mean 'help'? Surely you didn't think you'd find anyone alive."

He said, "No, I didn't think I would find anyone alive, but I had to keep going because I knew that I had to find someone."

"You had to find someone?"

"Yes."

"Why?"

"No one deserves to be out there alone in the sea. No one should be alone in death."

"Did you find someone?"

"Yes, I found a young girl."

Then he radioed for the Coast Guard and when they arrived he handed over the body.

I knew right away that he had said something that had

impacted me way deep down, beyond the calloused and cynical outer shell that I've created for myself because of the situations I go to. I started to cry. I'm not saying I never do that, but it's rare. It's rare when someone manages to penetrate me with his simplicity and stark honesty. He was struggling to answer my questions but he did his best because he probably thought that's what he was supposed to be doing. If I had been him and a reporter had shown up on my property, I probably would have thrown that reporter right off.

At that moment I felt such compassion for this fellow because I knew that he was not going to be able to overcome this for the rest of his life. I knew his life would never go back to what it used to be. I also felt very proud of him because he did what he thought was the decent thing to do as a human being. In many of the places that I've been I don't see a lot of that really happening.

For a journalist, when you're being shuffled from one crisis to the next, it's easy to become very hard and very disconnected from reality. I've found that one of the ways to remain sane is to seek out and latch onto children who are coping. I've done that in Afghanistan, Kosovo, Rwanda. They've grabbed hold of my heart and given me a sense of real purpose in what I do. On this day, a fisherman told me he had found a child in the water and I found it almost unbearable.

Susan Ormiston:

Afghanistan Corruption

Photo courtesy CBC

SUSAN ORMISTON HAS HAD BOTH AN INSIDE AND AN OUTSIDE CAREER. When she was inside, she anchored local newscasts and major network programs like *w5* on CTV and *the fifth estate* on CBC. When she was outside, she reported on the arrival of a royal baby, an assortment of wars, revolutions and disasters, and the biggest sporting events in the world—the Olympics in London and the World Cup in Brazil.

She started out in Saskatoon and over the years has been

based in Toronto, Halifax, back in Toronto, London and then back in Toronto again.

She was assigned to Afghanistan twice, and best remembers the first time—in 2007.

Between 2001 and 2014, more than forty thousand members of the Canadian Forces served in Afghanistan. At one point General Rick Hillier, chief of the defence staff, famously said their mission was to kill "detestable murderers and scumbags." Put more diplomatically, the mission was to support a democratic government in Afghanistan against attacks from al-Qaeda and the Taliban. The human cost to Canada was the deaths of 158 soldiers, 2 civilian contractors, 1 diplomat and 1 journalist.

Many fine reporters went to Afghanistan. Some stayed for just a few days. Some stayed for months at a time. Some went once. Some went multiple times. Most were embedded with Canadian troops because that made logistical sense. But the best reporters were always wary of reporting only what the authorities fed them. They always wanted to see for themselves.

My eyes were as big as saucers. We flew from Dubai on a private transport aircraft to Kandahar airfield. It was a fascinating trip. From the air I could see the vast desert and then Kandahar, which has more vegetation. I'm not a military reporter or a defence reporter. Everything was new for me. It was a university course packed into one month. Information just kept flooding in. I tried to absorb everything I saw, trying to add to what was then my limited knowledge of the geopolitics of Afghanistan and that part of the world. So it was exciting, even exhilarating.

I had done my homework before leaving Canada. I talked to a lot of other reporters who had been to Afghanistan. I made contacts within non-governmental organizations and the Canadian International Development Agency. I got briefings from the foreign affairs department. So I had spread my net widely, getting information and looking for story ideas.

The other thing I did before leaving Canada was to consider the danger I had volunteered to face. But I didn't think about it for too long. If you do that, you're going to talk yourself out of going pretty darn quick. The hardest part for me heading into a conflict zone is the night before I go. Back then my youngest was seven years old. I went into his bedroom the night before I left, and I looked at him and I thought, "Am I crazy? This is pretty risky. Is it fair?" All those things. But really you can't spend a lot of time focusing on that or else you won't go.

By the time I stepped on the plane I knew I had made the right decision. I was going to cover the biggest Canadian foreign story in a generation. The country was fighting a war, investing lives and money in a faraway land, something we had never done before in my lifetime. So for me it was a huge opportunity to seize the story, to go figure it out. I knew I had to report on what the military was doing, but I also wanted to report on everything else going on in that part of Afghanistan.

On that first day I was still pretty green, and jet-lagged, but everything started to happen very fast. A military public affairs officer picked me up and brought me to the media work tent. The CBC reporter I was replacing was going to leave on the same plane that brought me in, so there wasn't much time for a handover. It was, "Here's how this works. Here's how that works. Gotta go now. Good luck. And by the way, we've heard that there's been a Canadian casualty and we're waiting for more information."

Then she was gone and I sat down to try to figure out how to find out more about the soldier who'd been killed or injured somewhere out there in southern Afghanistan. I quickly realized that the public affairs officers were tight with their information and our deadlines didn't mean anything to them.

Most of the reporters who had been in Kandahar had, for various reasons, been confined to the base. Everyone called it "inside the wire." And that didn't interest me at all. I didn't want to sit in the work tent waiting for the public affairs officer to tell me what the military was doing that day. My objective was to get outside the wire. And I started doing that pretty quickly. This was a dynamic that the Canadian Forces hadn't dealt with much yet, and they were a little uncomfortable. I was embedded with the military, relying on them for food and shelter. But I wasn't in the military. So we were testing each other quite a bit on how we would work together.

When we went off base, I didn't formally tell anyone. I just told another reporter where I was going, and said, "If we're not back by five o'clock, send out the dogs." There was no use in asking the military for permission to go somewhere. I've always said, "Don't ask questions if you think you're going to get an answer you don't want."

We didn't have any security with us. It was just me and my cameraman, and a local fixer and a local driver. *[Foreign journalists hire fixers to help deal with local conditions. A fixer will know the local language and local customs, and will often have contacts in the government and bureaucracy.]* They would meet us at the gate of the base in their white Toyota van. We'd jump in and leave. I would always dress in Afghan clothing. I would wear a long black dress and headscarf, and sometimes I even wore a burka. It was the perfect cover for someone who looks like me. Under normal circumstances no one would mistake me for an Afghan woman. As long as I didn't have to speak I was okay. My fear was that someone would take issue with my driver or fixer and start asking me questions. And they would know immediately that I was a foreigner. We took the camera out as little as possible to disguise the fact that we were foreigners. We would hop out of the car, take our pictures and get right back in. Sometimes we had two minutes in the market to shoot my piece to camera and then get back in the car. In other areas we took the camera out for ten minutes, got our visuals and then drove away.

We put a lot of faith in our Afghan fixer and driver. I'd call them and tell them the story I wanted to do in the next few days. The fixer would then make some calls to his contacts and set us up with people we could talk to. But the two of them would often want to scope out the neighbourhood before we went. That would be the day before or even two days before. They needed to know what the atmosphere was. I learned very quickly that the ground truth changed every day, sometimes even every hour. I trusted my fixer and driver to tell me it would be too dangerous to go today—it may have been safe yesterday, but today it's too dangerous. Maybe there'd been an explosion or a prison break, or the fixer could have heard rumours of an impending Taliban attack. That would obviously change everything. Relaxed could become tense very fast.

About three weeks into my assignment I was getting tired. I was working every day, and because of the time zones, every day was like two days. When Canada was sleeping we were planning and shooting our stories. When Canada woke up, we'd go over scripts, do our editing and send our stories. So I was exhausted. But a group of Canadian parliamentarians had come to Kandahar and we had to cover them. They were confined mostly to inside the wire. And I remember thinking that they saw so little. They were coming to represent Canadians and to gather information they could relay to Parliament. They got great briefings but they didn't really see the war. And they knew it. One of them came up to me and said, "What's it like out there?" So here he was saying, "I can't get beyond the wire. You did. What's it like?"

We filed a story that night on the MPs. The next day was

supposed to be quiet. I always had a list of about six stories that I could pursue when nothing else was going on and one of them was on border security in Afghanistan, which was said to be very poor. Nothing dangerous was stopped at the border. Everything got in—drugs, guns, IEDs *[improvised explosive devices]* and Taliban. The only way to find out what was going on and why everything got in, was to get to the border. I asked the fixer, "Is that possible?"

He said, "Yes. We can drive to Spin Boldak. It's about an hour and a half from here."

I said, "Is it safe?"

He said, "Reasonably." So we arranged to go very early the next morning to avoid the heavy traffic. We were always aware that more people meant more danger.

I got to bed around 3 AM. I remember being in my cot thinking, "I can't do this. I am too tired." It's never good to go into a situation when you're tired. That's dodgy because you can't make good decisions and I just thought, "If I wake up tomorrow morning and it's pissing rain we're not going to go." But it wasn't raining at 6 AM. The cameraman was tired too, but he said, "Let's go." I would happily have crawled back into my sleeping bag. But duty called.

The fixer and driver were waiting for us at the gate. We piled into their car and I slept almost half the way because I was so tired. I was curled up in my black robe in the back with my scarves around my face. We headed south. Journalists weren't travelling around very much. The Taliban had really increased their presence in the area. The road was quite good because this border crossing was one of only two legal crossings between Pakistan and Afghanistan. That's why it was so strategically significant.

We got close to Spin Boldak and we could see it was a frontier town. It's a combination of medieval and somewhat modern. It was quite dank that day. It was cold and a little bit grey. We were ten miles from the border. We checked in with the border police. The commander set us up with his guys and we drove with them on the back of their truck with their guns out. By now it was about eight-thirty or nine o'clock in the morning.

We came upon a scene that rests in your imagination but that you doubt you'll ever actually see. It was complete chaos. The border was a couple of fence posts with a road that ran between them. There were border police checking documents, but I quickly understood why the border between Pakistan and Afghanistan was so porous. It was an artificial border. It really cut through a village. It wasn't like an international border where you're an American and I'm a Canadian. The Pashtu people lived in Kandahar and they lived on the other side of the border too, in Pakistan. They were one community. So it was no surprise that they had to go back and forth across the border all the time.

I had very little knowledge of all the history in the area. I was observing, talking to a few people, listening to my fixer. It was fascinating. And as a television reporter I was saying, "Oh my God, this is visually stunning. So many things to look at— trucks, donkey carts, people being wheeled across the border in wheelbarrows, a very primitive border patrol … I just knew this was going to be a great story. A story so few had seen. An important story because it talked about strategy and security. And I was there. The story became an illustration of why it's almost impossible to secure that border. There was not enough security to close it off. This was one of the holes in the defence of southern Afghanistan.

We were also able to see bribery and corruption at the border. We saw a big transport truck pull up. The driver hung his documents out the window. Then the border patrol guard motioned with his hand in a circle and the driver handed him some money. So we now knew bribes were part of the culture and we could illustrate it.

We stayed for about an hour and a half, probably longer than we should have. I just had to do a piece to camera before we left. I sat in the back of the car to do a very practical thing—put on my makeup. So there I was in the back of the Toyota, at the Pakistan–Afghanistan border, putting on my mascara and a little lipstick, and I had an audience. A group of little boys pressed their faces up against the backseat window, looking with big wide eyes at something they had probably never seen before. A blond putting on her makeup in a hurry.

When we finished at the crossing, we went back to the border police station. The commander, a man by the name of Abdul Raziq, invited us to stay for lunch. I thought that was a bit of a risky option but it was too tempting an option. We ate on a door that had been made into a table by propping it up on two smaller tables. Raziq sat at one end with armed guards standing behind him. We sat at the other end eating delicious lamb stew. The best lamb stew I've ever had. It was served on tin plates. I probably shouldn't have eaten it because of what it could have done to my system, but it was delicious.

The most interesting part of this was that Raziq was just twenty-nine years old. He was so young, very handsome, and had lots of charisma. He had grown up in this violent place. I learned later from my driver that there were persistent rumours that he had organized a mass killing of sixteen people just six months before. And here he was hosting us for lunch. I asked him about the bribes, and he said, "My men wouldn't dare take money." Which was complete bullshit. We had just seen it. In any case, it was just a fascinating look at this character who would later become the commander of the Kandahar police. He was an up-and-coming ally of US and NATO forces. Why? Because he had control of that border.

When we got back to Kandahar it was clear the military had concerns about where I had gone. The public affairs officer gave me a complete dressing-down. Where had we been? How did we get there? What did we think we were doing? We're going to have to talk about you roaming around Afghanistan. I said, "Yes, you're right. I'm sorry." But I wasn't prepared to go to Afghanistan and sit in an army base for six weeks. So we had to work things out. It's a simple thing. I have to go where things are happening. I have to be there. There is absolutely no way I can reasonably tell a story unless I am witnessing it. It's the essence of journalism.

Keith Boag:
Coalition Politics

KEITH BOAG HAS A PARTICU-
LAR FONDNESS FOR POLITICS.
He has covered seven Canadian
federal elections, ten leadership
conventions and two US presidential elections.

He's worked in television news
since he graduated from university.
He was a reporter in Ottawa, Kings-
ton and Moncton before he joined
CBC News in Fredericton in 1983.
Since then he's been based in Mon-
treal, Toronto, Vancouver, Cape
Town, Los Angeles and Washington.
The biggest chunk of his career has

Photo courtesy Jason Burles

been spent on Parliament Hill, where he was both a reporter and the bureau chief for CBC News.

He was the chief political correspondent for CBC News when the Canadian government made a decision that became the catalyst for historic and frantic manoeuvring in national politics.

October 14, 2008, was a federal election night in Canada. When all the votes had been counted, Prime Minister Stephen Harper and his Conservatives were the winners. But for the second consecutive election they had failed to win a majority of the seats in the House of Commons. The combined opposition of Liberals, New Democrats and the Bloc Québécois outnumbered the Conservatives 163 to 143.

The previous minority Conservative government had lasted more than two and a half years. There was no reason to think this minority would be any less stable. During this time, though, the entire Western world was close to panic because of a financial meltdown. There were real concerns that the global economy was going to implode. So just six weeks after the election, the Canadian government scheduled an economic update, a statement on how it planned to deal with the crisis.

....

It began for me on a Wednesday night. I was driving home from Parliament Hill when I got a call from an editor at *The National* in Toronto. She told me that there was a story making the rounds about the government's economic update that was coming out the next day. The story said the update was going to include a plan to eliminate public subsidies for political parties. And she asked, "Is that a big deal?"

I couldn't believe it. What that meant was that the Conservatives were going to introduce a measure to starve the opposition of cash. *[Since 2004 federal parties had received just over $2 a year for every vote they received in the previous election. It amounted to millions of dollars for every party.]* And they were going to do this at a time when they were running a minority government. That's just the kind of thing you don't do in a minority. You're supposed to play nice to keep the support of at least part of the opposition.

So I said, "That's a big deal all right."

I turned around, went back to the office, and we managed to put a short story on the newscast that said, "This is going to poison the atmosphere of this Parliament, which has been in session for only a week."

The next day we had the economic update, which made things even more difficult for the government. The grenade on party financing was in there. But there was nothing on the big question: What are you going to do as the country heads for recession? The prime minister had already gone on the record to say the situation was critical and it was time for stimulus spending, time to go into deficit. But the economic update had nothing. I thought that was incredibly unexpected.

By that night, I had sources in the opposition telling me they were talking about how they were going to stop the plan to end the system of public money supporting political parties. And one of the things they were thinking about was going to the governor general, Michaëlle Jean, and asking her to allow them to form the government.

The opposition said to itself that it couldn't force another election just six weeks after we'd had one. But it asked itself, "What can we do?" And one of the answers was, "We can try to form the government ourselves."

On Saturday, I ran into Kory Teneycke. He was the director of communications for the PMO [*Prime Minister's Office*], and he said, "We really fucked up. We never expected this was going to happen. And honest to God, we don't know what to do about it."

By Sunday, we found out that there was an agreement

among the opposition parties to form a government. The plan would make the Liberal leader prime minister and put some NDP members in cabinet. And the Bloc Québécois would support this. It wouldn't be part of the government, but it agreed to support the coalition.

The government then moved into high gear. They started getting their line of attack straight. They were going to attack the coalition for making a deal that included the Bloc Québécois. And that's when they started to misrepresent the truth. And they knew they were misrepresenting the truth. They knew there was a two-party coalition, supported by a third party. And they began to misrepresent that as a coalition of three parties, including the separatists, on the government side of the House, maybe even in the cabinet.

At this point it became very important for us to explain the reality. So whether Canadians liked the coalition or they didn't, they would have the facts to make a fair and honest judgment about it. They wouldn't get caught up in believing that this was somehow a coup d'état, which was what one cabinet minister called it.

I did a piece for *The National* that laid out the arrangement between the opposition parties. In detail. Who would be in cabinet. How many NDP. How many Liberals. Who would control the finance portfolio at this time of economic crisis. Where the Bloc Québécois would be in this. The story ran at the top of the broadcast. And it ran for four and a half minutes. Time is such a precious commodity in a TV newscast that most stories are the equivalent of a haiku. My story was a novel.

The government came up with the idea of asking the governor general to prorogue the House of Commons. That is, close the House down for a time so the opposition couldn't defeat the government on a motion of no confidence. Obviously, closing down Parliament just a week into a new session is practically unheard of. And with the global financial crisis going on, was this the best time to shut down the government? A reasonable question.

But once they came up with their prorogation plan, the Conservatives wanted to make sure that to the greatest extent possible, their rationale was heard. That went something like this: "We just had an election. The opposition parties are trying to take over the government. Stéphane Dion will become prime minister even though he's just been rejected by the country. And that is not the way Canada runs."

The government pounded home that message in every interview, every scrum, every chat with every reporter. Senior members of the government, including the prime minister, were saying things they knew were untrue. When cabinet minister John Baird said the Bloc Québécois was part of the coalition, and the Bloc would be sitting on the government side of the House, that was a lie.

Cabinet minister Jim Prentice said the opposition was doing something "irresponsible and undemocratic." That was a lie. The great fear the government had was that the opposition was not abusing democracy. They were in fact using the perfectly democratic means they had at their disposal.

Prime Minister Harper called the coalition plan "an undemocratic seizure of power." That was a lie. Who were they seizing power from? The PMO? Power doesn't really reside there when it comes to deciding who gets to form the government. Parliament has that power. And in this case, the majority in Parliament was ready to use that power. And the PMO was resisting that power.

This was one of those extraordinary times when you really had to say what was happening. There was no point in on-the-one-hand-on-the-other-hand journalism. It was too serious for that.

I thought the circumstances themselves were serious, but I continue to believe that when the government deliberately lies to you—doesn't spin to you, but lies to you, tells you black is white—then that's something you have to say out loud.

And we did.

It was something that had never happened in Canadian history before. And it required that you understood something about Canadian history to understand it was an important story. I'm not sure everyone got it in the first twenty-four hours. But we did. And we told our viewers it was important. We knew that all the opposition parties, particularly the Liberal party, saw the government's proposal *[to end their subsidy]* as an existential threat. And so the response to it was going to be extreme. They were going to do whatever it took to stop this.

Their motive was self-preservation, but they happened to be lucky enough to have all this happen in the midst of an economic crisis that the government was not responding to.

So all of these things made it complicated and dynamic and interesting, and those things appeal to me.

Every time we took to the air with another twist in the story, I remember feeling, "I'm ready for this. I know the context." I remember thinking, "There's nowhere I'd rather be." And that's a great feeling.

[The Conservatives persuaded the governor general to allow them to prorogue the House and so they survived. When the Conservatives won a majority government in 2011 they began chopping the public subsidy for political parties, and the subsidy was eliminated in 2015.]

Jeffrey Kofman:
End of a
President

JEFFREY KOFMAN'S CAREER IN JOURNALISM BEGAN in Stratford, Ontario. His first job was at the *Stratford Beacon Herald*. But after a summer of newspapering, he caught the television bug. He worked at Global TV and CBC in Toronto, with assignments taking him to London, Moscow and Washington. In 1997 he crossed the border to work for CBS News. He was based in New York until ABC hired him and moved him to Miami to be its correspondent for Florida, the Caribbean and Latin America. He reported from across the southern United States

Photo courtesy Jeffrey Kofman

and from Cuba, Colombia, the Dominican Republic, Haiti, Venezuela, Mexico, Bolivia, Ecuador—you get the picture. He's been based in London since 2013.

At some point he found time to handle five separate assignments in Iraq. On one trip he reported that some American troops were unhappy to be fighting there. The White House didn't comment directly on his report, but hinted that perhaps Kofman couldn't be trusted because he's a Canadian.

Among all his travels, it's the month that he spent reporting on the end of a rebellion in Haiti that is particularly poignant for him.

Haiti won its independence in 1804, but not without a fight. For thirteen terrible, blood-soaked years, slaves fought for their freedom. First they fought local plantation owners, then they fought the British, and finally the French. Sometimes revolutions based on the notion of freedom lead to democracy. Not in Haiti's case. For 186 years after independence, Haiti failed to hold even one democratic election.

When the first one was held in 1990, Jean-Bertrand Aristide—a former Roman Catholic priest, educated for a time in Montreal—became president. But he was overthrown by the military just eight months later. By 2000 democracy had been restored, at least nominally. Amid charges that Aristide had rigged elections for the Haitian senate a few months earlier, he ran unopposed for the presidency and started another term in office. But the serious grumbling about him never subsided, and by early 2004 an army of guerrilla rebels was marching to the Haitian capital, Port-au-Prince.

Of all the countries I've been to, including India, Pakistan and places in Africa, the most despairing is Haiti. Over the years it's given me sleepless nights. I've had a fair amount of exposure to rough places and danger, but nothing quite prepared me for Haiti. It was just a place that bumped along the bottom—a grinding existence.

We ran into trouble the day after we arrived. We heard there was going to be a demonstration a couple of miles from our hotel. We set out early in the morning, and even though it was so close it took us almost two hours to get there. Sure enough, we could see a demonstration a couple of hundred yards away. The crowd looked very angry. I told our driver to turn the car around and stay in the car with the engine running. I got out with my crew and I could see the mob getting more and more agitated.

Suddenly everyone was running toward us, throwing rocks. We ran for the car. The doors were open. The producer, the cameraman and I jumped in. The soundman, Rick, was struggling with the big boom microphone while he was running for the door. The mob was getting closer and our driver couldn't take it anymore. He put his foot down on the gas and drove off.

I yelled for him to stop but he wouldn't. He was shaking with fear. I looked behind us and I couldn't see Rick at all. All I could see was a Haitian guy being pushed into a car by another Haitian man who had a gun to his head. That car took off and in a few seconds it was right behind us. Our driver was monopolizing the road, not letting the car pass. I kept looking back and I could see one guy driving, a guy in the middle with a gun to his head and a third guy holding the gun. I kept telling our driver to stop. Finally he did, and the car passed us.

Then our driver just got out and walked away. He walked away.

We were absolutely terrified that something had happened to our soundman. We had no idea where we were. But the producer got into the driver's seat, turned the vehicle around and went back to where we'd last seen Rick. We didn't find him, but we found one of his running shoes lying in the road. I thought, "Oh my God."

By now the mob had disappeared and as we kept walking, there was Rick, smoking a cigarette, leaning against a tree. He had been smart enough to realize the crowd wasn't coming for him. It was coming for the guy who eventually got pushed into the car with a gun to his head. So Rick had just eased away and no one had even noticed him.

That's how our time in Haiti started. And then things began to deteriorate.

One day we wanted to go up to the front lines of the war. We knew the guerrillas had reached Gonaïves, so we started driving north. And what you see in Haiti as you're driving north is a barren landscape. It's like the hide of an elephant: just rugged and rocky, absolutely barren of life. Haiti, once a lush tropical paradise, has lost 98 percent of its trees. If you look at satellite images showing the border between the Dominican Republic and Haiti, you can actually see that on one side there's green jungle and on the Haiti side there is nothing. Because of the poverty in Haiti people have cut down trees to make fires for cooking or to get wood to build dwellings. There's been no successful effort to reforest, so the landscape of Haiti is essentially dead.

As we drove we came to a squalid little village called L'Estere. I remember seeing piles of scraps of lumber and people carrying lumber on their backs and on bicycles. They were scrounging for this lumber either to sell it or to build something. We went past a market area and I saw the most astonishing thing out of the car window. There were women standing in front of what seemed to be bags of charcoal. Maybe twenty women. And they were standing almost like players on a chessboard, as if they had been carved and placed there. They were standing in the hot midday sun wearing threadbare clothes. It was such a striking image. They were just standing there. We had to go and do our story so we just kept driving, but I made note of what I had seen.

When we arrived in Gonaïves we were swarmed by people on little motorcycles, ridiculously small mini-bikes with young males on them. We had to move really slowly so we wouldn't drive over any of them. We just wanted to make it into town and things were becoming increasingly claustrophobic.

We finally got to someone who said he was in charge. I told him we wanted to meet the guerrilla leader. There was a lot of back-and-forth negotiating and he said, "Okay this is the way it's going to work. We'll take you and your cameraman across the line. Everyone else stays here." The line was a series of shipping containers that blocked the road and there was an opening between them, perhaps ten feet wide. So they were proposing to take two of us on the backs of the ridiculously small mini-bikes through the opening. We were going to disappear on the other side, presumably get our interview, and if things went according to plan we would come out again.

I knew there was potentially a really good and important interview on the other side of the line, but I also knew that an American network TV journalist would be a very valuable person to hold for ransom. And these guys were very shady. I didn't trust them. There was no obvious chain of command. These were just guys with guns. It was getting very uncomfortable and very tense. Finally I just told them that we weren't allowed to separate our group, and they accepted that. We didn't get the leader, but I was still able to interview those guerrillas, take lots of pictures, do my reports to camera. We had a very strong story.

On the way back to Port-au-Prince we passed through the village of L'Estere again. I looked at my watch. We had time, so I said, "Let's stop here. I just want to find out what I'm seeing." I was just so curious about this very strange sight in the market—the women with the bags of charcoal. So the cameraman and I went over with the interpreter. And they were selling charcoal. It was a moment that just made me understand how life worked in a place so far from the realities that I grew up in.

I asked them what they were doing and how they made a living. They explained how they scavenged wood and turned it into charcoal. There was a market for it because charcoal burns more slowly than wood. You only need a little lump of charcoal to boil water, not a whole log. So that's what they were selling: lumps of charcoal for about two or three cents each. They were as poor as poor people get on this planet.

I asked, "Do you know there's a revolution happening in this country? Do you know who President Aristide is? Do you know there are guerrillas just a few kilometres from here?" One of the women showed me some money, the equivalent of five cents. "All I know is that I have six children and this is all I have in life. Those things you're talking about have nothing to do with my life."

It was a lesson for me on how the world really operates. We were talking about this geopolitical story, a guerrilla revolution, and yet the very people who should have been most affected by it were completely oblivious to it. Their struggle is so elemental, so much about basic existence. They are caught in such abject poverty. They are illiterate. They are penniless. They stand there day after day after day hoping they'll sell charcoal to someone and then they'll have enough money to feed their kids. Nothing nutritious of course, but something to fill their stomachs. For me it was just one of those moments that really rocked the foundation of everything I understood.

It was a profound and painful example of how the world is in the twenty-first century. These people were living what was at best a medieval life. An hour away there was staggering affluence in the United States. I think that moment allowed me to reach out through the TV screen and shake people and say, "Look. This is what it's like in this country only a stone's throw away from where you live."

One of the hardest stories to get on TV is the story of poverty. Editors don't like stories about poverty because poverty is depressing. When people watch stories about poverty they tend to change the channel because they don't like to be uncomfortable. But during that same trip to Haiti, I went with a Catholic priest to Cité Soleil, a slum where a million and half people live in squalor beyond belief. The stench from the open sewers is so overpowering that I couldn't breathe through my nose. Whether it was safe or not, I breathed through my mouth. Otherwise I would have passed out.

In a slum, a group of white people with a camera is a big deal, especially for children. So we were surrounded by children. They were wearing ripped and torn clothing. Filthy. Filthy. I was looking at a little girl wearing a Mickey Mouse dress who was playing with something, putting it in her mouth. It was a used condom and she was having fun stretching it. Your whole world is shaken when you see this.

There was also a boy, about thirteen years old. He was very curious and through our interpreter he was asking me questions. I asked him to show us where he lived. We followed him through a warren of shacks made of scraps of corrugated tin, salvaged lumber or sometimes cinderblock with plastic sheets. It went on and on. We finally arrived at the shack where he lived. He showed us a room that was maybe ten feet by ten feet. It had one double bed and a single bed. He told me twelve people were living in this house. I asked where he slept and he pointed under the bed. He said that's where he slept with his sister and brother on the dirt floor. I was almost shaking physically. It was absolutely devastating. As we turned to go he touched my elbow and said something.

I turned to the interpreter and I said, "What did he say?"

"He wants you to take him with you."

Nothing really prepares you for a moment like that. My heart just sank. I didn't know what to say. I asked the priest if I could give him some money, maybe put him through school. The priest said, "I'm not here to be your conscience. The problems are bigger than one child. I can give him some of your money, but I can't manage his education. I can't do that for every person in this place."

Even to this day I can still see that kid's face. I left that place thinking, "When you're born in Cité Soleil you don't have to worry about going to hell because this is hell on earth."

Back in the capital, I managed to arrange an interview with President Aristide. It was clear he was living in an alternative reality. Sitting in the grand presidential palace he told me all was well.

A couple of days later I returned to the palace to coordinate another interview the president had agreed to. This time he would be talking to an ABC anchor in Washington. When we arrived, the palace was chained shut. I asked the security guard what was going on. He had a look of terror on his face and he said, "No, no, no. Go away." So we went around to the back of the palace and immediately we had four or five guns in our faces and we were told to get out of there.

Just at that moment we started to hear gunfire all around us. We were on the inside of the palace grounds and the shooting was coming from outside, from the direction we knew there was an exit. It was frightening. It really was. At some point our driver found a way to weave his way out through a place that wasn't really an exit. He drove over a barrier and we were able to get out.

It was a really harrowing ride back to the hotel. There were all sorts of barricades. It was increasingly clear that Aristide was gone—he had left Haiti entirely. In fact, he had been flown out of the country overnight. That was history and I had watched it happen.

I left Haiti hoping that maybe people would understand it better. Understand that Haiti is a country in name only. You can see it on a map: it's half of an island. But there is no country in the sense of civic institutions and civil society. It's very hard, maybe impossible, to be optimistic about the future there—in a place that is so bereft of resources, of technical expertise, of basic law and order.

Eric Sorensen:
Obama
Nominated

Photo courtesy Eric Sorensen

THOUGH HE ONCE DID A TV REPORT WHILE PLAYING short-stop on his men's baseball team, Eric Sorensen is actually a better basketball player. Or at least he was as a younger man. In his graduating year at university he was named most valuable player of the Ryerson Rams basketball team. For all that, he's even a better journalist.

He started at a radio station in Welland, Ontario, and worked his way up. From Wingham and Peterborough in Ontario to Moncton, New Brunswick; London, Ontario;

and then to CTV Toronto. He became a reporter for CBC News in Saskatoon, then Yellowknife, before moving to Parliament Hill. He covered elections and international summits and followed three prime ministers across five continents. He spent eight years in Washington as bureau chief for Global News, covering important stories in the United States and around the world, including the funeral of Nelson Mandela in South Africa, the election of US President Barack Obama, and the Winter and Summer Olympics in Vancouver, London and Sochi, Russia. He moved back to Toronto as Global's senior national affairs correspondent in 2014.

Eric Sorensen was one of the thousands of reporters who covered election night in the United States when Obama won. But the night he remembers best from the 2008 election campaign is August 28, when Obama accepted the Democratic Party nomination in Denver.

On November 5, 2008, the *New York Times* carried a one-word headline: "OBAMA." The first African-American president of the United States of America had just been elected. The historic importance of this event cannot be overstated. In Obama's hometown of Chicago, his picture filled the entire front page of the *Sun-Times*. In a corner at the bottom it said, "MR. PRESIDENT." In London, the *Independent* put out a special edition at 3 AM. In Montreal, *La Presse* produced fifteen pages of special coverage. The *Toronto Star* headline captured both the enormous break with the past and the tremendous hope invested in the future—"A Dream Fulfilled."

One of the first stories that crossed my desk when I arrived in Washington in late 2006 was the possibility that the Democrats could choose as their nominee either a woman or an African American. I don't think I realized then just how far ahead Hillary Clinton was. We all knew Hillary. Obama was new. That's why I went to Springfield, Illinois, when he announced he was running.

It was a cold Saturday morning in February 2007. Obama was on the steps of the Capitol building and thousands of people were jammed into the square in front of him. I thought, "Wow! This is really something."

I was struck by how many foreign journalists were there. My position was right near someone from Japanese television. We were all caught up in the idea of the United States actually considering an African American for president. Jesse Jackson had tried in the 1980s but everybody knew then that was never going to happen. He wasn't a serious candidate. This was more real. But it was still something of a long shot given the resources that are necessary and the prejudices that had to be overcome. A lot of people were seized with the idea of Obama possibly becoming president. But there were people on Hillary's side for the very same reason. History was going to be made one way or the other.

At the outset, Hillary had control of the race. More people were behind her. More money was behind her. She was a Clinton. She had Bill on her side. I thought for Obama to win, he had to have everything fall his way. I didn't think he had any margin for error. His people had done the math and come up with a formula to get the delegates he needed. They targeted certain states and if he didn't win those he wasn't going to win the nomination.

I covered several of the primaries that year—a half dozen or so, including Indiana, Pennsylvania, New Hampshire.

Everybody at an Obama event was thrilled to be there. Everybody thought he was a new, young, African-American phenomenon who really could become the next president. He was a great orator and his speeches and his style—soaring—were new to us. People were likening him to Martin Luther King. He was a modern campaigner. He didn't seem old-fashioned in any way. He could be ironic. He could kid with people. He seemed young. He seemed very with it. People believed in him. Anyone who got close to him came away thinking, "He's got it." Hillary was not as good as he was at revving up a crowd, not quite as good at the street level as a retail politician. Still, a great many people believed in her too. They believed it was her time.

There were parallel campaigns going on. It was time for a woman. It was time for an African American. It should be a woman. It should be an African American. They were each making the case not just for historic change, but for the historic change that they represented. That was fascinating to watch.

Before too long all the experts began to say the arithmetic was beginning to look good for Obama and not so good for Clinton. By June, Obama officially had enough delegates to win the nomination. So at the convention in Denver there was no great drama or surprise, but it was a notable moment. People were there to witness history. What happened in Denver was so new: the idea of an African American being the standard-bearer of a major political party. Not only that, it looked as if he was on track to win the election. If you stopped to think about it, it was shocking. So when I arrived at the convention it was just full of people bursting with pride but who couldn't quite believe it was happening.

And that was enough for me to realize I was very lucky to be there. What a privilege it was. It was the kind of event where you shouldn't just let things wash over you. You should take a moment to stop and recognize the surroundings. But that's not why the convention has always stayed with me as a special memory. There were two other circumstances I recall vividly.

First, Henry Champ was there. [*Henry was a terrific reporter who had the rare gift of getting along with everyone. He had worked for CTV in Canada, then NBC around the world, and was now a reporter for CBC based in Washington. He died in 2012.*]

On the last night of the convention, the Democrats moved from an arena to an outdoor stadium so that eighty thousand people could hear Obama's acceptance speech. The stadium was bathed in light and sound, but behind all the cameras there was a small space that was relatively dark and relatively quiet. I found Henry sitting in a chair back there and he was exhausted. I went to him, knelt beside him, and he said, "I'm not sure I should be here. I'm so tired." He had finished his first cancer treatment a few weeks earlier. I thought, "He wants to be here. He wants to be working because this is news." He had gathered up his strength to go on camera and do his reports, and then he had come back to sit down again, to try to get his strength back. And I thought, "This is what we do and what an honour it is to be here with my friend who I admire so much." Henry wanted to be there even though he wasn't well. And together we witnessed history.

We had a front-row seat on a remarkable event. Henry wasn't a rookie reporter. He had seen a few things in his career. And here he was struggling to cover the news because he fully appreciated the enormity of what was happening. It was the last time we were on assignment together on the road.

The second circumstance involves my wife, Pam. She was a teacher at Dwight D. Eisenhower Middle School in Laurel, Maryland. It was a public school where almost everyone— the teaching staff and the students—was African American. Pam was always telling me stories of life at that school. My mouth would hang open at the insight she had into life in the United States and the experience of African Americans. What she kept hearing at school was that the Democrats were never going to choose Barack Obama because he was Black. And if he was chosen, he'd never be elected. And if he was elected he wouldn't live very long before he'd be killed.

Based on all the experiences that they had lived through, the people at Pam's school had concluded that African Americans didn't get a fair shake. Everything about their society—the attitudes they met on the street, the systemic things that African Americans dealt with every day—told them that Obama was someone and something that could never happen.

A few days before the convention, three teachers at the school asked Pam to ask me to pick up T-shirts as souvenirs. So one afternoon I had a minute and I strolled over to a stall where they were selling things and I found T-shirts with a picture of Obama on the front, with the date of his nomination. This is what they wanted.

I bought the shirts, tossed them into a bag and didn't think about them again until I got home. Then I gave the shirts to Pam and she gave them to the teachers.

She came home that night and told me the three teachers had agreed to wear the T-shirts just one time. Then they were going to take them off and frame them. Hang them in their homes. I said, "You're kidding." But it wasn't all that hard to understand. The souvenirs that I bought when I had a couple of spare minutes were so important to them because they had been purchased where an African American had been made the nominee of a major political party. You look at more than 230 years of history and see who had been nominated for the Democrats and the Republicans and of course they were all white. But now, at long last, an African American had been nominated and that had such meaning for them. These African-American teachers had been looking at life in the United States through a prism very different from the one I was using. I could see the history. For them it was more. It was justice. It was a turning point.

So those two things—buying the souvenirs that meant so much to others, and being with Henry when he was struggling to cover the news—made that story very meaningful for me.

Heather Hiscox:

Mounties

Murdered

Photo courtesy CBC

HEATHER HISCOX WAKES UP A LOT EARLIER THAN MOST OF US. Her morning begins at a time most of us still call night. But if she ever runs low on energy it's not apparent to anyone who knows her.

Her first job was at a radio station in Owen Sound, Ontario. After a couple of years she caught on with a radio station in Toronto. She then moved to a radio station in London, Ontario. Her first TV job was also in London. From there it was Global TV in Toronto, ASN in Halifax, CBC in Montreal, Global in Montreal, CHCH in Hamilton, and finally CBC National News in Toronto, where she now anchors the network's morning news.

When three Mounties were murdered and the killer was on the loose in Moncton, New Brunswick, Heather Hiscox flew in from Toronto—1,500 kilometres away.

Moncton is a city with a population of about seventy thousand. In the early evening of June 4, 2014, twenty-four-year-old Justin Bourque began walking down the street wearing camouflage clothing and carrying a rifle, a shotgun and a crossbow. Several people who saw him called the police. In Moncton, the police are the RCMP. Bourque knew the police would be coming, and when he saw them, he opened fire. In the space of about twenty minutes, he killed Constables Fabrice Gevaudan, Douglas Larche and Dave Ross. Two other officers were wounded.

Murder of any kind is extremely rare in Moncton. A police officer hadn't been killed in the city in forty years. But Moncton couldn't grieve right away. First there was the matter of capturing the killer. Bourque had run off, and no one knew where he was. That left the city very uneasy. The north end was locked down as police started their search.

....

I heard about the shootings that night when I was at home, getting ready for bed. I try to get to sleep at about 8:30 every night because I get up at 2:30 to go to work. I knew that three Mounties had been killed. So the next morning was going to be a busy morning. And it was. Our program is seen right across the country, but in some ways, on that morning, we did a local program for Moncton.

We sifted through all the information we were getting and were very direct in telling the people of Moncton what we knew about where it was safe to be, what was locked down, what was open and what was closed. But of course Canadians everywhere are shocked when three RCMP officers are killed. And if it can happen in Moncton, there's an understanding it could happen anywhere. It could happen in Moosonee, Ontario, or in Medicine Hat, Alberta, or in Maple Creek, Saskatchewan. So what we were reporting was important everywhere.

That morning we interviewed as many people as we could who knew something about what had happened and what was happening. By necessity, many of our interviews were done over the telephone. That's never our preference, of course, but the content of the interviews was strong. We talked to the mayor of Moncton, an RCMP spokesperson, people in the locked-down area, and of course our reporters. It was a strong program.

As soon as we got off the air, we began talking about whether I should head to Moncton to anchor the next day's broadcast. There was almost no debate. It seemed clear that this would still be the number-one story in the country. And there's just so much more you can do when you're on-site, so much more you can bring to the reporting.

I know people have the impression that when a TV network newscast comes to town it brings a cast of thousands and lights, cameras, satellite trucks. Some newscasts do require a huge amount of technical support, but we travel lightly. Two of us flew to Moncton. Just a producer and me. We didn't even take a teleprompter. Our technical set-up would be modest, and we'd use facilities that already existed in New Brunswick.

Our plane landed in Moncton just after suppertime. I tried to get a feel for the city right away. It's a cliché, but on the drive downtown from the airport, yes I talked to the cab driver. What were his experiences in the last few hours? What was his read on the story? What had he heard from his friends? Was his family in the lockdown zone? On the way to the hotel we could see all the signs that were beginning to appear on businesses. THANK YOU RCMP. WE SUPPORT YOU RCMP. Those messages would eventually be everywhere. We drove through the streets and saw almost nobody. It was seven or eight o'clock at night. Normally there would be plenty of activity in downtown Moncton. Police had ordered people to stay inside in other parts of the city, but even though this was not in the lockdown area people were still inside. They were nervous. The city had the feel of a ghost town.

We got to the hotel and decided to take a walk to get a feel for the main street. That's where we'd be broadcasting from in the morning. Normally the street would have been livelier, but not on this night. We went to the RCMP detachment a couple of blocks away. The flags were already at half-mast. Somebody had already been there to leave flowers, the beginnings of what would be a huge memorial over the coming days. So even in those few minutes we were able to gather a few vignettes. We were able to pick up on the details that we wouldn't have if we'd stayed in Toronto.

By the time we woke up the next morning they had arrested the shooter. So that obviously changed the tone of our story. It was no longer about a city in lockdown or a population scared of a man running around with guns and a crossbow. Now we could tell the story of who the shooter was, how he'd been arrested, what the course of justice would bring next. And now that Moncton could exhale, it was the story of the RCMP officers who had been killed, and of those who had been wounded. And we could show the sadness that hung over the city. We weren't far from the RCMP detachment, so we could see all the people arriving with flowers and cards.

We had talked by phone the day before with the mayor of Moncton, George LeBlanc. But now we could interview him in person and I think all Canadians got to see what kind of man he was. I thought he was a man who stepped forward and was a leader for his community. I told him that you don't expect a day like this when you sign up for municipal politics, a day when you're going to have to be the face and voice and strength for your community. And you could just see the weight he was carrying. He realized that he had to hold it together for his fellow citizens. He was reassuring. He captured the feeling of the community in terms of coming together and supporting those affected by the murders. I was very impressed and I think the country was too.

During commercial breaks or when a longer piece of tape was running, people would wave to us or toot their horns. I took that to mean that they appreciated our presence. I would never want them to feel that we were exploiting the situation. I'm very aware that local people might resent our presence. They might think, "These people are coming from Toronto, and they're going to try to explain what is going on here to the rest of the country." And they may not think we can do that properly. But in fact I didn't get that sense at all in Moncton. Instead we got many people saying, "You did a great job." I think they felt they got the information they wanted and needed and they didn't get coverage that was overly sensational.

So I felt good when we left Moncton. We achieved what we'd set out to achieve—that is, to give the most accurate and best information on a story that was quickly changing, and to convey its emotional impact in a way that was true to the people who were directly affected. And I hope as compassionately as possible.

A few weeks later I got a note from the mayor. He was generous. He wrote, "I want to express my appreciation to you and your team for the compassionate manner in which you reported on the tragic events here in Moncton. It made it just a little easier for the people of Moncton."

You don't often have your work validated like that.

David Halton:
Sadat to
Jerusalem

DAVID HALTON HAS JOUR-
NALISM IN HIS DNA. His father
is Matthew Halton, a legendary
CBC correspondent who was perhaps Canada's best-known reporter
during World War II. David wrote
Dispatches from the Front, a biography of his father.

It can't have been easy for David
to follow in his father's giant footsteps, but he carved out a brilliant
career of his own. While still at university he worked summers for the
Calgary Herald, the *Ottawa Citizen*
and CBC Toronto. Living in Paris on a
French government scholarship, he

Photo courtesy David Halton

freelanced for CBC and the *Toronto Star*. When he returned to Canada he was hired by *Time* magazine in Montreal.

He landed at CBC for good in 1965. He was based in Toronto, Montreal, Paris, Moscow (where he met his wife), Paris again, Montreal, London, Ottawa (where he was chief political correspondent for fourteen years) and Washington. He covered at least five wars, six federal elections and one impeachment trial of an American president. When Egyptian President Anwar Sadat decided to make peace with Israel, the first reporter he told about his peace initiative was David Halton.

Israel had proclaimed statehood in May 1948, and immediately found itself at war with the Arab countries that surrounded it. Other major wars followed, in 1967 and 1973. A ceasefire agreement, rather than a peace treaty, ended each war, so by 1977 there had been almost thirty years of conflict, with every prospect of more war to come.

The biggest country on the Arab side of the fighting was Egypt. If Egypt and Israel made peace, there would still be issues to settle, but large-scale war in the Middle East would be almost impossible. Of course, an Egyptian-Israeli peace seemed as likely as the cobra and the mongoose settling their differences.

In 1977 I was based in London, but in November I was in Jerusalem. CBC had no Middle East correspondent at the time, so it was quite common for me to travel there. I'd covered the Six-Day War in 1967. I was back four or five times in the early seventies. I'd interviewed the Israeli prime ministers of the era—Yitzhak Rabin, Menachem Begin. But I had never interviewed Egypt's president, Anwar Sadat.

We had asked the Egyptians for a Sadat interview four or five months earlier. But we heard nothing. There were faint rumours going around that Sadat might be ready for some kind of breakthrough with Israel, but there was nothing specific.

Then one morning the CBC London office called and said, "We just got word from Cairo that Sadat is willing to give you an interview. They say you should get to Cairo as soon as you can and stand by. They hope to arrange the interview in a day or two."

The only way you could get from Jerusalem to Cairo in those days was to first cross the Allenby Bridge into Amman, Jordan. From there I got the next EgyptAir flight to Cairo.

The story takes an interesting twist here.

I arrived in Cairo at dusk and the airport was chaotic— as it usually was. I went through customs and then two men came up to me and said, "We're from the foreign ministry press department and we're here to meet you and drive you to your hotel."

"Well," I said. "That's very kind of you."

So we got into the car with my bags and then I started to reflect upon things. I thought that theoretically no one should have known that I was arriving at that particular time and on that particular flight. So about halfway between the airport and the hotel I said, "How did you know I was coming?"

One of the men looked at me and said, "You are David Holden, aren't you?"

David Holden was the senior foreign correspondent of the London *Sunday Times*, a very prestigious figure.

"Actually," I said. "It's David Hal-ton, not Hol-den. I'm sorry, but I think you got the wrong person. I'm David Hal-ton."

They looked at each other and one of them said, "Well, we're almost at the hotel so we'll drop you off." Which they did.

None of this sounds relevant, but the next time David Holden flew in to Cairo he was murdered. Someone put a bullet into his heart on the road between the airport and his hotel. No one knows why. It's a great mystery. Some suspected he was working for British intelligence, MI6, or the American CIA.

One of my relatives in Alberta heard that David Holden had been assassinated and thought it was me. She called my wife in London with condolences. Fortunately I had talked to my wife just a few hours earlier so she was able to say that rumours of my demise were greatly exaggerated.

But I think I had a fairly narrow escape.

In any case, I waited in the hotel for a few days until finally a call came through to tell me that Sadat was ready for our interview. We went over to one of his several palaces by the Nile.

Word had spread that Walter Cronkite was getting an interview later in the day. We still didn't know what Sadat was going to say, but Peter Jennings—who was ABC's Middle East correspondent and a friend from childhood—was worried that Cronkite and CBS were going to beat him. So he had called me to ask if he could use parts of my interview if there was anything newsworthy.

I said, "Yes. Sure. Fine."

So Jennings came with us to the interview and he helped our cameraman with the audio. He was the most expensive sound technician in history. *[Just a few years later Jennings would become one of the most celebrated journalists in the United States. He anchored ABC* World News Tonight *from 1983 until he died of lung cancer in 2005.]*

Fortunately, just before the interview Sadat's press secretary said to me, "Be sure to ask him about plans to go to Jerusalem."

Without that prompting I may well have never asked the right question. As I say, there were rumours of some kind of peace initiative, but nothing this dramatic. So after a few general questions, I asked about going to Jerusalem and he laid it all out. Of course, I realized immediately the significance of what he said.

Walter Cronkite's interview was set for five hours later. But he was doing his by satellite, so the tape would be in New York instantly. The rest of my afternoon was spent in harried efforts to try to get our story back in time to beat Cronkite.

The problem was that we had shot the interview on colour film. In Cairo at that time they only had labs that could develop black and white film. We were told we could put the film in black and white developer but we obviously didn't want to do that for fear of screwing it all up. We found a colour film lab for Egyptian feature films. But it would have taken days to get through the Egyptian bureaucracy there.

Then NBC found out what we had, and they were going mad at the thought of being scooped. They made a last-minute effort to charter a Learjet to Amman, where they could handle colour film. But NBC looked at the time, did the calculations and decided that we'd miss their news deadline by thirty minutes. So that plan didn't work either.

It was exhilarating to have the news in the interview, but then so frustrating to try to get it on the air. I was the first journalist to talk to Sadat that day. He talked to just the two of us, me and Cronkite. But the absurd situation with the colour film meant that Cronkite carried the day.

I eventually flew to London and edited the film there.

Just six days later I was at Lod airport in Israel [today it is known as Ben Gurion International Airport] for some of the most moving scenes I've ever seen. Sadat walked off the airplane, greeted by Begin. I could see veterans of Israel's wars with Egypt—three or four generals—weeping. They never believed this was possible in their lifetime. Was this really happening? It was so emotional there. It was an immensely moving scene.

Later that day he got a tremendous reception, a huge amount of applause in the Knesset when he addressed the Israeli parliament. It raised great hope among Israelis that they could put war behind them. The boldness of Sadat, the showmanship—I'll always remember that. I thought he was acting incredibly courageously, going against the grain of decades of rejectionist Arab thinking.

Of course, Sadat would eventually pay for all this with his life. *[He was assassinated in 1981.]* But going to Jerusalem did bear fruit. The Camp David Agreement, negotiated with the help of US President Jimmy Carter in 1978, meant there was peace between Egypt and Israel. Still, part of the agreement, dealing with the Palestinians, never got off the ground.

So for me the Sadat-to-Jerusalem story was just extraordinary—that sense of having an orchestra seat for history unfolding, that semi-voyeuristic feeling that journalists sometimes have watching history in the making. It was truly exciting.

Don Murray:
Collapse of the
USSR

DON MURRAY HAS LIVED IN EIGHT CITIES IN SEVEN COUNTRIES, covered a dozen wars and reported from more than eighty countries. He started at the *Gazette* in Montreal and his first CBC job was in that city as well. When he was posted to Beijing he became the first CBC/Société Radio-Canada foreign correspondent to be responsible for both radio and television in both French and English. He also became conversant in Mandarin. After Beijing he was posted to Paris, and then Jerusalem. When he

Photo courtesy Don Murray

moved to Moscow he learned Russian well enough to interview Mikhail Gorbachev without an interpreter. He was posted to Berlin, and then to London for thirteen years, though he spent a great deal of that time in Baghdad.

He has written two books—*De Bourassa à Lévesque*, a history of Quebec in the late 1960s and '70s, and *A Democracy of Despots*, an account of the end of the Soviet Union and the beginning of the new Russia.

Don Murray was the CBC and Radio-Canada correspondent in Moscow when the Soviet Union collapsed.

The Union of Soviet Socialist Republics, as it was formally known, was born from the Bolshevik Revolution in 1917. Vladimir Lenin may not have intended to create a Communist empire that murdered millions and denied basic freedoms to everyone under its thumb, but that is exactly what the revolution did produce. Relations between the Russian empire and the West were never warm, but Russia was an ally in World War II. After the war, though, the USSR became the enemy, running puppet regimes behind the Iron Curtain in Eastern Europe, aggressively promoting Communism wherever it could around the globe. A Cold War began with the Western democracies. Both sides built huge nuclear weapon arsenals that, if let loose, would destroy the world several times over.

Then came Gorbachev. In 1985 he rose to power in the USSR and introduced two words into our vocabulary: *glasnost*, or political openness, and *perestroika*, or economic restructuring. Together, the policies transformed the very essence of the Soviet Union and its empire. Decades of repression and stagnation gave way to stirrings of nationalism in Soviet satellite states. In 1989 revolutions in Poland, East Germany, Czechoslovakia, Hungary, Bulgaria and Romania ended Communist regimes. By 1991 the Soviet Union itself was threatened and that Christmas Day it all came tumbling down. Gorbachev resigned and the Soviet Union became fifteen separate countries.

Don Murray's memories of the event are heightened by what had happened on another Christmas Day in another Communist capital.

It was 1980 in Beijing. I'd been in the country for about six months. The trial of the Gang of Four was just coming to an end.

[The Gang of Four was a group of Chinese Communist Party members who had great power during Mao Zedong's Cultural Revolution. When Mao died in 1976 the government declared the Cultural Revolution to have been an "appalling catastrophe" and put the Gang on trial for a series of crimes, not the least of which was killing almost thirty-five thousand people. The most prominent member of the Gang was Jiang Qing, Mao's widow.]

Foreign reporters, observers and diplomats got no closer than about 2 kilometres from the courthouse and could follow proceedings only through Chinese television. The trial would go on all day and we were shown edited portions on TV. The highlights were chosen to explain to the rest of the world that the Gang was guilty and that Jiang Qing in particular was a hopelessly renegade person.

This was highly scripted theatre, except Jiang Qing refused to play. She refused to admit fault. She refused to apologize. She refused to ask for mercy. Chinese television showed her on a couple of occasions and it was stunning for the Chinese to see. But those in power were sure it would confirm for everyone that she was vicious and dangerous. So dangerous that she wouldn't toe the line even when she faced the death penalty.

Since it was a show trial, it could have ended any time, and a verdict could come quickly. There were only about five thousand foreigners in Beijing at the time, in a city of ten million. I'd say half to two-thirds were gone by Christmas. But I decided to stay in case there was a verdict.

Of course, the judges weren't really the ones who were deciding. That was up to political leaders. The problem the Politburo faced was that Jiang Qing was accused of such serious crimes that they had to condemn her to death unless she apologized. And they clearly didn't want to do that. Some of the leaders must have wanted to execute her, but there was obviously debate and that delayed everything. (I had to wait until mid-January for them to finally come up with a verdict, which was "death deferred." It was a death sentence to be carried out in two years if she did not show remorse before then. And she never did. Eventually she committed suicide. So she defied them to the end. She denied them her death at their hands. She was a tough bird.)

So at the end of December there just wasn't that much to do. Christmas Day came along. There was a church that the Chinese authorities allowed to open for Christmas services. It was packed. I went to do a story for radio. There was terrific stuff—people praying, singing, talking. But it was 10 degrees below zero and I suddenly realized that the batteries I had were all drained by the cold. I had recorded a few sound bites, but missed the best parts.

It was so depressing. There I was on Christmas Day with this mess of bits and pieces of sound. I thought, "I really have chosen the wrong profession." I really thought I should just get on a plane and ask to be posted to Edmonton. Everything about China had been difficult and this was one last frustration that pushed me close to the edge.

I had already started doing battle with Chinese bureaucrats over my visa. In their eyes my visa allowed me only to do radio. No TV. I must have had the same discussion with the Chinese six thousand times. I'd say, "My visa allows for 'broadcasting,' which is radio and television."

They would say, "But in French your company is Radio-Canada."

"Yes. But in English it's the Canadian Broadcasting Corporation and that means radio and television."

This went on and on and on.

The restrictions on doing things were so immense it was hard to function. I had to give forty-eight hours' notice if I wanted to go outside Beijing. Of course when I did go, I was accompanied by three or four government people. It wasn't freewheeling. It was very, very heavy and deliberately made difficult.

Every foreigner was aware of being watched, and above all, the people you were dealing with were being watched, and they had real worries about the consequences. The regulation for any Chinese citizen was that they could have one unplanned meeting with a foreigner, which they then had to report to the police. Any further meetings had to be approved in advance by the authorities. People who ignored the regulations were often picked up by the police. People were scared to talk to me, and they were right to be scared. Living in China was as far away from the life that I had come to understand as I could possibly get.

So I was annoyed with the Chinese the entire time.

And then I realized that no one in Canada seemed to care. I stayed in Beijing that Christmas because there was news I thought was important. But I came to realize that had I left, no one would have noticed. I remember that around that time my telephone rang at three o'clock one morning. I thought, "My God, something terrible must have happened." But it turned out to be somebody on the foreign desk in Montreal.

He said, "How are you?"

"How am I? It's three o'clock in the morning. Why are you calling?"

"I thought we would just talk for a little while about how things are going."

He obviously had never even taken the trouble to figure out the time difference. It just became clearer and clearer that Canada didn't care about China. So it was a very bad Christmas.

Which is a stark contrast with my Christmas Day eleven years later, when I was a correspondent in Moscow.

When I arrived in 1988, the country was just beginning to open up. Foreigners still lived in compounds where Russians couldn't go. Correspondents still had to give notice when they wanted to travel anywhere outside Moscow. But all of those rules started to break down within six months of my arrival. Mikhail Gorbachev had created a Congress where people were actually elected and could speak freely and could go on television to say what they liked. It was astonishing. It was a complete overthrow of seventy years of history.

It was in the Congress one day in 1989 that Andrei Sakharov stood up and really made a difference. *[Sakharov was a nuclear physicist, the father of the Soviet hydrogen bomb, who spoke out for human rights and won the Nobel Peace Prize in 1975. At the time, Soviet officials refused to allow him out of the country to accept it.]* This was just a day or two before he died. He stood up and talked almost directly to Gorbachev and it was astounding to see. There had been crackdowns all around the country and Sakharov said, "You have to choose whether we want this to be a democracy or an empire. You can't have both." That's when the campaign to end the constitutional central role of the Communist Party picked up tremendous force. People were holding up signs saying END THE PARTY'S CONTROL.

Christmas night of 1991 was the night Gorbachev resigned. The Soviet Union collapsed.

I think we all understood it was unravelling, but to think it would literally end up being fifteen countries and crumbling to that extent—I don't think most of us saw that coming. My guess was that the Baltics would get away and maybe some of the southern republics too. But that they would all become independent countries? That was something I hadn't foreseen.

I filed my reports for radio and television. My wife and kids were back in Canada. They were staying with my parents. At six o'clock the TV news came on and my parents called everyone to watch my report. Everybody rushed into the room, leaving our eleven-month-old daughter out in the hall crawling around. In the middle of my story she came walking into the room, and that was the first time she had walked. She heard Poppa's voice and she stood up and walked. So that had nothing to do with journalism, but it adds to my fondness for the day.

Back in Moscow, I was able to go down to Red Square and look around. There were two or three Russians waving Soviet flags but it was as quiet as you could possibly imagine. The whole place was in shock, quite literally. I said to myself, "In my lifetime, nobody will ever see the end of an empire this big. It's only going to happen once, and I was here."

And unlike my Christmas in Beijing, this time the story I was telling really mattered to my audience. In Western terms, particularly in radio and television terms, it was good to have a story with a good guy versus a bad guy. Gorbachev was seen as a good guy. One of the problems with the China story was that nobody in the West could pronounce the names of the people involved, and everyone was so invisible. There were no good guys. They were all bad guys. Viewers and listeners could never understand what the characters were up to because it was so opaque. Gorbachev, on the other hand, was wide open. He appeared to be Western-friendly. He appeared to be a good guy.

As time went on, all the Western reporters in the Soviet Union kept trying to point out that he was not actually liked by Russians. Ordinary Russians were saying, "He's an idiot. He's ineffectual. The economy's a mess." Correspondents were insisting that Gorbachev wasn't a good guy and our newscasts shouldn't be presenting him as a good guy. But it didn't work. News editors wanted Gorbachev's travails. They wanted Gorbachev leaping over yet another hurdle that it seemed impossible to leap over. So people in the West understood the story in those terms and cared desperately about what was happening.

Mark Kelley:
The Worst
School

MARK KELLEY WAS BORN IN MONTREAL, went to university in Montreal and got his first job in journalism in Montreal. That was in the newsroom of radio station CKGM. Two years later he joined CBC News and has been there ever since. His first CBC job was with radio in Quebec City. He switched to television in the provincial capital, and then moved back to Montreal.

In 1998 he became the anchor of CBC's morning news program, based in Halifax. He stayed in that role when the program was moved to Toronto. Then he became one of

Photo courtesy CBC

the hosts of the investigative program *Disclosure*. He did documentaries for *The National* for five years, before anchoring a nightly program, *Connected*. Since 2012 he's been one of the hosts of *the fifth estate*.

In 2006, Mark saw a report from the Fraser Institute that aroused his curiosity and his journalistic instincts.

The Fraser Institute is often referred to in the media as "a right-wing think tank." The institute itself says its vision is "a free and prosperous world where individuals benefit from greater choice, competitive markets, and personal responsibility."

To that end, among the things the Fraser Institute thinks about is how well our schools work. It publishes annual rankings of schools in several provinces. The British Columbia list (called a report card) started in 2003. The institute says the report is an objective indicator of school performance, and says it "encourages and assists all those seeking to improve the schools."

I was flying home from a story in Quebec one day and I was feeling unsatisfied with the whole notion of daily news. We drop in somewhere, become a voyeur—you're in someone's life for two or three hours—and then we package that, put it on the air and leave. I was thinking, "There's got to be more to journalism than this drive-by model. We need to capture more of an experience. We're just scratching the surface."

As a journalist, I felt I had far more curiosity to be fed. And I thought people had more of a story to be told. Finally, I thought viewers would be far more satisfied if they could get a deeper experience from our stories. So that's why I thought, "Instead of going somewhere for seven hours, let's cover a story for seven days. Let's try to find a story that will lend itself to being covered for seven days and show something that would be more rounded and grounded than we can show by flying in and flying out."

So that was my idea. What it required was a real commitment from the news desk. A seven-day assignment is a great luxury in today's journalism.

In the summer of 2006 I was looking at the Fraser Institute school rankings in British Columbia. I had no intention of doing a story—I just happened to notice the list. What caught my eye was that there was, of course, a school that was ranked dead last. There it was—number 1,007. I wondered what it must be like to be a teacher in a school that's ranked dead last. Then I thought, "What's it like to be a student in the school when it gets out that your school is the worst?"

I didn't know if the story could go anywhere, but I picked up the phone and I called Roosevelt Park School in Prince Rupert, British Columbia.

Remember, it was during summer vacation, but the principal answered the phone. I told him I was curious about the list and I said I had this crazy idea. "Could I come out and visit your school for seven days and be a substitute teacher?"

His first response to me was, "How soon can you be here?"

Usually it can be very difficult to get into a school. You have to jump through so many hoops and over so many hurdles. You need waivers from the school, the board, parents, teachers—it can be endless. The principal said, "If you can you be here for the opening day of school, I'll take care of all the paperwork. I want you to see our reality."

The principal's name was Steve Riley and he was fantastic. He was an outgoing guy who had come over from England to visit Canada for a month or two, and fifteen years later he was still here. He had a passion for teaching. He had a passion for Prince Rupert. He fell in love with the place and he fell in love with the school. He was so outgoing and so motivated and so dedicated to doing everything he could for the kids.

When he saw the Fraser Institute rankings he was crushed. At the top of the list he saw private schools in Vancouver, and at the bottom of the list he saw his school. He said, "To put us on an equal footing is absolutely ridiculous. Our reality is completely different."

He was just so passionate about what his teachers were doing to engage the students and what the students were doing to lift themselves out of cycles and cycles of bad education. He wanted to put that on display. He wanted to show off what he was doing. It was counterintuitive to think that the principal of the worst-ranked school wanted to show off his worst-ranked school.

Principal Steve chose a Grade 5 class for me. He considered it to be a good illustration of what they had to deal with. Something like twenty-three of the twenty-seven kids in the class had special needs. And that was the story of the school. It was nothing like a private school in Vancouver where you have well-heeled kids coming from big houses, solid families, where everybody shows up with a bellyful of food and will go home to a warm house at the end of the day.

The class had a solid teacher, Penny Hazel. She was a teacher who had shown up with the intention of changing young lives and had been worn down by the reality of that school and of that environment. She had been worn down by the fact that there were so many special needs kids in one class and she was without a teacher's aide. In fact, that violated the union's standards. She'd been worn down by that. But she wouldn't turn her back on the kids, or turn her back on the profession, and was doing everything she could every day to inspire the kids. I would soon learn that trying to teach that class was very demanding, but she just couldn't give up on the kids because everyone else in their lives had given up on them.

I was amazed by her, and after a few days I talked to the principal. "Is she laying it on a little bit too thick for our cameras?" He said she was always like that. He was obviously proud of her and her dedication to the class.

For a while I was an extra person in the class. On Day 1 we just wanted the kids to get comfortable with me—a guy who's walking around their classroom. I'm the father of four kids so I have my own reality of dealing with kids and it was nothing like this. That day a bunch of straggler kids had come to the school. They hadn't been registered, but had just shown up. The principal just threw them into a classroom and had me read to them. What really hit me was just seeing twenty-five kids looking up at me with hungry eyes, just waiting to learn. Some of their parents had had experience with residential schools so they hadn't sent their kids to schools before because they didn't believe in them. For those kids, this was their first chance. They just wanted what every other kid gets—a good chance in life. This was clear to me in the first few hours I was at that school. And I knew from day one this was going to be an experience that would change my life forever.

Back in the Grade 5 class it was time for one kid to write his name. Scott was working on it, and having a lot of trouble. I realized that the things we take for granted—like simple literacy, simple comprehension, being able to pay attention—were absent. Nothing, nothing at all, at that school could be taken for granted on any given day. It was all a series of variables and wild cards. These were the obstacles you had to deal with every day if you were to have a hope of getting through to those kids.

I was heartbroken for Scott. Grade 5 and he couldn't write his name? A lot of things crystallized for me in that moment. I could see why so many First Nations kids had trouble integrating into mainstream society. What kind of future was this kid going to have? He would go through life hearing people ask, "How come you don't have a job?" and "How come you didn't finish school?" and "How come you're on the margins of society?" Well, you could answer all those questions right there.

I asked, "Why was this kid allowed to get this far in school? Why wasn't he held back?" And there was a good reason. Holding kids back creates a stigma, and if there is a stigma they won't show up for school. So the school wanted to keep kids of the same age together even though some were clearly achieving below expectations. They moved them along.

Principal Steve told me the real challenge for these kids would come once they left elementary school. In elementary school, they had each other and a lot of them were dealing with the same issues. But in high school they would be with kids from other backgrounds, and that's where they would stick out. And that's when they would just drop out.

The strategy might be completely different in any other school. But this was a strategy for success here—move the kids along, hoping that at some point they may be able to catch up to some degree. Not to the same standards we would have in the south, but catch up to some degree so that they would be functioning, they would be learning, they would absorb information. Hoping that there would be some sort of acceleration at some point. But they needed a foundation.

There were so many challenges that really had nothing to do with the school. Some of the kids had serious fetal alcohol syndrome. A lot of them had to go down for medication at lunchtime.

There was one kid, a sweetheart, I met. The teacher told me how one day she showed up to school and was particularly quiet. The teacher tried to coax information out of her.

"Are you okay?

"Yes, I'm okay."

Later in the day, the police came to the school and told the teacher that the kid's mother had overdosed in the bed beside her. The kid got herself up, got herself dressed and came to school. Didn't tell anyone. That's an example of what one kid went through.

Another kid had been in, I think, twenty different foster homes in her young life. She'd just been bounced from home to home to home. Another reality.

Kids showed up who just weren't focusing. I asked one, "What's your problem?"

"Well, I haven't eaten today and I didn't eat last night."

That was just one day, in one classroom, in Canada.

We had a project where kids were supposed to write what was special about them. And most of them couldn't think of a single thing. They'd never been told they were special. It was incredible. You think of kids as reservoirs of potential, reservoirs of imagination. But their reservoirs were empty. They'd never been fed anything. They had never been fed stories of travelling, of growing up to become a movie star or a hockey player. That was completely out of the realm of the possible for them. Their worlds were really small and really broken. And to see that at such a young age made me wonder what they were going to grow into if that's where they were in Grade 5.

It was Principal Steve who said it best. I never forgot what he said to me when I asked him, "What is your philosophy?"

He said, "We have to change the way the world sees these kids. And we have to change the way these kids see the world."

And that was it. That was my hallelujah moment. Where I said, "This is what it's all about."

That revelation came to me on Day 6, where I really understood. That's the payoff that you get when you spend that long on the story, the kind of thing I wouldn't have gotten had I been there a few hours instead of a few days.

I went in all gung-ho, thinking that in a few days we've got to change the kids' lives. We've got to change everything. The teachers, the real teachers, agree with that. But they are so utterly pragmatic that they know that change comes very, very slowly. Very incrementally. Have we taught Scott how to spell *Scott*? Have we done that today? Great. That's a great day. If we taught a kid how to spell his name. That's a great day. Are we going to get this kid passing Grade 5 math? Maybe not. You have to understand that change may come slowly, but change is always possible.

The thing about those kids was that they didn't realize what we saw. They didn't realize the difficulties they had to deal with because for them it was just their reality. It was amazing how the kids would come running into school, kids who had all these difficulties. The principal was trying to create a real safe haven, a happy place to be. I don't think the kids felt like outcasts. They weren't aware that they were at the bottom of the rankings, the bottom of the heap. The kids saw what they could get from school—the interaction, the attention, the friends. They were able to come to a place and be happy. That's what kept them coming back. And that's what the principal said was the key. "We've got to get them coming. Once we get them coming then we can start making change. But if they don't show up it's a lost cause."

Virtually all the teachers in the school were women. And many of those kids didn't have a father figure in their lives. So here I was, this young male standing in front of them and they started reacting to me, especially the boys. They were literally holding on to me. I would get there in the morning and the kids would come up beside me and hold my hand. Or they would grab my shirttail. They would just want to be around me.

The teachers told me it was all because I was a man who was communicating with them, giving them time, giving them attention. A lot of them really lit up. I didn't realize it at first. It had to be explained to me why they were forming what I thought was an unusually strong and quick bond considering I was a guy they'd never met before, from a place they had never been before—Toronto.

At the end of the seven days one of the boys, Austin, looked at me and said, "We won't forget you."

I did everything in my power to retain my composure. I was heartbroken. I just wanted to stay and help those kids. I've been to a lot of natural disasters in the world where I always have a sense of guilt when I get on the plane and leave, because I'm leaving people in their misery after I've told their story. And I felt the same here. But there was no natural disaster. This was Canada. This was our country. This was a community in our country. And this was their everyday reality. Leaving them there, I realized how lucky the rest of us are and how much our kids have in terms of opportunity.

I always say that the value of being a journalist is being the translator of an experience. And that experience was so powerful. I knew my job was to translate that experience to people, to give them the experience of what it was like to be a kid or a teacher in that school. And how important it was for schools like that to get encouragement, to get nourishment, to get support. These schools shouldn't be labelled the worst, but should be labelled the most exceptional schools for what they are doing with the hand they were dealt.

I think people see the school rankings and if they think at all about the school at the bottom they imagine lazy, do-nothing kids who don't really care and who skip school all the time. They imagine lazy teachers. They imagine a group of people who are a waste of time and money. That they are somehow undeserving when it comes to allocating resources. I suppose everyone's first reaction might be, "Let's give our resources to the best. Why waste it on the worst?"

That's what fuelled me. To tell the real story of that school and share it with Canadians. It was the story of a school that was trying to give every kid what he or she deserved—which is a chance. And it was having some success. I felt so proud to be a journalist because I got to tell that story.

Neil Macdonald:
Finding a Nazi

Photo courtesy CBC

NEIL MACDONALD WAS MEANT TO BE A REPORTER. There was a very short, best-forgotten period, when he worked as an editor, nailed to a desk, at CBC News. But he couldn't sit down long enough to be any good at it. He wanted to be out in the field, chasing down stories. And he surely did that well.

He started as a copy boy at the *Ottawa Citizen* when he was nineteen years old. He eventually worked as a reporter at the paper, and at the

Gazette in Montreal and the *Vancouver Sun*. He's been at CBC News since 1988, based in Ottawa, Montreal, Jerusalem and Washington.

It was when he was working for the *Ottawa Citizen* that Neil Macdonald was assigned full-time to report on the Deschênes Commission.

In 1985, stories had begun to circulate that hundreds—perhaps even thousands—of Nazi war criminals were living in Canada. The government decided to find out if that was true. So it appointed Jules Deschênes, a justice of the Court of Appeal of Quebec, to investigate.

To cover the commission properly I wanted to know everything I could about the Nazis who had made their way to North America. So I made friends with the people who were running the Office of Special Investigations in the US Department of Justice. They were really good. They were state-of-the-art Nazi hunters. I went to see them in Washington quite a bit.

I also spent a lot of time in the National Archives in Ottawa. I started reading the transcripts of war crimes trials that Canada held after the war. Most people don't know it but Canada, as a wartime power, held trials. Canada convicted Kurt Meyer, for example. He was an SS officer, found to be responsible for the execution of eighteen Canadian prisoners just after D-Day. *[The SS were Hitler's elite, fiercely loyal and often murderous soldiers.]*

There's a mountain of information like this in the archives. I came across the notes of one researcher. It was a list of the people he wanted to track down because they had supposedly committed war crimes against Canadian soldiers. And one name on the list was Wilhelm Mohnke.

When I started to read about Mohnke, I didn't realize the stature of this guy. He was almost an original Nazi. Joined the SS in 1931. He became a general, in charge of a Panzer division in Normandy. Canadians had the misfortune of running into his guys after the D-Day invasion. These Germans were hard-core. They'd been on the Russian front. They were fanatical. They were Hitlerites from the time they were children. There were accounts that they killed five or six Canadians for every one of them killed. There were also accounts of Mohnke having lined up Canadians who'd been captured on the field of battle and machine-gunning them. Then after the war he just disappeared.

I had all that in my head when I heard from my American friends in Washington that there was an SS reunion taking place in a town called Nesselwang in the Bavarian Alps. So I went. I flew over, rented a nice car, a convertible, drove to Nesselwang and checked into a guesthouse.

The SS reunion was something else. These Nazis were real Nazis. Not neo-Nazis. Nazi Nazis. There were two major groups: the *Waffen* SS, combat troops, and the "Death's Head" SS, the ones who ran the concentration camps. And a few were *Leibstandarte*, Hitler's personal guard.

They had locked themselves inside a hotel. I was on the outside with a bunch of European journalists. The reunion had also attracted a lot of neo-Nazis, skinheads and the like. And in response to that, a lot of German leftists had shown up to protest. So lots of Communists were there, and people from the universities. But all on the outside. That hotel looked impregnable.

I remember going back to my hotel and sitting in my room and thinking, "Jesus Christ, this is hopeless. What am I going to do?"

Then I went to the bar, and this very attractive woman came over to me. She asked if she could sit down and have a drink with me. I thought she might have been a hooker. But she turned out to be a professor from the University of Munich. A

Communist. And she offered to translate and help me. I said, "Sure." She wouldn't even take any money.

And she turned out to be an absolutely brilliant translator. She kept her face perfectly impassive even though she felt these people were devils. We ran into these Nazis around town and made a few contacts even though they were very suspicious of reporters. I soon found out the town was really a Nazi haven. It was a town from which the Nazis had originally emerged. The owner of my guesthouse was looking over my shoulder at the notes I was writing and he started telling me these men weren't evil. He said they were patriots.

When the Nazi reunion officially ended, I just stuck around. The other media people packed up. I was still there with the translating professor. And no one else from the media. One of the Nazi guys we had run into, a travel agent from Frankfurt, invited us into the hotel for one last night of festivities.

I'm tall. I have blue eyes. I had been in the military. I don't have blond hair, but I had passed Aryan muster with these Nazis. And some of the guys started telling me their ranks and letting their guard down.

So I asked if anyone knew Wilhelm Mohnke. It got quiet for a bit. But then one of them got drunk and he told me that Mohnke never came to these reunions, but he lived outside Hamburg. He even told me which street he lived on.

I had to go to Vienna after that to keep an appointment with Simon Wiesenthal, the most famous of the Nazi hunters. And I had some business in Munich too.

Then I drove up to Hamburg. I went right to the university because that's where you can always find the best fixers, people who can translate and give you the lay of the land. I hired a very earnest, very smart young man. He really understood the local customs as well as the language.

We found Wilhelm Mohnke. We contacted him by phone. And we told him what we wanted. We told him he could tell his story or not. But either way there would be a story. I always find it quite helpful to tell people the story would get done one way or the other. I say, "You can participate or not, but if you don't then you leave it all to me."

So he said yes. And this was on a Sunday. He said, "I will see you Thursday morning at nine."

Right at the appointed hour, I arrived at the house with my student. Mohnke's wife answered the door and she offered us desserts and coffee. He was wearing a suit. Sitting at a desk.

So we started talking. I laid out the Canadian government's case against him.

He listened and it became clear that he didn't give a shit about who he was killing during the war. It was all a means to an end. At one point he said to me, "What are you, a Protestant?"

And I said, "Yes, Scottish."

And he said, "You know, if it had been necessary to eliminate Scottish Protestants, we'd have done that."

Now this was his way to justify the Holocaust, and I'd heard it before. Nothing personal in all the killing, just a consequence of war. It scared the living daylights out of my student because he'd never met a real Nazi before.

And this was a real Nazi. At the end of the war he was in Hitler's bunker. He might have overseen the burning of Hitler's body. That's how close he was to the top.

I asked him again if he'd killed Canadian prisoners. "Did you do it?"

He said, "For the record, I never had any Canadian soldiers machine-gunned. But do you not think the Canadians were doing that?"

He was making the point that the Allies shot prisoners, but there are no war criminals on the winning side.

The other thing he did was pull out a scrapbook. He had kept some documents. Some even signed by Hitler. But one of Mohnke's documents was his order to have a German soldier executed for raping a French girl. This was supposed to show me that the German army functioned like Knights of the Round Table. They had some code of honour. I think he was trying to say if we shot anybody, well everybody was doing it, and this document shows we were honourable too.

He told me the story of his life after the war. He'd been arrested by the Russians. Spent six years in solitary confinement at Lubjanka prison in Moscow. Freed in 1955. He returned to Germany, where he had very good contacts. And he got a job dealing with trucks and trailers.

So I wrote up the story and there was a big reaction.

The justice minister at the time was John Crosbie. He was asked why we weren't arresting Mohnke. He'd been a free man for thirty years. Canada was very embarrassed. But the Germans weren't going to hand him over. And our government said there would be trouble proving a case against him now because of the lack of surviving witnesses, even though I'm not sure that was true. You can find witnesses.

Wilhelm Mohnke was probably the closest thing to a pure fascist I had ever met. He was hypnotizing. You finish reporting a story like that, and it was like that Leonard Cohen poem "All There Is to Know about Adolph Eichmann," where Cohen describes how ordinary Eichmann was and asks if you were expecting talons or green saliva.

It reminded me of that.

So when it was over I realized I had managed to do what the Canadian government hadn't managed to do in thirty years—find Wilhelm Mohnke. Which forced you to ask if they had been trying very hard, if they really wanted to prosecute any of these guys.

Mohnke wasn't hiding. He had never changed his name. He had a good job. And he used all that as evidence that he wasn't guilty of anything. He was sort of saying, "If I'm such a big war criminal, why am I here?"

I was only twenty-eight years old. It was a hell of a big story. And I had done it by myself.

Lisa LaFlamme:
Naimatullah's
Cancer

LISA LAFLAMME WAS AN OVERNIGHT SUCCESS IN ONLY ONE SENSE: she worked a lot of overnight shifts. A lot of them. She started in Kitchener, Ontario, working from 4 AM on Saturdays and Sundays. She worked part-time for seven long years before she got a call to come to Toronto and do some anchoring when CTV launched its all-news channel. At the same time she did consumer reports for the network.

She then worked on Parliament Hill, anchored *Canada AM* and then became CTV's national affairs corre-

Photo courtesy CTV News

spondent, which let her loose on major stories at home and abroad. In 2011 she became the chief anchor and senior editor of CTV *National News*.

Sometimes, not very often, but sometimes, a story just walks up to a journalist. It happened to Lisa LaFlamme in 2006 when she was on assignment in Afghanistan. But no matter the cliché, stories don't write themselves. A reporter has to recognize what's happening and cover every possible angle to make it come to life, and to draw the bigger picture around it.

I spent a lot of time in Baghdad from 2002 to 2006, so I was comfortable with a war and military environment, but I'd never been to Afghanistan before. When I arrived in Kabul I was exhausted. I was taken to a house where I'd stay overnight and my local fixer, Mohammed, said to me, "I'll bring you your flight ticket from Kabul to Kandahar tonight."

I said, "I'm so exhausted. Just bring it in the morning."

I went to sleep and the next thing I knew Mohammed had busted into the room, right through the door, pulling me up from the bed and slapping me and shaking me. There was a faulty heater in the room and I was overcome by carbon monoxide. It took me hours to begin to feel normal again. Mohammed had saved my life. If he had listened to me and waited until the next morning to bring the plane ticket, it would have been game over. I had been in the country for just a few hours and survived a near-death experience, not because of a war but because of a faulty heater.

Stranger still, when I got to Kandahar, my head still feeling very blurry, the first thing I heard was that two Italian aid workers had died that night of the exact same thing—

carbon-monoxide poisoning from a faulty heater. It was hard to get it out of my mind. I thought a lot about it as I slept that night, "I've survived so there must be a reason I'm here."

In all my time in Baghdad I had never been embedded with the troops. I was a little nervous with the concept. But I was at Camp Nathan Smith, not the big air base in Kandahar. This was a much smaller camp. It meant I could cover the kinds of stories I wanted to do more readily because I was right in the city, not forty minutes outside as the air base was.

The media was set up in an old fruit-canning factory. There were about eight cots lined up. I was the only woman at the time and there was a little area where I could change privately. But really, I was so exhausted by the time I got there I didn't care. I could have slept on the head of a nail.

I was going to be on this assignment for a couple of months. So I wanted to find a healthy mix of both military stories and people stories. I took any opportunity they gave me to go out on a convoy. I was out for days at a time sleeping in gravel pits in the middle of what they called the kill zone when they tried to get the Taliban. But I always lean to stories that tell the human side of anything. So when we came back to the camp I tried to do a story on a hospital or a school.

To do those stories I had the help of another fixer, Jojo. He was my lifeline. This nineteen-year-old kid was just an incredible guy. He was willing to go anywhere or do anything and we really did cover amazing stories. I know we pushed the envelope. And we had to push because that was the only way we could explore whether the Canadian military's work was helping or not helping.

(Five years after I met him, Jojo was killed. He pulled up at a stop sign in Kandahar City and was shot in the head at point-blank range. He was obviously seen by the Taliban as a collaborator, working with the Western media. He had never carried a weapon. He was just a kid.)

I had been in Afghanistan and at the camp for about a month when, one Saturday morning, I walked outside and saw an unusual sight. I ran to my cameraman and said, "Get your camera. Just shoot. I have no idea what this is, just shoot." I could never have dreamed what would unfold.

I saw this man in full Afghan garb, limping terribly—an old, old man. And with him a little boy with a scarf, his mother's scarf—though later I would discover she was dead—wrapped around his face and this big bulge on the side of his face. They came up to the gate and because they were not seen as a threat the guard let them through. They went right into the medical tent and we just kept following and recording. The doctor unwrapped his scarf and there was just this horrifying massive abscess on his cheek and jaw.

The doctor was such an incredible man. He even spoke the local language. He'd worked in Canadian emergency rooms and he knew it was bad. He knew it was probably cancer and there wasn't much they were going to be able to do for the boy, whose name was Naimatullah. But they did what they could. First of all just taking off the scarf. There was blood and it was very painful for the boy. He was screaming and the grandfather was sitting in a chair not knowing what to do, but realizing these people were the best hope for his grandson.

The medics gave him some drugs and laid him down on a gurney. Over the next few hours word of Naimatullah spread through the camp and people just kept coming into the tent. A lot of the soldiers had toys their own children had given them to remember them by, and now they were handing them over to Naimatullah. It was very powerful to see that.

A local Afghan doctor was called in and he said the only palliative care hospital in the region was in Pakistan and it cost a hundred dollars a day to stay there. That was an impossible amount for Naimatullah's grandfather. The Canadians concluded the boy would die at home, probably in some pain. They gave him some drugs and reluctantly sent him on his way.

But one soldier decided to write to his church in Edmonton to see if they could raise some money for the boy. He seemed hopeful, even confident, but there were no guarantees.

I decided to go home with Naimatullah and his grandfather. And oh my God! What a slice of the tragedy that is Afghanistan. We walked into a mud compound, very dark. Suddenly I saw a person in a corner. It was Naimatullah's father, hopped up on heroin. He was on his haunches, leaning up against the wall. He was physically shaking. He looked maybe twenty-five years old, but I really don't know how old he was. He couldn't even speak. There were poppy fields all around the neighbourhood and they hadn't done any mass eradication programs. Most of the people there were addicted.

The grandfather seemed heartbroken. His son was in this terrible state, and now his grandson was very sick. This old man would eventually be the only man left in the family. The next two generations were lost generations.

A little later I found a rehab centre for heroin addicts, but it was just more evidence of what Afghanistan needed. There was a massive lineup when I went there. The treatment consisted of strapping down patients on boards lying on the grass in the open air, binding their hands and legs to the board and waiting for them to get through the shakes.

We put Naimatullah's story on the air that night, and I'm told the newsroom phone started to ring off the hook. People wanted to do something. The military was also getting calls. The base commander called me over and said, "You know we're not an effin' charity. What are we supposed to do with this?"

Well, they started a little think tank at the camp to figure out what they were going to do. Then the Edmonton church did indeed raise some money and it started to hear from other churches that wanted to contribute. Within seven or eight days there was $18,000. I was stunned by that. It was encouraging and inspiring that Canadians cared so much.

The Canadian doctor told me that if Naimatullah's cancer had been caught early, it could have been treated. So I went to an Afghan hospital to show why early treatment there had been impossible. The woman who ran the hospital showed us around. The facilities were filthy, filthy, filthy. There were wards full of children. There were lovely, well-meaning, well-educated people on staff ready to help but they needed drugs, they needed medicine, they needed equipment. They needed all the things that were hard to get in a place like Kandahar. I have a searing memory of a dental chair that looked like it came right out of *Silence of the Lambs*. The chair had straps to tie the patient down because there was no anaesthetic to put anyone out.

Behind the hospital there was a dump—a seething, filthy, rat-infested dump with piles of surgical needles and bloody bandages. And little kids played soccer there, or climbed in the waste.

Before long the grandfather and Naimatullah came back to the Canadian camp. Again there wasn't much the doctors could do. They sedated the boy. But with the money that had been raised they started making arrangements to send Naimatullah to Pakistan, to the palliative care centre in Lahore.

That hospital required an adult to accompany the boy and to stay with him as well. Originally a Canadian civilian on the base was going to go, but to his credit the grandfather pushed to say it should be a family member. And that's how he ended up in Pakistan as well.

It took about three weeks, maybe a month. I was out of Afghanistan when Naimatullah died. That poor, beautiful boy. I knew he was going to die but I sobbed when I heard the news.

Honestly, it was like a knife in the gut. But he died in a very clean children's cancer hospital. He was in a clean bed. He had clean jammies on. That was some comfort.

And since all the money raised back in Canada wasn't used on Naimatullah, there were other children who benefited from his legacy.

We saw the best of Canadian intentions on display. I'm sure it created a lot of goodwill in Afghanistan. That grandfather would have gone back to the people in his district and told everybody what the troops were doing. So there were elements that were very positive in the battle for hearts and minds. But it wasn't a conscious battle for hearts and minds. I saw those conscious efforts—troops going into villages to hand pencils to the kids. But this outreach to Naimatullah was the real thing.

As a reporter you never want to be just a reciter of the facts. Another goal is to expose something—expose abuses, expose needs. Here was a story that showed Canadians what Afghanistan needed, and what the military was doing to provide. It became very personal for me. I always think of myself as a human being first and a journalist second. I felt like I was doing some good. I remember this story so vividly because it mattered.

Peter Mansbridge: Under Vimy Ridge

Photo courtesy CBC

THERE IS SURELY NO ONE IN CANADIAN JOURNALISM WITH A MORE UNLIKELY CAREER PATH than Peter Mansbridge. A high school dropout (nothing he is proud of, but something he does not hide), he was loading bags onto an airplane in Churchill, Manitoba, when he was asked to announce the next flight. A CBC manager, Gaston Charpentier, was in the airport, liked the voice and hired him. That he would one day become the personification of CBC News, its chief correspondent, was a prediction only a madman would have made.

It didn't happen overnight. Peter went from Churchill to Winnipeg, Regina and Ottawa before landing in Toronto. He has anchored *The National* since 1988, as well as major news specials, including federal elections, the 9/11 attacks, the Pope in Canada and the death of Pierre Trudeau. He has never forgotten the importance of getting out into the field to report. He's done that from world capitals and war zones, and from every province and territory. He even did a live broadcast from a Canadian icebreaker moving through the Northwest Passage.

Peter Mansbridge also anchored CBC News coverage of the nine-tieth anniversary of the battle of Vimy Ridge, when the Queen re-dedicated the monument after it had undergone repairs. He made a return visit in 2014.

Canadian soldiers fought as Canadians for the first time on the morning of April 9, 1917, more than two years into the horrible sav-agery of World War I. Previously they had fought as members of the British Army. But on that morning in northern France, the four Canadian divisions came together for the first time. More than 15,000 infantry-men charged the German positions at Vimy, positions that the French had tried to capture at least twice before, incurring more than 100,000 casualties, but failing.

The Canadians had planned with meticulous thoroughness. They came up with an innovative "creeping barrage" strategy for artillery—a thunderous assault of shells that moved just ahead of the troops, and forced the Germans to keep their heads down. After three terrible days of combat, the Canadians stood atop Vimy Ridge, 7.5 kilometres long. A total of 3,598 men had been killed; more than 7,000 had been wounded.

After the war, to show its gratitude, France ceded Vimy Ridge and the land around it to Canada. A soaring monument now stands there, that cannot but stir any Canadian who sees it. Figures on the monument represent faith, justice, peace, honour, charity, truth, knowledge and hope. A female image, *Canada Mourning Her Fallen Sons,* takes your breath away.

....

My grandfather fought at Vimy. He was originally British, but he was living in Canada when the war broke out. He signed up and he went overseas in the Canadian military. He was wounded at Vimy Ridge and taken back across the Channel to a Canadian military hospital in Folkestone, England. That's where he met my grandmother. She was a nurse whose husband had just been killed in the British military.

It didn't take long for them to get married, and my father was born the next year, in 1918. The three of them came back to Canada after the war. They lived in Toronto but my British grandmother just couldn't stand it, so they went back to England. That's why my dad ended up in the Royal Air Force in World War II. So that's a very personal connection I have to Vimy.

My other connection is in the place I live—Stratford, Ontario. The war memorial here was designed by Walter Allward. It's the last project he worked on in Canada before he was selected to design the Vimy monument. So it's nice to think of the one in Stratford as a mini-Vimy.

We were in France in June of 2014 to mark the seventieth anniversary of the D-Day landing. Because 2014 was also the hundredth anniversary of the start of World War I, CBC was planning a special program, and we thought that since we were already in France it would be a good time to also go to Vimy and do some shooting for the special.

On June 6, then, we were in Saint-Aubin, a town along the beach where Canadians landed on D-Day. The emotion of that day is pretty special and you feel proud as a Canadian. I walked the beach, thinking about what it must have been like for those guys. We were on the air for five or six hours—a long day. That night our CBC group got together for a small party.

The next morning most people slept in. They would get up in time to drive to Paris and then fly home. But I was up at five o'clock that morning, and at my door were the producer, Stephanie Jenzer, and the cameraman, Pascal Leblond. We got into the car and, in a way, we began travelling further back in time, going from World War II to World War I. We arrived in Vimy around lunchtime. I could see the monument, of course, before we got there. It's a staggering sight, high on the ridge, visible from kilometres away.

We had agreed to meet at two o'clock with people from the Durand Group in Britain. They're volunteers with an interest in military history and expertise in underground exploration. They were going to take us into the Goodman Subway, one of the fourteen tunnels that had been dug before the battle at Vimy to allow troops to move forward to their attack positions under cover, out of sight of the Germans and safe from artillery. There are other tunnels at Vimy that tourists can go into. You can get some sense of what it must have been like in 1917. But they're not that deep, and they're perfectly safe. The Goodman Subway is the exact opposite—very deep and not so safe.

We met the group at two o'clock and they drove us through the restricted areas where people aren't allowed to walk because there are still, these many years later, unexploded shells from World War I. They took us on a little trail in a couple of vehicles, deep into the woods, through the barbed wire. We got to a little log cabin that I had to stoop to get into. There were a half-dozen men inside—the underground exploring group. They are the only people allowed to go into the Goodman Subway. They've been at it since 2000, but it's still unstable. There have been collapses. A man had been killed there just a year or two before. But they had obviously determined it was relatively safe for us to go down. You know, it's funny: in the limited amounts of time I've been in war zones or tricky situations, you think about danger a lot before you get there, but when you're there you're so overwhelmed by what you're in that you don't think about it.

They gave us a safety lesson, told us it might feel claustrophobic. They said if we felt frightened to speak up and they'd get us out of there right away. Then they strapped us into some gear, put hard hats on our heads, and we started walking into the forest. All of a sudden I saw a metal door in the ground. We opened that, and a ladder dropped down. It's eight metres down, far enough and dark enough that I couldn't see the end of the ladder from where I was standing. I was hooked up, and men outside were holding me by ropes as I went down. There were the three of us from CBC, and one guide named Nick Pryor.

He was a beauty. He had a British accent and he spoke breathlessly. He always sounded like he was extremely excited. He lost his breath telling the simplest story. But that's charming on the air and it only heightened the experience.

I'm six feet tall so the first thing I noticed was that in most parts of the tunnel I had to be hunched over. In a hundred years the average height of a man has changed. They built the tunnel to this height because most of the people back then were much shorter. If the soldiers had to stay down there for any length of time, they wouldn't have wanted to be hunched over.

The walls of the tunnel are like chalk. They look just like the White Cliffs of Dover. That's their colour. They haven't changed in a hundred years. Nothing down there has changed. It was like walking back in time. The only light was from a flashlight that Nick was carrying—a kind of lantern. And we had lights on our helmets. So I had to bend over and shine my headlamp down to see what Nick pointed out. There was stuff all over the place. There were bits and pieces of rifles, hatchets, communication lines running along the floor of the tunnel. I saw a water can, a food tin and various tools—all rusty. And there was live ammunition on the ground. Nick picked something up and he said, "Peter, this is a live grenade." The next thing you know, he passed it to me and I was holding a live grenade that was all rusted. I didn't hold it for long. They're trying to keep everything just as it was, so we just put it back down and moved on.

I saw where the military dumped their water supply into a pit. There was another area they used as a toilet. I saw where the soldiers slept when they were in the tunnels for a long period of time. Nick said the tunnel had been used before, during and after the attack on Vimy Ridge. Very exciting.

Suddenly he said, "Look at this wall. It's not in any of the other tunnels that have been discovered. We've never seen anything like it."

It was our guys' names. They looked like they'd been written yesterday. That's how well preserved they were down there, because of the temperature. Some looked like they were done in pencil. Some looked like they'd been etched in. I didn't see anything that looked like ink.

I tried to imagine how the names got there. Somebody had to have been the first to do it. Some guys were standing there in the hours before 5:30 AM, when the signal was to come to charge out of the tunnel. They had nothing to do except stand there or sit there, so somebody put his name down. And a pattern developed. In some places there's a soldier's name, then their regimental number and the regiment's name. Sometimes they added where they were from. It's usually just the province. Sometimes there's a town, but it's mainly provinces. And then in some cases—not many but a few that I saw—the guy drew something.

Someone from Nova Scotia drew a fish. A guy from Quebec drew a canoe. A guy from Ontario drew a maple leaf. A guy from Manitoba … we weren't all in agreement as to what it was. It looked to me like he had drawn a wheat field. And from British Columbia there was a guy who didn't draw anything— he carved a face into the wall. Whether it was his face or his buddy's face, we don't know.

At that point it got quite emotional. I think the men were telling, in a couple of lines and a picture, their life story as Canadians at that time. It may well have been the last thing they ever wrote. Did they go out the end of that tunnel and become one of the thousands of Canadians who were killed or wounded? You look at all this, and you just don't know.

I was sixty-five years old when I went down there and of course no one that old was down there during the war. But I tried to imagine what eighteen-year-olds must have been thinking at that moment. Canadians hadn't yet been in a big battle. And the war was a slaughter. It was butchery. Those guys were fodder for machine guns and cannon. They probably took some comfort in the fact that they were underground, safe from shelling. But they surely knew the odds were that they were going to join the brutal statistics. You can't be down there without imagining what it must have been like for those young guys.

And the walls made it personal. Those names and places. The casualties weren't just numbers anymore. A living Canadian actually wrote his name here just before he went into battle. To look at it and to touch it—I felt a powerful connection between me and that soldier.

It was such a tremendous privilege to be there. It would be a major project to make the tunnels safe enough for tourists to go through. As far as I know there are no plans to do that, and I'd be very surprised if there ever are. This was the first time they'd even let a media person down there.

I've had amazing opportunities in my career to see so many things, and meet so many people who define us as Canadians. But I have never been to anything quite like Vimy. When I came out of that tunnel I can truly say I had never felt more Canadian. There I was in France, visiting something almost one hundred years old, and it was incredibly moving.

Joyce Napier: Interview with the Devil

Photo courtesy Joyce Napier

JOYCE NAPIER IS A JOURNAL-IST WHOSE CAREER PATH ISN'T EXACTLY RARE, but it's not typical. She has worked in both of Canada's official languages. She started in Montreal, first as a freelancer for *The Globe and Mail*, then full-time for The Canadian Press. She switched to French for a job at *La Presse*, then back to English again to work at CBC News. She started that job just three days before the École Polytechnique massacre and was the first CBC reporter on the scene.

In 1991 she made what was supposed to be a short job swap with a colleague from Société Radio-Canada, and Joyce has been with SRC ever since. She has reported from Jerusalem and from Washington.

On July 4, 2005, Joyce Napier was waiting in a Radio-Canada television studio in Montreal when Karla Homolka—probably the most notorious female serial killer in Canadian history—was released from prison. Homolka had chosen to be interviewed in French only, sensing that Quebeckers would be more willing to accept her than English-speaking Canadians who had probably followed her case more closely.

On the scale of horror, Homolka's crimes are off the charts. One of the people she killed was her own sister, Tammy. Homolka drugged her so that Homolka's fiancé, Paul Bernardo, could rape her. The unconscious Tammy choked on her own vomit and died. (Bernardo was despicable as well. As the "Scarborough Rapist," he had assaulted at least eighteen women over a three-year period.) After Homolka and Bernardo were married, they kidnapped, tortured and murdered a fourteen-year-old girl, Leslie Mahaffy. Then they kidnapped, tortured and murdered a fifteen-year-old girl, Kristen French.

When the pair were arrested, police assumed that Bernardo had been the prime instigator of the crimes. Indeed, Homolka claimed Bernardo had forced her to participate. Homolka was then told if she agreed to testify against Bernardo at his trial, she could plead guilty to her role in the murders and be sentenced to just twelve years in prison. She took the deal. Only then did police find a stash of videotapes that told the truth about what Homolka had done. It was clear evidence that she had committed unspeakable crimes quite willingly. But it was too late to undo "the deal with the devil."

....

I was a Washington correspondent for Radio-Canada at the time. But I was in Montreal filling in for someone who was on vacation. It had been arranged well before anyone knew we'd be getting an interview with Karla Homolka. Four days after I arrived, though, I was told that there was a possibility we'd be getting her. This was Thursday and she was going to be released from the penitentiary the following Monday. Every media outlet in North America was trying to get an interview, so we were among hundreds that had been in touch with Homolka's lawyer.

I had no part in securing the interview. None. All the credit goes to a producer and a researcher. It was their efforts that paid off. On Friday I was told definitively that Homolka would be coming to us directly from prison. I was told it was very hush-hush. I was to speak of it to absolutely no one. In fact, very few people knew about the interview even within Radio-Canada. The technical crew that eventually taped the interview—the cameramen, the audio operator, the director— didn't know what they were coming in to do that day. It was very *Mission: Impossible.*

I spent the weekend reading about the case. I had been living outside the country during the Bernardo trial and had not followed it closely. I wanted to have my facts straight. And I soon did. I had the facts. I knew that the Canadian justice system had made a serious mistake. I knew this Homolka woman had managed to manipulate the justice system and make us believe for a while that she was not what she was. It took me until Sunday to understand the psychosis of the case. Until then I was just a journalist who had to do an interview, a big interview, but still just that—an interview. I didn't realize the emotional side of it right away. The outrage is what I didn't measure, the outrage of Canadians.

On Sunday I realized how extraordinarily closely everyone would be watching the interview. And I admit I started to have doubts about whether I was the right person to do it. I knew I was good on foreign affairs. I had acquired many years of experience. I'd covered big stories. Gone to wars. I knew this was different. I knew that if I screwed this up it would damage my reputation. I thought about calling my boss and saying, "Perhaps you want to get someone else to do this. I'm a reporter. I don't have the kind of discipline you need for a long interview. What I normally do is very different." It was as close to a panic attack as I've ever come. But I didn't make the call, and when I woke up Monday morning I told myself I was going to do it and I wasn't nervous anymore. I just made up my mind that I was going to do it.

When Homolka arrived I was ready. I had my makeup on. I had put it on myself that day. I didn't want anybody fidgeting with my face. I was in my bubble. I was extremely focused at that point.

Homolka's lawyer had engineered an elaborate plan to drive away from the prison without being seen by all the reporters waiting on the outside. They were in a van, hiding in the back under carpets. They drove right to Radio-Canada, taken into the bowels of the building where deliveries usually arrived. It was an industrial environment. And then they were rushed into the studio. We had a very austere setting. Just a black curtain surrounding us.

The lawyer was on the verge of falling apart into a million pieces. It was surprisingly touching. I wanted to take her hand and tell her everything was okay. She was a young woman. Her client was a serial killer. Maybe she had a problem with that. Or maybe she was thinking about what she had just gone through—an escape from hundreds of reporters and producers and satellite trucks. If that had gone wrong she could have been trapped and the situation could have gotten out of hand. [In a strange twist, Homolka would eventually marry the brother of this lawyer. She's had three children with him.]

So that was the scene when Homolka stepped into the studio. I was ready and focused. Her lawyer was falling to pieces. Homolka looked at the makeup table with the powders and brushes all laid out, and the bright lights around the mirror. And she said, "Don't you have a hairdresser?" I looked at her and said, "No. We just have a makeup artist."

She said her hair got a little messy when she was in the van, hiding under the carpet. I was thinking, "Your hair got a little messy? That's what you're thinking about now?"

At that point our makeup artist, a young woman, realized that she was going to put makeup on Karla Homolka. She did it, but she told me later she had wanted to mess up the job because Homolka was a horrible person.

We shook hands. She had a soft, moist handshake. But the thing that struck me was the look in her eyes. Maybe I read into her eyes what I knew about her. But I thought there was a look in her eyes that was very disturbing. It was dark and blank. There was no expression there.

Then we started the interview. It was going to last twenty-seven minutes. My objective was to make her talk for twenty-seven minutes because I thought that's what people wanted to hear. They didn't want to hear me lecturing her. It wasn't about me. I thought if I struck a pose of neutrality, I might draw her out. I don't think she rehearsed her answers, but she was always careful to be in control. I don't know what would have happened had I waggled my finger at her and started lecturing or hectoring. This was a cold, calculating woman. I was sure I wasn't going to break her in twenty-seven minutes. I knew what I was dealing with. I knew what I was up against.

From the very beginning I thought it was obvious that Homolka didn't have the basic human ability to distinguish between right and wrong. She's a psychopath. She's a sociopath. Here was someone who did horrible things and yet she was so matter-of-fact in her tone. I've met people whose hearts are full of remorse and regret. Roméo Dallaire is one of those people. I interviewed him about what he considers his failure to stop the genocide in Rwanda. He broke down in the interview. He's a man whose heart will forever be filled with remorse. But Karla Homolka is not like that at all.

About halfway through I asked, "Your relationship with your family is difficult?" And she said, "In what way?"

For a split second I said to myself, "In what way? She's asking, 'In what way?'" And I said, "Because you killed your sister."

She had committed that unthinkable crime and yet she didn't think there was any reason for her to have a difficult relationship with her family. That was the pivotal answer. It revealed exactly who she was—a psychopath living among us.

At the end I asked, "What is the first thing you'd like to do as a free woman?"

Her answer was, "I'd like to have an iced cappuccino. An iced cappuccino from Tim Hortons."

The interview was her first and maybe only chance to tell Canadians she was a thoughtful, remorseful, introspective person. And the extent of her immediate ambition was to have an iced cappuccino. That said a lot.

When it was over, she stood up and walked out of the studio. No handshake. I had to be civil, but I didn't have to be friendly.

The next day, a lot of the media blasted me. Columnists wrote critical things, and that's their right. And these many years later, I know why. I wasn't emotional enough for them. Was I outraged at the deal Karla Homolka had struck? Of course I was outraged. But I was one person and I hadn't reflected the outrage of millions of people. When I read the criticism in the newspapers, I saw that they wanted me to have beaten her up a little bit more. And maybe I should have been more aggressive. But I didn't want to become the story. And I don't like to show my feelings on television. When I was in Jerusalem and a man blew himself up in front of my children with a bomb, I didn't want to go on TV and explain how I felt. I just can't do that.

Look, my daughter was the age of her victims at the time, so I had no love for Karla Homolka, not even compassion for her. I didn't necessarily feel hatred for her, but I did feel she shouldn't have been a free woman. She should have been locked up forever. I had met creeps before her. I was a crime reporter for five years so I knew there were all sorts of ways to kill people. I had often been in courtrooms and listened to gross testimony. So, evil? I was accustomed to it. I once went to a maximum-security prison to do a story and as I sat in the cafeteria a man who had killed three people offered me a slice of pie. So I had met creeps before. But Karla Homolka was a dark human being. A dark dark dark human being.

Laura Lynch:
Zimbabwe Crisis

LAURA LYNCH HAS A LAW DEGREE, AND SHE WON A NIEMAN FELLOWSHIP at Harvard. But those two facts are footnotes in a journalistic career that has taken her around the world. She started in British Columbia—in Vancouver and Prince Rupert. She has also been based on Parliament Hill and in Washington, London and Toronto. From those points she's travelled to every corner of the planet, mainly for CBC.

Since there are only two countries on earth that start with the letter Z—Zambia and Zimbabwe—

Photo courtesy CBC

Laura is likely one of the few journalists to have reported from both. In 2007, a trip to Zimbabwe proved to be a highlight of her career.

The story of Zimbabwe starts out as a familiar one: a country in Africa where the white minority is in complete control and the Black majority is denied its rights. The Black opposition is declared illegal and its leaders tossed into prison. Eventually, the white government concedes that the status quo is untenable. It releases a charismatic Black leader from prison and he becomes president in the first democratic election.

That was the story of South Africa, of course. But it was also the story of Zimbabwe. When it was run by whites the country was called Rhodesia. Robert Mugabe spent eleven years in prison, and then became president. But there the similarities with South Africa end. Robert Mugabe was no Nelson Mandela. Mandela became a symbol of tolerance and harmony among all people. Mugabe became a tyrant. He has been president since 1980. By 2007 his policies had driven Zimbabwe into an unstable, often violent state. The people were impoverished by hyper-inflation so staggering that Zimbabwe's currency lost all meaning.

When I was doing my Nieman Fellowship in 1999/2000, one of my classmates was a Zimbabwean journalist. He came to Harvard shortly after being released from Mugabe's jails, where he'd been tortured. He'd had the guts to publish a story about an attempted coup on Mugabe. He came to our class as a psychologically damaged person. At the end of his year in the United States he could easily have won asylum and stayed. But he chose to go back because he wanted to run for office and try to make a difference in his country. Sadly, he died before he could do that. But that's why the Zimbabwe story was personal for me.

It was never easy to get into that country, but in 2007 the

Mugabe government had completely locked things down. It wasn't letting in any journalists. The economy was going further and further down the toilet. People were suffering physically and there was a lot of violence going on. I thought it was time to get there and try to tell stories that needed to be told about what was going on inside. It was obviously risky. There was an awful lot of preparation to make sure we'd be safe when we got there. Weeks of preparation. We knew that if they discovered we were journalists, we would go to jail.

I decided that the only way I was going to get into Zimbabwe was as a tourist. That wasn't much of a stretch because there were lots of tourists going there. Some to hunt, some to see Victoria Falls. Our story was that the cameraman, Richard Devey, and I were friends who were going birdwatching. We thought that would explain the camera. I would tell the border agents that I was a lawyer, which I am. Richard would tell them he was a musician, and in fact, he used to play in a band as a drummer. So our stories were easy because they had some truth in them.

We booked rooms at the best hotel in Harare even though we knew we weren't going to stay there. The border agents were likely to ask where we were staying, so we had to have reservations somewhere. We would end up in a safe house instead. We never went close to the hotel. That hotel would have been teeming with government agents and spies. If we had gone there we may as well have waved our hands and said, "Come get us." At the safe house we could just try to blend into the neighbourhood. One night we went out for dinner. Another day we went shopping and bought paintings just as tourists would.

Another precaution was to land in Bulawayo, Zimbabwe's second city. We knew that security was much tougher at Harare airport than at Bulawayo. Richard had put his tripod inside his nylon bag, but he was quite nervous that the authorities would immediately think it was too professional for a birdwatcher.

We had flown in from Johannesburg and because there was a lot of theft there, people routinely wrapped their luggage in stretch plastic. We had done that, but the legs of the tripod stuck out from Richard's bag. Sure enough, the border people wanted to have a look. They tore at the wrapping, but it was too thick. So off they went to find some scissors. But with the way things were in Zimbabwe at that time no one could find a pair of scissors, so they let the bag through.

We had arranged for a security guard to meet us outside the airport. Immediately we were smacked in the face with the reality of Zimbabwe. Because there was a fuel shortage, the back of the truck was filled with fuel cans, to make sure we had enough for our trip to Harare. We also had to get through police checkpoints where people would be routinely stopped and fined for some imagined violation of the law, which was just the way the police would try to make some money in a place where nobody had any money.

We got to the safe house that our Zimbabwe security man had arranged. And now the best-laid plans fell apart. The security man had a lot of contacts in the country, so well in advance of our arrival I had sent him a list of the some of the stories I was interested in, and the people I wanted to talk to. He had not done a single thing about arranging anything. He was not journalistically inclined. That sent me into an absolute panic. We had five days to do our work. That's not a lot of time when you are operating under cover. So we went one step at a time. What could we do?

We drove around Harare and Richard shot pictures surreptitiously from the car window. There were extraordinary lineups everywhere—at banks, bakeries, gas stations. You might have expected the lineups to turn into demonstrations or protests, but the people were so beaten down. They just waited and waited. They just felt they had no other option.

We needed some scenic shots of the city, so we drove to a

park that rises above Harare. Richard pretended to be taking pictures of me when he actually was shooting past me, toward the city.

We went out to interview people under cover of darkness. We were always careful to check that we weren't being followed. At times I asked myself if we were taking too many precautions. On one level the things we were doing sounded absolutely ridiculous. From an espionage novel. But I just kept reminding myself that not only were Richard and I taking a risk: the people to whom we were talking were taking a risk. Our local fixer was a young Black Zimbabwean. He had direct knowledge of what the regime was capable of. He'd been tortured. He showed us his scars. So this wasn't make-believe. It wasn't a game. It was real. People's lives were at stake. So I thought it was probably a good idea to be paranoid.

In fact, just a few months after we left Zimbabwe, Barry Bearak of the *New York Times* was arrested for, as he put it, "committing journalism." He had also entered the country as a tourist. He was held for thirteen days with another journalist from the *Sunday Telegraph,* in a jail he described as "filthy. The odor of human waste infected the air."

The risk of being sent to one of those awful prisons was real. Which is why we were so careful.

There was no power in large parts of the city so it was very dark on the roads from Harare to the outlying townships. Once we got to our destination and out of the car, we moved as fast as we could. Richard and I are white and we stood out like sore thumbs. All it would have taken was for someone to tell the wrong person we were there, and suddenly the police would have arrived to pick us up. Because there was no electricity, Richard sometimes used a miner's lamp on his hat to light a scene. Our pieces had a moody look because of that, but it wasn't art—it was necessity.

I managed to connect with a doctor who was the head of

Physicians for Human Rights. We went to his house to talk to him. We arrived at the prearranged time, but he wasn't there. He had gone out to get food for his family. And that could take hours and hours. So we waited a long time for him. The crushing reality of living there just kept coming back.

We went to a hospital and we filmed children who were dying from a very preventable disease. At the mortuary the coffins were piled up as they tried in vain to keep up with the dying. We went and filmed in a cemetery. That was risky because it was in daylight. We had to move quickly filming the headstones, trying to show just how many people had died in recent months and how young they were.

I found out about a small village where people's homes had been knocked down by the regime because they had voted for the opposition in previous municipal elections. The situation there was so dire and so desperate. People living with next to no shelter. Old people who were ill. Children who had lost their parents because an AIDS epidemic was wiping out large parts of a whole generation. Walking through mud with no shoes. And the only thing they had done, the only crime they had committed, was to not vote for Robert Mugabe. That brought it all home. The reality of Zimbabwe.

We had done all the work we could in Harare. But I wanted to interview the Opposition leader, Morgan Tsvangirai. So the plan was to wake up on our last morning, go to his home and then hightail it down the road to the airport in Bulawayo. That was the time I was most nervous we'd be discovered because government security would be watching his house. We went into his compound and did the interview and he was obviously glad to see us because there were so few journalists in the country. Then we got out as fast as we could.

All our work would have been wasted if our videotapes were seized at the airport. While we were in the country we had hidden them in boxes of Tampax, confident that no one would touch them. Now we had to get them out. We concocted a plan for that even before we arrived. We would send everything back by courier to London. We were assured that would be safe.

Did anything change because of my stories? It's hard to measure what the impact was. It would have opened some people's eyes in Canada. And since my stories were picked up by other broadcasters around the world I'd like think they helped accelerate international efforts to crack down on Mugabe. Zimbabwe got under my skin. It should have been an African success story. It was a country with so much potential. The literacy rate was high. It had industry and agriculture. It was the breadbasket of Africa and it was turned into the basket case of Africa. It was hard to watch it crumble, especially under a leader who started with such promise. Mugabe came to power saying that he would rule for everyone. Then he proceeded to go after his own people again and again and again, relentlessly. I feel so sad for so many people who thought their lives were going to get better and instead became immeasurably worse.

As a journalist, I had a responsibility to go to Zimbabwe and tell the story that Robert Mugabe did not want told. He didn't want the world to see what he was doing. And as long as no one was bearing witness, Mugabe would get what he wanted. At least I had done something to hold him to account.

Kevin Newman:
John Glenn's
Shuttle Launch

Photo courtesy CTV News

KEVIN NEWMAN'S FIRST JOB IN JOURNALISM WAS AS A SPORTS REPORTER for Global Television, even though he says he had "almost no interest" in sports. A year later he found himself at Global News in Toronto and he was plenty interested in that. He was posted to Parliament Hill for the network and then CTV hired him to report on Atlantic Canada from Halifax. He went back to Parliament Hill for CTV and then moved to CBC in Edmonton. But CBC moved him back to Ottawa for another round of political reporting, then to Toronto to host *Midday*.

He spent seven years at ABC in New York—as the anchor of *World News Now*; the news anchor of *Good Morning America*; the co-host of *Good Morning America*; and finally as a reporter for *Nightline* and *World News Tonight*. He came back to Canada in 2001 to become the first anchor of *Global National*, based in Vancouver and then Ottawa. In 2010 he returned to CTV in Ottawa, and then moved to Toronto in 2013 as part of *W5*.

At two and a half years of age, Kevin Newman was too young to pay any attention to American astronaut John Glenn's first flight into space. But in 1998 he was at the Kennedy Space Center for Glenn's sequel.

Both of Glenn's flights were huge media events. The first was in 1962, when he became the first American to orbit the planet. That earned him a tickertape parade in New York City, even though two Russian cosmonauts had been in orbit before him and one had done five times as many orbits as Glenn.

His second trip, thirty-six years later, was on the space shuttle *Discovery*. At seventy-seven years of age, he became the oldest person ever to fly into space.

I was a total Apollo junkie. I got unnaturally excited every time there was an Apollo launch. I guess the first one I tuned in to would have been Apollo 7 in 1968—the first one after the disaster of Apollo 1. I keenly remember that one. I remember researching how they were testing what it would take to get to the moon.

[Apollo 1 was destroyed by a fire on the launch pad during a test, less than a month before it was scheduled to lift off. Three astronauts were killed. It took NASA more than eighteen months to correct what had gone wrong and launch the first manned flight in the Apollo Project—Apollo 7.]

I'd always been a bit of a *Star Trek* fan growing up. But

this Apollo program just seemed heroic. It seemed impossibly ballsy. Whenever there was Apollo coverage on TV I would be there from the beginning to the end. It was probably the first time I experienced live breaking news coverage, where you could be taken somewhere and experience it in real time with the people who were at the location. I guess it was intoxicating in some way. I felt that it was bringing me from suburban Mississauga, where I lived, to a place I wouldn't be otherwise.

I thought the astronauts were the men that I would never be. They were almost unreal. I was nine years old. I wasn't interested in character. I wasn't interested in nuance. I didn't want to begin to understand them. They were just guys in a rocket going into space. I think I knew myself well enough to know that I was too chicken to be an astronaut. Maybe that's why journalism worked for me. We're not actually doing the stuff. We're observing the people doing the stuff.

I tended to watch the coverage on CBS. There was something about Walter Cronkite's enthusiasm and his childlike wonder and sense of adventure that I found so compelling. I thought he had the most amazing job anybody could ever have. He would be sitting at that desk and there would be a rocket behind him. It was all so captivating. I was totally transfixed.

Interestingly, as time went on, I became more fixated with the people who were sitting beside Cronkite. The people explaining it were usually some of the original astronauts in Project Mercury—Wally Schirra, Scott Carpenter.

Much later, when I watched *The Right Stuff*—the movie about the original seven astronauts—I recognized and connected to the people being portrayed not as astronauts but as the colour commentators on the moon shots.

I remember wondering what it took to be that Cronkite guy. I don't think I had the awareness as a nine-year-old, but when I think back, I realize it really was the beginning of my understanding that journalism could be a ticket to be a witness to history, and that you can credibly claim to belong somewhere when amazing things are happening.

In July of 1969 I was ten and I was so excited by the moon landing. I knew it would be dark by the time Neil Armstrong put his foot on the moon, and I was getting more and more excited waiting for the sun to set. Then I could go down to the basement and watch this thing happen.

I remember that grainy picture—Armstrong going down the ladder. For some reason I couldn't figure out what I was seeing. I wasn't sure where his body was. I was so frustrated. My brain couldn't process it initially. It was only when he jumped down and planted his foot on the surface of the moon that I got it all. I was pretty stoked about it and I remember getting up the next morning and racing out the front door to pick up the newspaper. The *Toronto Star* had the biggest headline I had ever seen—"MAN WALKS ON THE MOON." Stunning.

As I grew up, I continued watching. I always found the extraordinary danger associated with space flight compelling. I remember Apollo 13. *[What should have been the third landing on the moon in April 1970 was aborted on the way to the moon when an explosion in an oxygen tank made a landing impossible and put the safe return of the astronauts to earth in serious doubt.]* I was really anxious following that, understanding what was at stake and imagining what it would be like to never come home. So I continued to watch the space program. I was hooked for life.

When Marc Garneau became the first Canadian in space in 1984, I went down to the Kennedy Space Center to cover the event for Global News. The cameraman, the soundman and myself were all guys in our twenties. We were thrilled. We took a tour one day around the space centre. We saw the original Apollo mission control. I saw all the stuff I had grown up seeing on TV. It was incredible.

The shuttle launch was something else. I could feel the blast—a rush of air pushing up against me. And then I heard the extraordinary crackle of a shuttle launch. I remember thinking two things. One was, "Holy shit! Man is capable of incredible power." And second, "Who in their right mind would sit on top of that?" I was twenty-five at the time, and to that point it was the best assignment ever.

Eventually shuttle launches became more routine. When I was the news anchor for *Good Morning America* I sometimes handled live coverage of a launch from the news desk in New York. Nothing fancy.

When it was time for John Glenn to ride the shuttle, I was the host of *Good Morning America* and I pushed to be involved. It was a classic American story: John Glenn returns to space. It was the kind of story that played right into everything US morning television did. It was Americana. It was an adventure. It had tension. It would be one of those dawn-to-dusk days in American television news where our program would start the day, set the stage. Then Peter Jennings would take over to anchor coverage of the launch later in the day. There was a great appetite for everything John Glenn did because he was so iconic.

We had to find a way to make the story our own. I pitched the idea that I should interview John Glenn. A week before the launch I flew down to Houston mission control, which was a dream come true.

I sat in a room in front of John Glenn, and the weird thing was that he knew me because he watched our show. I was totally the fan. I was barely a journalist. I did manage to ask him whether he felt it appropriate that a man his age and of his stature as a senator should be taking up space on the shuttle. He answered it easily because he was obviously prepared for it. We had a good conversation, a good interview. The one mistake I made was bringing a book that he had written years before to Houston to get him to sign, and then completely forgetting. I am still pissed off at myself about that.

It wasn't until an editorial meeting three days before the launch that I was told our producers had lined up Wally Schirra, Gene Cernan and Scott Carpenter as the expert panel that would sit with me for our live programming. These were the same guys I had watched—as a kid—sitting with Walter Cronkite. Now I was going to be at the desk with those three former astronauts, which was pretty cool. I was very excited.

There was one more thing I did: I asked if we could get a pass for my eleven-year-old son, Alex. He was kind of into space. I had triggered his imagination with Lego space battles and that kind of stuff. And I thought that if I wanted to experience this launch with anyone, it would be with Alex. We got the pass, and he and I flew down.

We got to Cape Canaveral and went to see our ABC set. There was a full mock-up of the shuttle. I brought Alex inside and he sat in the co-pilot seat playing with the toggles. He had the time of his life. It was really very special.

We went back to the hotel room. I got my research, crammed for a bit and then went to bed.

On launch day we got up at 3:30 in the morning. Our astronaut panel, icons of my youth, showed up happy to be there, excited to be on television again for the launch of someone they knew personally. They were solid men. It was almost like a sports team reuniting. They didn't see each other all that often so now that they were together it was fun to see them ribbing each other. They were laughing at how fat they had all become, how bald they had become. I could tell they had an intimacy with each other.

We went to air and it was one of the easier shows I did, because I was knowledgeable, interested and enthusiastic.

When you have all those things as a host you know the show is going to work. And the show really did work. It was a really good show. I had this enormous out of body experience. There are times as an anchor when you have to make sure not to over-think yourself—just live in the moment, don't go outside yourself because you're not going to be able to function.

But this wasn't one of those times. This was a moment when I gave myself the luxury of standing outside of myself as I was broadcasting, thinking, "Look what you're doing here. Look who you're with. Look how far you've travelled. How amazing is this?"

When the show was over I pulled my son onto the set and introduced him to the astronauts. It was probably the best moment I ever had in journalism because I got to introduce my son to my own childhood heroes. And to me that encapsulates what journalism can be. We get to be witnesses to our time. We get to be witnesses to the adventure of our time. And for those of us who are fathers or mothers, there are occasions when we can pull family into our experience and give them the benefits of our profession. To say, "You just met somebody you never would have met if I wasn't a journalist."

As journalists, we ask our families to give up a lot. They're expected to put up with all the demands on our time. So I really felt that in that story I was able to give something to my child that he wouldn't otherwise ever have had a hope of experiencing.

For the launch, we got on a bus that took us to a VIP area even closer to the launch pad than the media area. I was twice as close as I had been when Marc Garneau went up. The blast was much more profound. I felt the heat and pressure up against my chest. I had a little camera and as the shuttle was going up I was shooting Alex watching it, his mouth agape and speechless.

We always look for an arc to run through a good story, something to tie everything together. Look at the very clear line in my story—through my fascination with space, its intersection with live television, and the role of the anchor and the role of the storyteller. It all came together that day. And on top of that I was able to give back a little to my family. It was insane.

Paul Workman:

Liberating

Kosovo

Photo courtesy CTV News

PAUL WORKMAN'S FIRST JOB IN JOURNALISM WAS AT THE *OTTAWA CITIZEN*. But in less than two years he made the jump to television and has been a fixture now for more than forty years. He started with CBC News in Ottawa, then moved to Regina, Edmonton and Montreal. Among the major stories he covered in that time was the 1983 murder of JoAnn Wilson and the subsequent trial and conviction of her former husband, Colin Thatcher, and the 1989 massacre of fourteen women at the École Polytechnique in Montreal.

He became a foreign correspondent in 1990, first in Jerusalem, then in Paris. In 2006 he went to CTV News as its correspondent in New Delhi, and then became the network's bureau chief in Washington. He covered both Iraq wars, the war in Afghanistan, the fall of the Berlin Wall and the assassination of Benazir Bhutto.

In 1999, Paul was in Kosovo at a time of great upheaval.

When Yugoslavia broke up, there were two provinces in Serbia—one of the newly independent republics. In the province of Kosovo, the largest ethnic group, Albanians, began to agitate for independence.

By early 1998, there was a full-scale war raging between Kosovo and what was now left of Yugoslavia, the republics of Serbia and Montenegro. A year into the war, the Serbs began a campaign of "ethnic cleansing," murdering at least six thousand people and perhaps twice that number. In addition, more than 1.5 million ethnic Albanians were forcibly expelled from Kosovo.

By March 1999, the West had seen enough. The North Atlantic Treaty Organization (NATO) began a bombing campaign against the Serbs, the first time it had ever used force. In June, it began to prepare a ground invasion. But that was made unnecessary when Serbia agreed to withdraw its military from Kosovo.

....

Early in 1999 I was in Macedonia with my producer Edith Champagne. She read something somewhere, just a couple of paragraphs, about how people were beginning to leave Kosovo, forced out of their homes. This was the beginning of the expulsions, very early on. To her enormous credit, Edith said we should go there.

We had an old, lumbering armoured vehicle. So we packed up and made what was essentially a pretty dangerous drive over the mountains to get into Albania. It took hours and hours. We finally got to a small Albanian town around five or six o'clock at night. And what a sight there was. There were wagons coming toward us pulled by tractors. Entire families, their possessions piled high. Grandmothers. People walking. Animals. Carloads and wagonloads of people.

As we kept going we saw masses of people, these ethnic Albanians, coming across to safety in Albania. Terrible scenes. People brought their old parents out in wheelbarrows and went across fields because the Serbs had blocked the roads. It was really quite astounding, quite moving. There were extraordinary moments, extraordinary pictures and unforgettable memories of people suffering terribly.

It was raining and it was muddy. It was incredibly difficult to work. There was one restaurant/hotel and we didn't have a room. We bunked in somebody's house for a while. But we stayed with the story.

We were the only Canadian crew anywhere near the place. The only other journalists there were from CNN and from French television. And we had the story pretty much to ourselves for days, until everybody else caught on to the fact that there were tens and tens of thousands of ethnic Albanians pouring out of Kosovo. Eventually 800,000 to 1,000,000 came pouring out. We stayed for more than a week, and because I had spent so much time watching this refugee procession, I grabbed onto Kosovo as my story. I wanted to own it.

Many weeks later, when the NATO bombing campaign started in Yugoslavia, I was waiting in Macedonia again for whatever was going to happen. Either the NATO force would go in to fight a war or it would go in to keep whatever peace was arranged. No one was sure which it would be.

I had been there for three or four weeks when a Canadian team of reconnaissance people, about a thousand strong, arrived in the country. It was a very state-of-the-art reconnaissance unit. Of course I met the Canadians when they came in, and spoke to the commanding officer, Major Paul Fleury of the Edmonton-based Lord Strathcona's.

"Look," I said to him. "If you go into Kosovo, I want to go with you."

He said, "I think we can arrange that."

These were the days before embedding became common. But he promised, and I took him at his word. Then things began to move politically. The Serbs agreed to sign a treaty, and that meant there would be no ground war. It meant a NATO peacekeeping force was going to move into Kosovo.

Late on a Friday night, I found out the Canadians were going to be leaving for Kosovo the next day. I tried to get in touch with Major Fleury to say, "Okay I want to go with you. You promised I could go." But I couldn't reach him. He wasn't answering his phone. I was pissed off.

He had been very amenable to the idea of my coming along. He had not received permission from National Defence in Ottawa. This was just something he said he would do. But now I couldn't reach him.

I got up early the next morning and got into a taxi. I was on my own, with no producer or camera crew. The taxi took a back road, a road parallel to the one I thought the Canadians must have been moving along toward the border with Kosovo. Then we drove back down the other way and found the Canadians. I jumped out of the car and found Major Fleury.

"You promised you would take me into Kosovo."

"Yes, I did," he said. "How much stuff do you have?"

So I showed him what I had: a backpack, a camera, a little tripod and a sleeping bag.

He said, "Come on up."

So I joined him in his command vehicle. The Canadians were among the first NATO troops to go over the border because they were ready. And they had the equipment to move into the country, see what was going on and report back to the other troops who were following.

But the convoy moved very, very slowly. The first night we stopped short of the border and set up camp. The next day we moved out again and we crossed into Kosovo around dawn. Major Fleury opened up the hatch of our vehicle and let me poke out the top with my little camera. And there I was, taking video of the Canadian troops moving into Kosovo in a line of armoured vehicles. I was the only journalist there, coming across the border.

There was no resistance. The Serbs were docile. There was always the possibility that someone would get angry and start fighting or that somebody would fire weapons in the wrong direction and start something. But by and large it felt safe.

I stayed with the Canadians for two or three days. At night we camped out in the middle of roads because they were worried about land mines. When you travel with soldiers, you bond with them. You like them, you joke with them and you get to understand what they are going through.

When we started to move into villages that had been under Serbian control it was like a scene from 1945. People came out of their houses with bouquets of flowers, bottles of wine. They were shaking hands, getting their pictures taken, climbing on the Canadian armoured vehicles. And the soldiers really felt that they were liberators. It was an extraordinarily emotional time for them because they were doing something that was very important.

It was emotional for me as well. I was observing everything and taking pictures and thinking, "This is what it must have been like for the war correspondents who came into Europe on D-Day and marched into those French villages, greeted like heroes and liberators."

In some ways it all went back to my childhood. I used to watch *The Twentieth Century* with Walter Cronkite in the late

1950s and early '60s. He had these terrific war stories with terrific war footage and as I got older and interested in journalism I always thought that D-Day was one of those stories that I regretted not being able to cover as a journalist. Seriously. I wanted to be Robert Capa. I wanted to be Matthew Halton. *[Capa was a still photographer for* Life *magazine. Halton was* CBC's *best-known war correspondent.]*

It was probably the first time since the Korean War, perhaps even World War II, that a CBC journalist travelled with Canadian forces into what was essentially a liberated war zone. It really felt like I was a true war correspondent. For the first time.

And being a journalist was the only way that I would have been able to experience and witness what I did.

We are witnesses. That's what we are. That's what I've always considered my most important role. To witness, if not history, then current events. Witness whatever suffering, whatever happiness takes place on the ground in these situations. It really was one of those moments where I thought, "Yeah, this is why I got into journalism."

Céline Galipeau:
A Curse in
Afghanistan

Photo courtesy Société Radio-Canada

CÉLINE GALIPEAU HAD BEEN WORKING AT HER FIRST JOB in journalism, at a Montreal radio station, for just a little while when she came to the conclusion that she had a terrible voice. She thought that a move into television would at least give her an opportunity to mask the voice with pictures. So she went to a much smaller city, Trois-Rivières, to begin anew. That seems to have worked.

In less than a year she was back in Montreal, this time at Société Radio-Canada, where she was a reporter and part-time anchor. She was then posted to Toronto for the network before beginning a series of overseas assignments. First, she reported from London. Then she took on Moscow for both SRC and CBC. Céline was then posted to Paris, before moving to Beijing, again reporting in French and English for the public broadcaster.

She came back to Canada to anchor the weekend editions of SRC's nightly news. Since 2009 she has been the chief anchor of *Le Téléjournal*.

Céline Galipeau's coverage of an almost unbelievable state of affairs in western Afghanistan was searing—and a sad reminder that democratic freedom was still an empty promise for far too many people.

When the last Canadian soldiers left Afghanistan in 2014, Canada's ambassador to that country said that the families of military members who had been killed in the war could take some comfort from "the knowledge that the sacrifices of lost loved ones has been worthwhile, that they made a difference."

Maybe.

Canada and Afghanistan are separated by 10,000 kilometres. But that physical separation is dwarfed by other considerations. Human rights for example.

....

It was 2007, more than five years after the fall of the Taliban. We were being told that things in Afghanistan were still difficult but getting better. Canada was in the country for a purpose, and one of those purposes was helping Afghan women. And I could see that we were helping some. I remember going to Kabul on earlier trips to Afghanistan and I could see women in the streets. Women were going back to schools and universities. Some of them were working. But at the same time, life for most Afghan women was still really hard. That's what I wanted to show.

In the West we were talking a lot about the burka and the

veil, the external symbols of women's oppression. But for Afghan women oppression went way beyond symbols. I had heard about women who were so desperate they committed suicide by self-immolation. To me that was awful. It meant so much pain. It meant such a hard death. Why would women do that? I wanted to do the story, but I didn't know if I'd be able to. I wasn't sure we'd have access to it. The phenomenon was most widespread in Herat, in the northwest corner of the country. I didn't know if we'd be able to travel there because it wasn't very safe.

Most Canadian journalists at the time were covering Kandahar because our military was there. I had been in Afghanistan three times before, but this time I wanted to try to show what was going on in the rest of the country. In Kabul I did stories on the reconstruction, corruption, how everything was quite chaotic. But I wanted to get to Herat.

The roads around that city were just too dangerous for driving. Even flying wasn't too safe because Ariana, the Afghan airline, was flying old Russian planes. But we decided to risk it, and we made it to Herat. When we landed it looked like a beautiful city.

We made our way to a hospital and I spoke with a doctor. He said he was treating eighty women who had tried to kill themselves by setting themselves on fire. He was short on medicines and I think he thought our reporting might help relieve that situation. So he agreed to organize things for us, which wasn't easy.

I had a cameraman and my translator was also a man. In Afghanistan, a man is not allowed to see a woman. In these rural areas women stayed in the house almost all the time because no one was supposed to see them. If they did come out they wore burkas, so no one saw them. If another man saw them they were considered spoiled. In some cases that was enough to get them killed.

When a woman went to hospital, she had to be accompanied

by a man from her family. There was no other way for her to be in a public space. So all these men who were watching over the women were all over the hospital. They sat in the corridors, usually on the floors, and they just waited. They waited until they could take their woman back home or until the woman died. So when the doctor agreed to let us in the ward where the women were, he first had to get all the men out because they never would have allowed us to take pictures inside. They never would have allowed us to get close to the women to talk to them.

The doctor told all the men to leave. But they were all outside as we came in, and they were angry. They realized what was happening. There were about a thousand really angry men outside the hospital screaming at us.

We went in and we were allowed to stay for maybe an hour. I didn't really know what I was going to find. There was a special area reserved for the burned women. Oh, it was so despairing! It stays with me even today. I can still remember those women in pain. It's always hard to see someone suffering but this was extraordinarily difficult. The women were all lying down and they were all crying. Not crying openly, more like weeping quietly. Most of them were burned over 60 or 70 percent of their bodies. They had some ointments and some bandages, but nothing more, nothing for the pain. We were in a country of opium and these women had nothing to help them.

All the women were young. I think you had to be young to do something like this to yourself. I think you had to be young not to realize how painful this was going to be. Because you don't die immediately when you burn yourself. It takes time. The burns get infected after a while and the women die in terrible pain.

This was a story about self-immolation, but in fact some of the women had been burned by their husbands. When they wanted to get rid of their wives, they just set them on fire. And if by chance they survived, they'd bring them to the hospital. No one would ever say what happened. There's so much shame, there's so much fear. It's difficult to get the truth. Even for the doctor and the nurses. The doctor talked to the women, encouraging them to talk to me, but it was very difficult.

I got close to a woman named Sarah. She told me she was twenty years old. She had burns over 60 percent of her body and she had her child next to her. She explained to me that she was forced into marriage when she was seventeen to a man she didn't know, a man her family had chosen for her. She started her new life with him and he started beating her. Her in-laws were also very hard on her and they beat her as well. She felt that she wasn't a wife—she was more like a slave to this family. That often happened, apparently, in the rural areas. The women were married off and they become in charge of cooking and cleaning. This young woman was so desperate that one day she had had enough. She doused herself with cooking oil and then she lit a match.

I tried to get her to explain why she had done that, and I realized that she had done it because it was the only thing she could do to say, "No." To say, "Enough." It was the only thing she felt she could do to rebel. It was quite something to realize women could be so desperate that the only thing they could do was kill themselves like that.

I asked her what she was going to do when she got out of the hospital and went home. "Will you go back to your own family?"

She said, "No, I cannot go back to my family because they don't want me. They are ashamed of what I have done. I have no choice. I have to go back to my husband's family."

I looked at her and said, "Aren't you afraid?"

She said, "Of course I'm afraid, but what choice do I have?"

Like all the women, Sarah depended on her in-laws even for medicine or antibiotics. The families didn't want to pay because the woman was worth nothing when she came out. If a woman survived through the hospital stay and was brought back home, very often their families killed them because they were deformed. They were useless. I know what I'm saying sounds harsh and brutal, but it's the reality of Afghan women. Unfortunately, they weren't worth much.

I talked to another woman whose name was Sahebjan. She was eighteen. Her story was quite awful because she had been married to a cousin and he started beating her the night they got married. One day he tried to kill her, he tried to strangle her. And then he gave her a container of gasoline and told her to burn herself. And so she set herself on fire. But she didn't die. She was in the hospital and her mother was with her. She told me she wanted to die. She didn't want to live. That the abuse from her husband was so harsh she just couldn't stand it anymore. She just wanted to die. She said, "It's just unbearable. Let me die."

When I left the hospital I felt so powerless. What could I do? At the same time I was thinking, "What can we do in a country like this? How can we help a country that treats its women like this? How many years is it going to take to change the mentality? To change something so entrenched? How can we change a country that thinks women are worth nothing?"

Afghan men were not treating women like this because of the Taliban. This was happening before the Taliban, and during the Taliban, and men were going to treat women like this after the Taliban.

Canada and other Western countries were trying to help Afghanistan. But I became very pessimistic about achieving success. Most of us don't know what is really happening in that country. The only things we usually see are the military, the politicians. We are so proud because now there's a parliament and there are women in parliament and that is a good thing. But for ordinary women things are quite different. In a sense violence comes from everywhere to these women. From their fathers. From their husbands. From their brothers. From their fathers-in-law. From their mothers-in-law. And they're absolutely powerless.

It was such a discouraging story to tell, but as a journalist I felt that I had at least given a voice to those young women who didn't have a voice—women who had no choice in life except to try to kill themselves in this most horrific way. I thought I could at least give them a voice to explain what they were going through, explain the situation of most women in Afghanistan.

I'm Canadian. I was allowed to work. I was allowed to study. I never had any problem. I knew it was still a problem to be born a woman in certain countries, but I never knew how bad, how terrible it was still for so many women. From then on, everywhere I went I started to do stories specifically on the fate of women—in India, in China and elsewhere.

We usually talk of war in military terms: Who's winning and who's losing? How many are dead? We tend to forget what happens to ordinary people going through extraordinary events. Ordinary people who live terrible lives, who will never get statues built to honour them. Ordinary people who are victims.

Of course, my story didn't change anything. But at least people would know about those women, and people would realize that we still had a lot to do in that country to be able to say we did something for democracy and we did something to help ordinary people.

Laurie Graham:
No More Coal
Mining

LAURIE GRAHAM'S FIRST JOB IN JOURNALISM WAS AT A RADIO STATION in her hometown of Sydney, Nova Scotia. After six months, she joined CBC in Sydney and stayed with the corporation for twenty-three years. She was based in Halifax, Toronto and on Parliament Hill. In 2013 she joined CTV News as deputy bureau chief on Parliament Hill.

Photo courtesy Laurie Graham

She has covered several election campaigns in Canada and also reported from countries around the world, including Russia, Haiti, the

Netherlands, South Africa and the United States. But she says her heart has never left Cape Breton.

Laurie Graham was the reporter who broke the news that the federal government was closing the last coal mine in Cape Breton.

Coal mining went back a long way in Cape Breton. The first deposits were discovered in 1672 and underground mining began in 1720. For more than two hundred years coal provided a livelihood—albeit a difficult one—for countless men and their families. But by the end of World War II, the coal-mining industry was in decline. It picked up for short periods of time—during the Organization of Petroleum Exporting Countries' oil embargo of 1973, for example. But the long-term prognosis was clear: the industry was dying.

It was a long, painful death, especially for the miners who needed the work. Governments tried several schemes to make the industry viable, until their cupboard of ideas was bare. In May 2001 the federal government gave up the fight.

....

I'm from Cape Breton and once you're from the island, you're from the island. I've always understood that it's an industrial area. My family was more steel than coal. My grandfather was a steelmaker. My uncles all worked at the steel plant. I didn't have any coal miners in my immediate family—my dad was a fireman and my mother was a teacher—but I always knew that coal and steel were what kept the island alive.

I was a local reporter for about eight years in Cape Breton. Coal was a big part of the news. There were always problems with the industry. Governments kept saying, "We can't keep pouring money into it." But there was a tremendous amount of denial in the mining community and disbelief, because mining was in families for generation after generation. It wasn't just fathers and grandfathers and uncles—it was a great-grandfathers and great-uncles too. Communities were born out of coal.

It was death by a thousand cuts over a long period. People would be laid off, but then a mine would get a new contract so everyone would come back to work. Then there would be another down period. Then some country would say it needed more coal to be shipped. Great! Now people came back to work.

Governments always worried about the political impact of what they did. So they were reluctant to do anything definitive that might lose them seats at election time. But the miners never thought governments did enough. It seemed they were always angry with every politician, provincial and federal. "We need these jobs," they'd say. "They should be helping us. They should be finding more contracts."

The best example of their anger happened in early 2000. The federal government laid out a plan for shutting down the industry that was going to take about a year. There were a bunch of guys who were going to fight this by taking over a coal mine. They went underground and occupied it. They wanted the government to talk to them, to negotiate with them. They said they weren't leaving. They just wouldn't let the mine shut down.

Of course, the media arrived to see what would happen. We were all outside and these guys were underground, but we found a way to talk to them. They had a cellphone and we set up a contraption with a microphone and I interviewed them from the back of our van. Just listening to their voices was kind of haunting.

It went on for about two weeks. There were about ten men underground. But on the outside there were maybe four hundred people supporting them. Friends and family. A local priest was there and he called the occupiers heroes. So it was a community that was fighting. They finally got a commitment from the government to try to work out a more generous severance package, and I got word that the men were coming up.

The families who had been in the parking lot suddenly came out of their cars and started to form a wall. I knew that was a sign the men were on their way. And I knew they weren't going to stop to do any interviews. They would never identify themselves because they could be jailed for taking over federal Crown property.

I went to my cameraman, Lyle Hart, and I said, "Lyle, this is going to happen very quickly. Park yourself. Find your spot and get ready."

Sure enough, as the guys came up the families and friends locked their arms and gathered around and shielded them. The miners just ran. It really was a great moment. I remember another reporter being caught off-guard when all this happened, but I was from Cape Breton. This wasn't my first time at the rodeo. This was not my first hangout with coal miners. They knew exactly what they were doing. So the story wasn't just about the miners who took over a coal mine. It was about the whole community and they felt they had won. They hadn't won a lot, but it was something.

One day more than a year later, I was in Halifax and got a phone call from a source in Ottawa I considered to be reliable. He told me that the next morning the minister of natural resources was going to be in Cape Breton to announce that the last coal mine, the Prince Mine, was shutting down.

I was completely floored. To get out of the mining business altogether was huge. I hung up and I checked the story with another source in Ottawa and got confirmation.

There were fewer than five hundred men working in the mine at that point, but in a small community that's a lot of people. And so long as people were working, the possibility was in their heads that things could turn around. They could make themselves believe that the mine would win a new contract to keep things going. So whether it was a hundred people working, or two hundred, or five hundred, it meant there was hope. This was the day that all hope was gone.

I started driving to Cape Breton, but I hadn't yet convinced the national news desk that there was a story here. Just 440 jobs were being lost. Why did that matter? Didn't everybody already know that coal mining was dead?

That's when I realized the value of fighting for a story, and the value of really knowing a story. Knowing the emotion behind the facts. Knowing the emotion of closing down an industry. I argued that we weren't just going to report the facts. We were going to report on what shutting down the mine meant to a way of life.

I drove right to the mine gate. The miners had to come through the gate at the end of their shift. And there they were! It was a scene straight out of the movies. The men carrying their lunch pails, dark faces covered in coal dust because they'd been underground for twelve hours. I told them the news, and the reaction was awful. It was disbelief. Devastation. Anger. Frustration. Tears. Some said they were going to fight the decision. But others were more subdued: "I don't know what I'm going to do," "I don't know how I'm going to feed my family," "This is the only job I know."

Some of the guys were in their forties. They had small kids. And these were good-paying jobs.

The minister was in Sydney the next day and made the announcement, just as I had reported. Now all the emotion started to play out. It was going to take six months to shut down the mine, and I used that time to tell the miners' stories.

I knew a man who had been a coal miner forever. He had young kids, including a son. And that to me was key. Someone close to retirement age was one thing. But this guy had a young son. Was he ready to accept this was real, that the mine was closing? I talked to him about how difficult it was, and I asked him what he was telling his son.

He told me he had grown up in a family where everyone just went underground. His great-grandfather, his grandfather, his father, his uncles, his brothers all went underground—no questions asked. But, he told me, one of the most important things in his life was reading to his son every night. He always had a book to read to his son.

I asked, "Why is that?"

He said he didn't blame anyone, but when he was a boy nobody ever read to him. He said, "If I can read him books he'll understand the value of reading, the value of books and the importance of education. I want my son to have an education and I don't want him to go underground."

And that is a moment I will never forget. Very poignant. He didn't know what he was going to do for himself, but he was making the turn for his son. And that's what any community has to do when it relies on an industry that is going to die.

That's not to say that Cape Breton is a place that doesn't believe in education. There's a university there. But in mining communities the path underground was just assumed. Some kids didn't finish high school. Some may have finished high school but going on to university never entered the conversation. And now for some, the light went on. It was the moment for me when I realized everything was changing.

(More than ten years later I was going through the Sydney airport and I ran into that miner. He was working security. We looked at each other and I said, "Oh my gosh." And he said, "I see you on TV." I asked him if he missed the mine. He said, "Every day." Even though it was such a hard life, he still missed being underground. And his son was in high school.)

The shutdown of the mine was pretty anticlimactic when it happened. The fight was over and it was time to move on.

But it's never time to forget. The island has taught me so much and I never want to forget my roots. The miners taught me to carry myself with pride. My husband is from Cape Breton as well. Any time we think we're having a rough time there's an expression we use to put things in perspective: "At least we're not underground." You think you've got it bad? Why don't you go to work in the dark for twelve hours, doing something that can actually kill you, and that later in life likely will kill you? Go ahead, try that.

I was a young network reporter in 2001, trying to make a difference and trying to help people across the country understand my region—really understand it. Lots of people look at Cape Breton and think of employment insurance. But it is a hard-working community. They want to get up and go to work every day even if it means doing dangerous jobs. I don't think this story ever leaves the back of my mind. It's a constant reminder of who I am and where I'm from.

Martin Seemungal: A Free Election in South Africa

Photo courtesy Martin Seemungal

NOT MANY NORTH AMERI-
CAN NETWORK TV REPORT-
ERS have spent as much time in
Africa as Martin Seemungal. He has
covered some of the most heartbreaking humanitarian crises of our
times, along with wars and environmental disasters. His first posting in
Africa was to Johannesburg for CBC
News in 1991. The CBC then moved
him to Cape Town and Nairobi.
He became an ABC correspondent
in 2000 in Nairobi, then moved to
Rome. In 2007 he went to Baghdad
to report for CBS. He began working for PBS in 2008, became CTV's

Middle East correspondent in 2011, and went back to PBS in 2014, based in Johannesburg.

He had begun his career in Kingston, Ontario, and moved to Ottawa first for CTV, then CBC. He reported for CBC in Toronto before his first posting overseas.

Martin Seemungal was working for CBC News as the South Africa correspondent during a dramatic period in that country's history.

For most of the twentieth century South Africa was a country like no other. Eighty percent of the people who lived there were Black. But they had almost no political power. The government was all-white. Blacks could not vote. But the oppression went much further than that. Beginning in 1948 the government imposed a system of racial segregation it called apartheid. Black South Africans were forced to live apart from whites, and they needed documents authorizing their presence in a white area. Millions were moved from their homes into so-called homelands. They were forced to use separate public facilities, were forbidden to marry outside their race, and they lived with high unemployment and terrible poverty.

The government enforced apartheid with ruthless and sometimes violent determination. Black protest often ended with police gunfire and bodies in the street. Black leaders were exiled, executed or imprisoned. The best known among them was Nelson Mandela, who spent more than twenty-seven years in prison. Only the most optimistic of optimists saw even a glimmer of hope that change was possible.

But then it happened. Mandela was released from prison, and the country began a political process that would culminate in 1994 with the first multiparty, multiracial, democratic election in South African history, and the election of Mandela as the first Black president.

....

It's difficult to talk about Election Day 1994 without the three years that led up to it.

When I arrived in 1991, Nelson Mandela had been free for about a year. He was trying to control the terrible violence that was going on in the townships. The government knew the country was going to go to full-fledged democracy, but it wanted to divide the Black vote. So it started to plant Zulu–Inkatha people in townships dominated by Mandela's African National Congress (ANC). There was tremendous violence between the two groups. That's when "necklacing" attracted great attention. The ANC would find an Inkatha collaborator, put a tire around their neck, then set it on fire, killing them in a gruesome and horrible way.

And within the white community most Afrikaners were very right wing and didn't want any part of Black-majority government. So there was unease, restlessness and anxiety everywhere you looked. There's a certain romance now when people talk about the first free election. There's a tendency to think it was all inevitable. But it wasn't. In the lead-up to the election there were many times when I thought it was all just going to fall apart.

People forget about the referendum in 1992. A whites-only referendum. Black people still couldn't vote. President F.W. de Klerk put a proposal to the people essentially asking if they believed in the concept of one person, one vote. Did whites agree that the government should proceed with negotiations leading to a multiracial democracy? People forget how pivotal that battle was. I remember that everything was hanging in the balance. The vote was yes *[70 percent to 30 percent]* and that was a big step forward.

But it seemed that the violence would never stop. There was a feeling among some that the government was stoking the violence, or at least certain elements within the government were stoking violence. There was always the worry that the government would find a reason not to go through with the big plan.

Whenever the ANC held a demonstration to demand their rights, they ran into the police. Sometimes the police would just open fire and mow people down. I'll never forget covering my first massacre. One minute I was standing there covering a demonstration, and the next minute the police were firing tear gas and then opening fire. Twenty-five or thirty police officers just started shooting. Pump-action shotguns. It was like a firing squad. Finally I heard some policemen yelling, "Stop firing. Stop firing." When the gunpowder cleared, the bodies were just lying there. That's the kind of stuff I got used to dealing with.

They were constantly having demonstrations in the townships just so people could vent. "We want democracy! We want the vote!" Seventy thousand or even eighty thousand people could march. There was a Black element that was impatient with the pace of progress. There were people within the ANC who didn't agree with Mandela. They were thinking they'd been on the bottom long enough. "It's our turn," they would say. "There's no in-between. We're going to take power, and we'll use guns if necessary." Mandela talked them out of the guns. Black South Africans had been marginalized and treated as third-class citizens; they had lived in squalor in urban Black townships and they had been put into pseudo-independent homelands. But Mandela and others in the ANC persuaded them that violence was not going to help their cause. It was quite astounding that most demonstrations were peaceful.

There was one demonstration that started peacefully but ended badly. It became a pivotal event in the lead-up to the election and we were the only ones to capture it on camera. We were filming an ANC demonstration when I looked down the road and saw a huge column of AWB cars. [The Afrikaner Weerstandsbeweging (Afrikaner Resistance Movement) was a far-right political organization firmly opposed to any devolution of power to Blacks.] These guys were thugs. They had guns, shotguns, pistols. They were yahoos, but quite frightening. I turned to my cameraman and said, "This is not good. Let's take cover." So we got behind an armoured vehicle with a 50-calibre machine gun on top. The vehicle belonged to the police in the Black homeland of Bophuthatswana. I thought we'd be safe there.

We started filming the AWB guys. They were cursing and swearing at us. Just as the last car passed by us—a green Mercedes-Benz—a pistol shot went off. One of the AWB guys was taking potshots at the ANC. And the 50-calibre machine gun opened fire. It was like a scene from some gangster movie. All I could see were bullets flying. The AWB car was being peppered with bullets. Eventually the shooting stopped, the car door opened and one guy slumped out. He was dead. The other two guys were wounded. They came out with their hands up and they were just terrified. They said, "Don't shoot us. Don't shoot us." We filmed all of this. We interviewed the two wounded men. And then we left to send our report back to Canada.

About two hours later another reporter dropped by my office and said, "Hey, Martin, did you see the three dead AWB guys?" I said, "No, you've got it wrong. We filmed the whole thing. One guy was dead and two survived." But he insisted all three were dead. I kept saying, "That's not possible. The other guys were wounded and their wounds were not life-threatening."

Then he said, "I've got the photo right here. Three dead." It turned out that after we left one of the more radical elements of the ANC, or the Bophuthatswana homeland police, took out an AK-47 and executed the two other guys. The execution was filmed by a Black cameraman working for CBS.

Well, our footage and the CBS footage made it to South African television and was played over and over again. Everyone saw what had happened. I talked to a newspaper editorialist about it and he said that moment was incredibly important. Because that was the moment when white South Africa realized the futility of resisting change. They saw that Blacks had guns and they could get more guns if they had to. And the whites said to themselves, "There's way more of them than us. So a lot of us are going to die in any fight. And the whole country could easily go down the drain."

That was the moment, two months before the election, when white South Africans committed. Conservative Afrikaners, who were trying to come up with all kinds of excuses about why not to have an election, now said, "We've got to do this or it's going to explode, and there'll be nothing left for anybody."

Still, there was serious doubt about ever reaching Election Day. There was a bomb that went off a week or two before the election in Johannesburg. That was just the kind of thing everyone was afraid of—something that would force the cancellation of the election—because of what we had all gone through and what we had all witnessed. There had been so much violence, so much carnage, so many massacres, so much death. It just seemed that delivering a peaceful, free and fair election would be very difficult.

But we did make it to Election Day. People started lining up to vote at four in the morning. I remember arriving at a polling station at the crack of dawn and seeing this endless line of people, just standing there waiting patiently for the polling station to open. At first I just sat in the car watching. I got tears in my eyes watching these people, knowing what they had all gone through, and not just them but all their ancestors. It was very emotional. I got out of the car to talk to some people.

"Why did you come so early?"

"I've been waiting my whole life for this."

"This is a moment that makes me feel like a human again."

The line snaked back forever. But everyone was so calm. It really struck me that those people knew that they were carrying the weight of decades of oppression. They remembered the brutality that went on and on and on. But now their moment had arrived. They were so very dignified. They knew they had earned this right. They had paid a huge price to get here. Many of them had lost family members over the years to the violence. And they were going to calmly, patiently, graciously take what was rightly theirs.

Some people stood in line for eight or nine hours. No one complained. I remember thinking, "Where does this patience come from?" And that made me think about Mandela and what he had gone through in prison. I think he set the example. He said, "We have to forgive. We have to move on. We're going to destroy this country for everybody if we don't forgive and embrace white South Africans as our fellow countrymen." And that message really got through. I think people carried that with them that day. They said, "If Mandela can go to prison for twenty-seven years, I can stand in line for nine hours. It's the least I can do."

I went to white polling stations as well. Generally speaking they were dour. Whites were largely still suspicious about what was going to happen. But the liberal whites, who had fought for this day, were in some ways happier and showed more emotion than I saw in the Black areas. I once talked to someone who thought that apartheid was as detrimental to whites as to Blacks. At least to the white psyche. There was a guilt about apartheid that whites always lived with. So some of the white people I talked to were so thrilled. When they voted they were freeing themselves. They were throwing off the chains of apartheid that had weighed on their shoulders as well. No longer were they going to be the minority oppressing the majority. "I feel freer than I've ever felt living in South Africa"—imagine a white person saying that!

It was a few days later when Mandela was inaugurated, and for me that was the moment when there was no doubt the new South Africa had arrived. It was the end of what had gone before, and the beginning of something new. That was the huge celebration. It was full of symbolism. First Black president of South Africa, the new flag of South Africa. But to me one of the biggest moments was seeing these old Afrikaner generals of the air force, army and navy standing there after Mandela was inaugurated. As he walked past they snapped to attention. I was only 30 feet from where this was happening and I could see their expressions. They were poker-faced and emotionless, but I wondered what they were thinking. When they joined the military as young cadets could they possibly have seen a day when they would be saluting a Black president? It was very powerful.

I've covered wars and famines and assassinations. They were big moments in history. But I could cover more stories like that tomorrow. I will never cover another South Africa in my life. It's impossible because of what the country stood for. This was a story of the victory of good over evil. I'm not saying the whites were evil, but apartheid was evil, and what it stood for was evil. To cover that story was an amazing privilege that I can't ever forget.

Nahlah Ayed: Revolution in Egypt

Photo courtesy CBC

NAHLAH AYED WAS BORN IN WINNIPEG, BUT WHEN SHE WAS JUST SIX YEARS OLD her parents decided to put her in touch with her roots and moved to a Palestinian refugee camp. She came back to Canada as a teenager and began an education that would make her a journalist with unique credentials to cover the Middle East.

But first she worked in the nation's capital as a freelance contributor to the *Ottawa Citizen*. Then she became a producer for CTV in Ottawa, and then Toronto. She moved back to print for five years at the Canadian Press bureau on Parliament Hill. In 2002 she joined CBC News. Her first posting was in Amman, Jordan—though she was in the Iraqi capital, Baghdad, most of the time. She was based in the Lebanese capital of Beirut for five more years, before she was moved back to Canada to report from Montreal and Toronto. Her memoir, *A Thousand Farewells*, was published in 2012, and in 2013 she went back overseas, first to Egypt, and then to CBC's London bureau.

Nahlah Ayed was in Egypt to witness the end of the Hosni Mubarak regime.

Mubarak became Egypt's president in exceptional circumstances, succeeding Anwar Sadat after Sadat was assassinated in 1981. Mubarak came to be the ex-president of Egypt in exceptional circumstances as well, pushed out in a revolution in 2011. That revolution was part of what came to be called the Arab Spring, a series of protests—some peaceful, some not—from Tunisia, Jordan and Yemen to Libya, Syria and Kuwait. All the protests pushed for more political freedom. Some succeeded in obtaining small concessions. A few succeeded in removing top leaders.

Egypt is by far the most populous country in the Middle East. That's why what happened there was so important. That's why the world was so riveted by the struggle for power between a man who had ruled unfettered for thirty years and the throngs of people in the streets with their hearts set on democracy.

....

When the Arab Spring started in Tunisia, I watched it from London. When we all finally realized what it was about and they were able to bring down the regime, I immediately called the assignment desk at CBC back in Canada and said, "Watch Egypt." I don't remember my thought process but I just knew this desire for change was going to be infectious and that Egypt would be the next to go.

I flew to Cairo three days after the big protests started there. I arrived on what would be called the Day of Wrath. It was Friday. I was desperate to get into town before the Friday prayers ended because I knew the moment they ended, the mosques would empty and all hell would break loose. Which is exactly what happened just as I arrived at the hotel.

Thousands and thousands and thousands of Egyptians were on the streets and there was tear gas everywhere. It was chaos. The hotel was overrun by people trying to get away from both the wall of tear gas and from the police. We were just trying to get our equipment into the hotel when all this was starting to happen. I tried twice to leave the hotel to get out and report, but we just couldn't. There was too much tear gas. I could not breathe. I literally could not walk out. I did some interviews right in the hotel lobby because there were so many people there who had run from the police.

I finally got out of the hotel as night fell. I saw lots of police. And that's when it got really, really bad. The shooting started and the fighting started on the streets. Completely crazy. It was a bloody day.

For the rest of the time there we went out every single day to cover the protests. We covered both sides—anti-Mubarak and pro-Mubarak. The pro-Mubarak side started blaming foreign journalists for fuelling discontent and they started beating up some journalists. So we had to find a way to get the news without putting ourselves deliberately in harm's way. We went around surreptitiously or quietly, or we stayed a little farther back from the heat of the action. Sometimes we took circuitous routes to places to avoid the pro-Mubarak mobs.

One day, when we were trying to avoid a particular area, we took a water taxi across the Nile to go to the other side and went all the way around to try to get back to our hotel. Sadly, under a bridge, we ran smack into another pro-Mubarak protest. There was a group of us in the car. People surrounded us and I heard them saying in Arabic, "Should we cut their heads off now or later?"

They started questioning us: "Why are you here?" "What are you doing?" All of us were screaming at the driver to back up and leave. But he said he couldn't. He said, "They're going to hurt me." And he kept telling the protesters that he had nothing to do with us.

I finally got out of the car and walked over to a policeman. I said, "Here's my passport. I'm a foreigner. We want to get to our hotel."

He walked me over to an army guy and I told him the same thing. He felt that because I spoke Arabic he could make me responsible for all the supposed wrongdoings of the media and he felt free to yell at me. He spent ten minutes yelling. "Why would you bring foreigners on to the streets?" he wanted to know.

"Because we are trying to do our jobs. And I'm not bringing them. They are my colleagues trying to do our work."

But after dressing me down for supposedly breaking some rules, he arranged for us to walk through the crowd to our hotel. We must have passed twenty tanks, which is when I realized why that spot had attracted the army, the police and the thugs. We were at the radio and television building. That's one of the first places the army surrounded because they were worried about what would happen if the other side controlled radio and television.

Speaking Arabic was useful that night, and usually it was. There were many times it alerted me to danger I otherwise would not have known. And it opened doors because people love to communicate in their own language and so it helped me get to the heart of what people were trying to say. But there were definitely times I wish I didn't speak the language. I heard all the insults they thought I didn't understand. Sometimes at a government department or some official office I would insist that I didn't speak Arabic because I knew I would be treated better as a non-Arabic speaker. And Arabic is not spoken exactly the same way everywhere. So inevitably when people heard me speak they would say, "Where you from?"

My answer was, of course, "Canada." But they would always say, "Yes, but where are you really from?"

I would dodge the question, so they would ask it a different way. "What's your father's name?" Or, "What's your grandfather's name?" They can gather so much information just by the construction of your name. They would always try to figure out which side I was on, though I was trying to be as neutral as I could be. I didn't want to start a discussion about my background. I wanted to know what they thought.

Over those fifteen days in Cairo I saw a lot of extraordinary things. One day when I was at the hotel, I heard a roar in the sky. I thought I knew what it was, but I couldn't quite believe it, so I ran to the balcony. Fighter jets flying over the capital of Egypt! F-16s in a circular formation over Tahrir Square. Who thought that was a good idea? I never thought I would see the day when fighter jets were deployed over Cairo. It was the most bizarre sight.

Every day brought something else. Another day I looked over the balcony and suddenly a car exploded.

Cairo is a chaotic place at the best of times. Once the protesters owned Tahrir, it became Utopia. It was organized. It was clean. There were people picking up garbage. There were orderly entrances where you were checked and your bag was checked. It was extremely welcoming to a foreigner and the foreign media. I had never been welcomed so warmly in Egypt, where most people think foreign media are spies. For the first time in the Middle East, I felt wanted as a journalist. People were volunteering to speak to me. English speakers were waving their hands and saying, "I'll give you an interview." It was so unusual, it was almost bizarre.

Much later stories came out about women who were sexually assaulted in Tahrir. *[The most infamous was the assault on CBS News correspondent Lara Logan, who was attacked repeatedly by two hundred to three hundred men.]* I was shocked when I heard about it. I'm not crazy about crowds, but I had walked up and down Tahrir a thousand times and never felt unsafe. My issue is that I'm short. I can't see over the heads of people. I was at the edge of the crowd the night Lara Logan was attacked. I was with our security person. The cameraman wanted to wade into the crowd and get more shots. I said, "It's dark. I can't see past my nose. I'm not coming with you. I'm going to stay here." I told the security guy to go with the cameraman because he would need help. The security man said, "You're just going to stand here?" I said, "Yes, I'm fine."

They were gone a half-hour and when they came back I was talking to the same group of young men that I had been talking to when they left. I never felt unsafe.

The day I knew Mubarak was finished was the day I heard that train tracks had been blocked by protesters. The protests in general had not interfered with daily life. Tahrir was just one part of the city. The rest of Egypt seemed to be operating normally. But now the train tracks had been blocked, so I went to check it out. We drove through a really dodgy neighbourhood and ended up on a major thoroughfare where there was a hostile-looking crowd. Our fixer said, "You have exactly five minutes to do what you have to do. Then we're getting out of here."

I looked over at the tracks and saw not young male university students, not middle-class kids—I saw what looked like ordinary Egyptians. They were people who did menial jobs, difficult jobs. They were standing on the tracks stopping anything from coming or going.

That's the moment when it was perfectly clear to me that Mubarak could not survive. I thought Egyptians could deal with almost anything. Sometimes there are waves of crime. Sometimes the traffic is impossibly bad. The weather can whip up strange things like sandstorms. But if the trains were blocked it meant that bread would soon be impossible to find. And you cannot keep bread from the people. The majority of Egyptians live from hand to mouth and day to day. They literally earn a dollar in the morning and they go buy bread with that dollar in the evening. If you stop that, and people are on the brink of going hungry, that's a terrifying thought. There was no way that could be allowed to happen. Mubarak would have to be removed from power if that was the only way to get bread to the people.

Two nights later, I was at the hotel overlooking the crowd in Tahrir Square. We knew an announcement was coming so we were listening to the TV. I was with another CBC reporter, Margaret Evans. We had both spent decades covering the region and when the news came that Mubarak was gone, we just looked at each other and we both had tears in our eyes. It was just one of those moments. We knew how big a deal it was. It wasn't that I was a cheerleader as a journalist, hoping that change would come because people deserved it. It was just that I had spent much of my life trying to understand the Middle East. My investment in the region told me something was going to happen, so when it did, it felt like vindication.

After the announcement I went into Tahrir Square and into the crowd. I had never seen a happier crowd. I have never seen such jubilance—even at an Arab wedding, which is saying a lot. It was extraordinary. People just wanted to talk. They were singing. There was a woman I was trying to interview but all she wanted to do was ululate. These were people I was not accustomed to seeing let loose. Egyptians are known for their music and dancing. But this was something else.

Especially for the women. They were middle-aged and older, fairly conservative. But on this night they were out there completely carefree—dancing and singing and chanting at the top of their lungs. I have never seen anything like it. The atmosphere was euphoric.

For the first time in their lives they had a reason to celebrate. They didn't want to think too far ahead. They just wanted to milk that moment for as long as they could. The one thing that marks almost everybody who lives in the Middle East, except the really rich and those who are mobile, is that it's a series of disappointments. You have your personal life and then there's a second layer you have to contend with. Depending on what bomb went off where, which two countries are fighting, it's kind of this constant second pressure on your life beyond what we all have to contend with. I think for those people, for the first time, they had a reason to let go. Something had gone right and they didn't care about tomorrow.

It was the first time in my Middle East experience that secular, democracy-minded, fairly well-educated young people were the story. Everybody always wanted to talk about the kids who were growing beards and joining al-Qaeda. The media focused on who was behind the latest explosion or who was joining Hezbollah. The voices of these young people were lost in the cacophony of negativity.

These young people looked at the rest of the world and saw others their age doing so much better. They wanted to know why they couldn't have a normal life. Why couldn't they have a car? A great job? A government that cared about them? This was their time. There's something that gives you a great amount of satisfaction as a human being and as a journalist watching people try to take matters into their own hands.

Mubarak would never have stepped down if the army hadn't forced him to. It was the only institution in Egypt that could hold the country together. As a journalist you had to feel a little disquieted when people were celebrating the army taking over and it's now the guarantor of your human rights and your safety. There is obviously something fundamentally wrong with that. But it was impossible not to be caught up in the excitement on that night.

I get the most satisfaction from my job on a day when I'm able to answer the question *why*. Almost anybody could be a reporter if all you want is someone to tell you what's going on, who's doing it and where. But *why* requires an investment. I realized I had thought about the *why* in Egypt for years. This was not some spasm of violence. What do these protesters want? I knew the answer because I had lived among those people. I had travelled to Egypt a million times and I knew. Everything clicked into place. I actually knew what the hell I was talking about.

Don Newman: Crossing the Floor

DON NEWMAN KNOWS POL-ITICS. That's why his long-running afternoon program on CBC's news network was so aptly named—*Politics*. He covered it in the nation's capital, in every province and terri-tory, and around the world as well. But as he so often showed, he could handle any breaking news event, from a hostage-taking to a plane crash, with intelligence and aplomb.

His first journalism jobs were in Winnipeg, in newspapers and television, when John Diefenbaker was prime minister. Don moved to Regina, and then back to Winnipeg

Photo courtesy CBC

for most of the Lester Pearson years. *The Globe and Mail* brought him to Toronto at the beginning of the Pierre Trudeau era. He got a close-up of that era when the *Globe* moved him to its parliamentary bureau in 1969. He joined CTV in Ottawa, and then the network moved him to Washington just in time for the re-election of Richard Nixon, and the Watergate catastrophe that followed. CBC hired him away for the Jimmy Carter years, then posted him to Edmonton for part of the Peter Lougheed era.

In 1981, Don moved back to Ottawa for CBC and became one of the network's political mainstays until his 2009 retirement. The title of his memoir comes from the words he used to begin his program every day, *Welcome to the Broadcast*.

An early highlight of Don Newman's career was being the first journalist to reveal that federal politician Hazen Argue of Saskatchewan was planning to change parties.

Even though this kind of thing has happened well over two hundred times through Canada's history, in both federal and provincial politics, it's still news when a politician decides to leave one party to join another. Sometimes it's small news. But sometimes it's very big news, and such was the case in 1962 when Argue deserted the federal New Democrats to become a Liberal. It stirred up accusations of disloyalty and opportunism. Winston Churchill, who changed parties twice in his career, once said, "Some men change their party for the sake of their principles; others their principles for the sake of their party." Which kind of man Hazen Argue was is still debatable.

···

The story really started in 1958. In the federal election that year the CCF *[Co-operative Commonwealth Federation]* won just eight seats. So the Canadian Labour Congress and the CCF decided to get together to form a new party, a coming together of big eastern labour and prairie populist socialism. The new party would be called the New Democratic Party, the NDP. But it would take a few years to organize everything, so the CCF continued to exist. Hazen Argue was one of the CCF-ers who managed to hold onto his seat in the election, and he sort of bullied the upper echelons of the party into making him the leader of the party until the NDP got going.

He then decided that he should be the first leader of the NDP. But the behind-the-scenes organizers wanted Tommy Douglas, who was the premier of Saskatchewan. Apparently they tried to talk Argue out of running so they could have a coronation at the founding convention in 1961, but Argue said, "Hell no, I should be the leader." So he ran against Douglas and against the establishment machine, but he was swamped at the convention.

Argue knew he would lose the leadership race, so at the same convention he ran for a place on the national council of the party. But the powers-that-be were so annoyed with him that they made sure he didn't get elected even to that. So he went from being the last leader of the CCF to being basically nothing. He was just another member of the caucus. He wasn't too happy.

At this point I was still working in Winnipeg, at my first job. But I was looking around for another job and I got one in Regina at a station that had both radio and TV. I got there on Thanksgiving weekend, just before the legislature was coming back into session. There was a reporter with more seniority who was covering the major business of the legislature every afternoon. My job was to go to the committee meetings in the morning, which I subsequently learned was the best place to cover any legislature anywhere in Canada. That's because it's more laid back and you get to meet all the MLAs [Members of the Legislative Assembly] as they gather around the coffee pot. After a short while I knew most of them pretty well. A lot of the liberal MLAs stayed at a hotel in downtown Regina that had a coffee shop that stayed open late at night. I would often go there after work and one night one of the MLAs said to me, "You know, Hazen Argue is negotiating to join the Liberal party in Ottawa."

I couldn't believe it. This was a provincial Liberal telling me about something going on with the federal Liberals, and even though they were close, it was possible something had been communicated poorly. Maybe the story wasn't true.

I knew the history. Argue had been a CCF MP since shortly after World War II. The Liberals had been in power most of the time since and Argue had been a strong critic of the Liberal government. And he'd been a prominent critic as leader of the CCF. So it seemed to me it would be very unusual for a guy who had just run for the party leadership of the NDP to suddenly show up in another party. I said, "Really?" He said, "Yes. He wants to run in the next election as a Liberal."

I still thought the whole thing sounded pretty weird. But a few nights later I sat down with a couple of other Liberals. I was going to ask if they had heard that Argue was negotiating with the federal Liberals, but instead I decided to bluff a little. I asked one of them, "Are you part of the negotiations for Hazen Argue to join the Liberals?" And he said, "Oh no. It's the federal guys who are doing that." Three other MLAs said the same thing, so now I was convinced that the story was true.

I was just twenty-one at the time. But I was confident that the guys who had passed on the information were salt-of-the-earth farmers from Saskatchewan. I heard it from enough people. And I had heard it from different people, not just guys who hung out with each other and could have heard the same story at the same time from someone who didn't know what they were talking about. So I was confident enough to tell the news director of the station what I had learned. He told me to find one more source. I went out one more night, asked my trick question again, and got another confirmation. I came back to the news director and he said, "Well then, put it on the air." So I put it on the air.

I reported that Hazen Argue was in negotiations with the Liberals to cross the floor of the House of Commons. The Canadian Press wire service picked up the story and in Ottawa they asked Argue for comment. He denied it. Said it wasn't true.

I was pretty new to reporting and I thought, "That's unfortunate. I still believe my story is true, but this is tough—to have your scoop denied."

Then the story kind of disappeared for a bit. A few weeks later, though, there was a by-election in the provincial riding of Weyburn to replace Tommy Douglas in the legislature.

I went down there to cover it when the campaign was going on, and I went to cover the results on election night. The mayor of Weyburn, Junior Staveley, ran for the Liberals. And a man named Oran Reiman, a schoolteacher, ran for the CCF/NDP. The results started coming in, and lo and behold, there was Staveley winning. For more than twenty years the riding had been held by the CCF and Tommy Douglas, so it was quite an upset. I went to Staveley's headquarters and did the usual stuff, including an interview with the winning candidate. Then I went over to Reiman's campaign office and as I opened the door and walked in I could see everybody was pretty disappointed and everybody was getting drunk.

Hazen Argue recognized me right away. He grabbed me and pushed me out the door into the cold outside and he shouted, "I should kill you!" I was about maybe 150 pounds and he was a burly farmer. He said it more than once: "I should kill you!"

"What do you mean?"

"You son of a bitch. Reporting that I was negotiating with the Liberals."

"Well," I said. "I have good sources and that's why I reported it."

Which got me another, "I should kill you!"

Then he stormed back into the campaign office. I collected myself for a minute or two and thought, "I came here to interview Oran Reiman, so that's what I'm going to do."

I opened the door and went back in. Argue was in another part of the room and he may not have seen me. I went up to Reiman and said, "Mr. Reiman, can I get a few words with you for our listeners?" He said, "No. Fuck off!" He wasn't a very good loser.

On the way back to the newsroom I realized that Argue threatening to kill me kind of confirmed my story. He wouldn't have been angry had I been wrong. He was so angry only because I was right.

That's where everything stayed until three months later. I worked seven days a week at the station. On a Sunday afternoon in March I had just finished reading a radio newscast when the phone rang. I picked it up and a voice said, "Hello, Don. It's Hazen Argue." My first thought was to wonder if he had come to Regina to kill me.

I said, "Yes, Mr. Argue?"

"I've just been listening to you on the radio and I thought I'd call you. I'm in Regina and I'm going down to my riding in Assiniboia tomorrow and I'm announcing that I'm joining the federal Liberal party, and I'm going to be the candidate in the riding whenever the federal election comes."

I said, "That's very interesting. I'm going to put it on the radio."

He said, "Yes, I wish you would."

I hung up and started tapping out the story on my typewriter. But I thought, "This is a pretty big story. I'd better call the news director and tell him about it." So I did.

"Wow!" he said. "That's great. Call him up and ask if he wants to do a half-hour on TV tonight."

So that's what happened. We did a thirty-minute interview

program with Hazen Argue. At the end of it he thanked me and never mentioned the ugly scene when he'd threatened to kill me.

In fact, I never talked to him about our confrontation ever again. We went our different ways for a few years, but when I got to Parliament Hill and he was a senator and then a cabinet minister under Pierre Trudeau, we'd run into each other and say hello to each other. Neither of us ever brought up his floor crossing.

I guess it was a bigger deal for me than for him. I'd been in journalism for only about a year and I thought, "This is really what it's about. I'm going to be able to break the news. I'm going to be able to report things people don't want you to report but that is in the public interest." And then to be proven right much later is really very exciting. That's when I decided to make the commitment to journalism.

Tom Kennedy:
A Life in Haiti

Photo courtesy CTV News

TOM KENNEDY BEGAN HIS CAREER AT CBC MONTREAL AT A PIVOTAL TIME in Quebec and Canadian history. The Parti Québécois was about to win its first election, which would lead to the first referendum on separation. Tom covered the Quebec story for ten years and was then posted to a place where the politics is easier to decipher—China. He reported on how the country was slowly opening up to foreigners and particularly foreign investment. He was in Tiananmen Square on the night in 1989 when the Chinese government cracked down on students demanding democracy.

He moved back to Toronto for a year, though he travelled frequently—including to Panama, when the Americans invaded and arrested Manuel Noriega, the gun-running, drug-smuggling, murderous general who was in charge of the country. Then Tom went back to Quebec to cover the buildup to the second referendum. CTV then lured him to its London bureau, and for more than a decade he covered lots of wars and two papal conclaves. He returned to Canada once more to work on documentaries for CTV's *W5*.

In 1994, Tom Kennedy was one of the reporters sent to Haiti to report on an invasion that never was.

US President Bill Clinton had decided to send twenty-five thousand troops to Haiti to overthrow a military regime that had removed a democratically elected president from power three years earlier. The invasion plan was no secret, and as the troops left the United States, former president Jimmy Carter flew to Haiti to try to negotiate a peaceful resolution. Remarkably, he succeeded. When the American military arrived, there was no war to fight, but the troops stayed to work out the details of a peaceful transfer of power.

....

I got to Haiti just before the Americans got there and stayed for about two weeks. It was chaotic when I arrived, and clear that democracy was going to come back one way or the other—either through the force of an invasion or through the power of Jimmy Carter's persuasion. So people were beginning to wreak revenge on those who had wielded power in the preceding years.

I went out with a cameraman one day and we were on a hill looking down a country road that was down a long incline. We could see quite far, and about a kilometre away we could see a mob sort of trotting along the street with machetes. The cameraman put the camera down on the ground to get a steady shot. He was down on all fours taking a shot and the mob kept coming right at us, waving those machetes. I said to the cameraman, "Maybe we should leave." But he was enjoying the beautiful picture he was seeing and he said, "No. It's a great shot, great shot." I turned to our driver, who was a Haitian, and asked, "Do you think they're coming at us?" He said, "I can't be sure, but I don't think so."

So we stayed there and as they got closer and closer to us we stood our ground, wisely or not, and they finally turned. They went to a house and started beating on the windows, trying to get in. Obviously one of the regime's enforcers lived there and they were going to hack him into pieces. But he wasn't there. His wife was there, but they didn't kill her.

So that was the atmosphere the entire time I was there, even after the American military arrived. Pretty much every morning when we went out there were bodies lying along the road. Some of that may have been "ordinary" murder, but most were revenge killings against the people who had been running the place.

One morning there wasn't much going on so I took a driver and a cameraman and we just drove around the city to see what we could find. Finding nothing, we decided to go out into the countryside. We moved just northeast of Port-au-Prince. There was only one road you could drive on, barely. You had to go very slowly because the road was in desperate shape, just a wreck, potholes everywhere. And there was jungle on either side of the road.

Off in the distance I could see a crowd of people. I figured they had found more bodies. But as we got closer I could see some American military vehicles parked there.

We drove up and when I rolled down the window a soldier poked his head into the car and asked me if I spoke Creole.

I said, "No. But my driver does and he also speaks French. And I speak French." I figured he needed translation, so I said, "We can translate for you. What's the problem?" That's when he said something completely unexpected: "There's a woman here having a baby."

We all scrambled out of our car, and there she was—a woman about twenty-seven or twenty-eight years old. She was lying flat on the ground. Maybe two dozen people formed a circle around her—young people, old people, women, men. There was no sense of privacy at all. I guess you can't expect privacy when you're giving birth in the middle of a country road, but still.

It was a really hot day, and the Americans especially felt it. They had all their gear and they were wearing body armour and helmets. A medic was down on the ground with the woman, who was obviously in the advanced stages of labour. The medic wanted to set up an IV drip, but he wanted to explain what he was doing so the woman wouldn't be scared. He wanted us to tell her. So we did the three-way translation. He spoke to me in English. I translated it to French for the driver. And he spoke to the woman in Creole. The IV went in and I was holding the IV bag over the woman while she coped with her contractions.

Thankfully, it didn't last too long. We were there for only about thirty minutes before the baby was born. It was a girl. The mother was in surprisingly good shape, smiling and very happy. There was a female soldier there who picked up the baby and wrapped her in a blanket. Everybody then walked over to an American Humvee. The mother sat in the back while the American female soldier carried the baby in the front passenger seat. And they drove off.

I stayed behind to interview the soldiers and the medic who had helped the woman give birth. And to talk to some of the people who had crowded around to watch the show.

I was told that the woman had been on her way to a local

clinic to give birth. There was no transportation so she was walking. After about a mile or two she had just collapsed on the road.

The medic was very memorable. He had reddish hair and a really pale complexion—the kind of skin that burns in a second when you're out in the sun. And he was really sweating because he had all his heavy gear on. He was from the American South. That was obvious from his accent. I asked him if he had ever done anything like this before and he said, "No, sir. Ah been trained to treat bullet wounds but not to help a lady give birth to a baby."

I guess we were at the spot where she had given birth for another twenty minutes or maybe a half-hour, finishing up our shooting. By then all the soldiers had left. We got in the car and went to track down the clinic. We had rough directions and we eventually found it. The clinic was kind of a cement boxy structure. There was an American Humvee parked out front, so I knew we were in the right place. The clinic didn't have much in the way of facilities. There was no security or reception desk. I just walked in.

I wandered around inside and in due course came upon the woman who had given birth. She was there with the baby in her bed. She was beaming and she was very, very happy. I went over to her and our driver was translating from Creole to French and back to Creole. She confirmed that she'd been walking down the road to the clinic when she collapsed. Then she asked me if I knew the soldier who had helped her. I said, "No."

"Do you think you could track him down?"

"Yes, I probably can. What do you want from him?"

"I want to know the name of his mother."

I left the hospital room and went out front. The Humvee was still there, so I went up to the Americans and got them to radio around to try to find the medic. It didn't take long to find him. They got him on the radio and told him that the woman who had given birth wanted to know the name of his mother.

I heard him answer, "Helen."

I went back into the hospital and said, "His mother's name is Helen."

She looked at her baby, then looked up at me, and said, "This is Helen." She named the baby after the medic's mother.

The story has always stuck with me. There was so much turmoil at the time. Violence, people being killed. There was still some sniping going on. So for this to happen in the middle of all that was quite something.

I also remember wondering what the future was going to be like for this child. What if I came back in twenty or twenty-five years and I tried to find a young woman named Helen. What would her life be like? Haiti is so poor. There's just so much hardship. In a lot of ways Haiti is the most depressing country in the world. Could Helen overcome all that?

Life expectancy for a baby born in Haiti in 1994 was about sixty years. If she wasn't killed in the earthquake in 2010, and if she didn't die of AIDS, which is a big problem in Haiti, then she's probably alive. And she's probably a mother herself now. But unless she defied the odds, she's probably dirt poor, just like her mother was.

Mark Phillips:
Rwanda
Genocide

Photo courtesy Brian Kelly

MARK PHILLIPS WAS A RED-HEAD WHEN HE STARTED IN JOURNALISM. The grey hair has grown in around the world. His first job was as a producer at CBC Montreal. He became a reporter there, and soon moved to the network's parliamentary bureau for four years. He went overseas for CBC in 1980, posted to London, where CBS News saw the quality of his work and hired him away.

He has worked for CBS ever since, based in London, Moscow, Rome, Washington and now back in London again.

When 800,000 to 1,000,000 people were killed in Rwanda over a period of ten days, Mark Phillips was the first TV reporter for a North American network to witness the horror. He was based in London for CBS News at the time.

It's fair to say that in 1994 most people in the Western world couldn't have found Rwanda on a map. It may even be true that most people had never heard of it. But on April 6 of that year—buried deep inside newspapers, or near the end of some television newscasts—there was a story reported more for its peculiarity than for its apparent significance. A plane crash in Africa had killed the presidents of not one but two countries: Cyprian Ntayamira of Burundi and Juvenal Habyarimana of Rwanda.

Habyarimana was a member of the Hutu tribe. That put him in the company of 83 percent of his country. But another tribe, the Tutsis, dominated the upper echelon of Rwandan society. Hutus immediately blamed Tutsis for the death of the president. They accused an army of rebel Tutsis, the Rwandan Patriotic Front (RPF), of shooting down the plane. The RPF blamed Hutus for attacking the plane to provide an excuse for what was to follow. To this day, we don't know the truth.

What we do know is that Hutus went on one of the most savage and mercilessly brutal killing frenzies in recorded history. No Tutsi in Rwanda was safe. Man, woman, child. It made no difference. They were hunted down and slaughtered, usually chopped to death by machete.

．．

I had done a fair amount of work in Africa. Mostly North Africa or Southern Africa. I hadn't really done much in Central Africa. I was no expert on Rwanda. I knew only what everybody else knew—that this was an ethnic Hutu–Tutsi conflict. I'd read about the history. But other than that, I was just dropped into the story. And that's not a unique circumstance.

The cameraman, soundman and producer came from South Africa. We met in Uganda. Then we drove toward the Rwandan border to hook up with a group of RPF fighters. At this stage, the rebels controlled that part of the country, but there was still serious fighting going on. We had entered the great unknown, a big black hole. We really didn't know what we were getting into.

On the first night with the RPF, we camped out in a series of huts. And as we were talking to them they were actually eating the bugs off the walls. It was quite clear at that point that this was going to be a different kind of story.

As we moved farther into Rwanda it was obvious that something terrible was going on. Every place we came to was pretty well empty. Whole populations had fled and not returned. We went to one or two places where refugees had gathered and in many of those places, the men were all gone. The women and children had bandaged hands and arms. That's where you get wounded when people are chopping down with machetes on you and you're trying to defend yourself by putting up your hands and arms.

The horror increased as we got closer and closer to the capital, Kigali. We saw evidence of the burned-out villages. We saw people with injuries consistent with the stories we were hearing, and we then started to come across what we later came to call ethnic cleansing.

Whole families had been killed and were just lying bloated and rotting in the fields or along the roads. There were clumps of burned, hacked-up bodies. There were bodies in various states of decomposition. There was a gruesome scene in a river that was full of bloated bodies caught in little eddies going round and round.

They weren't the first dead bodies I had seen. But they were the first mutilated bodies I had seen. I was at Sabra and Shatila in 1982 [refugee camps in Lebanon where at least seven hundred *to eight hundred civilians had been killed in a day and a half]* and had seen evidence of man's glorious history in several places, but never to this scale. I don't think it matters much how many you see. I don't think you get over it or find a way to prepare yourself for it. But I've never seen carnage to the extent I saw in Rwanda.

As the rebels advanced a lot of the attackers had run away. That led to a sight I will never forget. Before the Hutus crossed over a bridge at one river with floating bloated bodies in it, they left their machetes behind. And so there was a huge pile—a massive stack of machetes, 20 yards by 20 yards, maybe 10 feet high. Machetes, a lot of them still bloodstained.

All this murder was going on, but I can't say I felt particularly unsafe. At one point the rebels took us right to the front line near Kigali. They had some light artillery with them and there was an exchange with government forces that still controlled the capital. In my experience it's artillery that worries you because you can't really protect yourself from it. You can jump in a hole if it's small-arms fire, and you can move back from dangerous areas. But with the reach that artillery has, if you're in an area that is being shelled, and it's happened to me quite a few times over the years, that's what makes you very nervous.

The RPF was quite happy to have us with them. These guys thought they were the good guys. They wanted foreign coverage, and we were the first foreigners they had seen. They looked after us. But that only goes so far. In these situations you only have the word of the people you're with as to what's around the next bend or through the next thicket you are approaching in a densely wooded country. So there's anxiety. But the longer you stay in a situation like that the more confidence you get—perhaps misplaced—that things will be all right.

One day I was supposed to meet with one of the RPF commanders. The roads in Rwanda are terrible, basically tracks, and we spent the better part of the day bouncing along the hills to get to this place where General So-and-so was supposed to come and see us. We set up the camera in a clearing. The cameraman lined up his shot and as the sun moved across the African sky he kept adjusting until the sun was practically gone. Eventually it was completely dark and the general never showed. The producer, who was an old hand, tossed his last cigarette butt in the general direction of the fifty others he had smoked that day and he said, "It never pays to plan." It's a line I've used fifty or sixty times since then.

We were in Rwanda for about a week and in those days there was no way to put our material on television except to carry it all out. We knew we were sitting on hot stuff. We had to retrace our route across the border back into Uganda and then wait for a flight to London. You're always nervous that someone else will get the story.

I don't want to sound too wizened here, but I've often found that on a story like Rwanda, I'm much more affected watching the footage after the fact than I am when I'm living through it. In real time, once you are over the shock of discovery—the shock of seeing twenty, thirty, forty bodies or more, all the carnage just lying around—then you start getting busy. You're taking notes. You're thinking about what you're going to say and you start to write the piece in your head. You're shooting the on-camera bits. You're deciding what you need to shoot, and where you have to go next, how safe you are, and all the rest of it. And it's some time afterward that you kind of get hit in the head by what you've actually witnessed.

When you think of the word *holocaust* you think of Auschwitz and bulldozers, that kind of thing. In this case we saw large piles of bodies. It's not on the same scale. Still, how do you measure a holocaust? There was no shortage of visual elements. We had one shot of a whole family just lying by the roadside and they had been chopped up and they were all holding hands lying in a ditch. It was a pretty gruesome scene.

It sounds trite and self-serving, and maybe only another journalist would really understand my meaning, but if you're a foreign correspondent, then Rwanda is exactly the kind of story you hope at some point in your career to come across. It was just me and my crew. And a story I was discovering on my own. To find myself in a place with a story that big, it's a kind of Livingstone moment. Knowing that I'm the first person who's going to tell the world about what the hell has gone on. And I had better figure out a way to do that.

Gillian Findlay:
Lottery Scam

Photo courtesy CBC

GILLIAN FINDLAY TOOK A JOB ANSWERING THE PHONES IN THE CBC Vancouver newsroom while she was still in university, but she kept her eyes open for bigger opportunities. When she saw a research job, she took it. That led to occasional reporting assignments, and eventually to a full-time job as a reporter.

She moved to Toronto to become the health reporter for CBC's *The Journal*, even though she had never covered health issues before. That soon opened the door to the program's documentary unit. She then jumped back into daily news for the network, first in Toronto (where she was the lead reporter in its coverage of the Ben Johnson scandal) and then in the London bureau. ABC hired her for its Moscow bureau in 1994, and then moved her to Jerusalem. She returned home to CBC in 2002 to be part of *the fifth estate.*

When an elderly man felt he had been short-changed by the Ontario Lottery and Gaming Corporation (known as the OLG), Gillian Findlay and *the fifth estate* set out to discover the OLG's dirty little secret.

Winning a lottery is hard enough. While exploring the universe aboard USS *Enterprise*, the non-emotional, ever-logical Mr. Spock never bought a lottery ticket. He would have known how ridiculously slim his chances were of winning. We may know the odds as well, but we play willingly. Winning the Lotto 6/49 jackpot? One chance in 13,983,816. If you buy fifty tickets a week the laws of probability dictate that you will win the jackpot once every five thousand years.

But let's say you defy the odds, and your numbers come up. It happens all the time, of course. And it happened in 2001 to Bob Edmonds, a seventy-seven-year-old man who lived in Coboconk, Ontario. He won a quarter of a million dollars. He should have lived happily ever after, but that's not what happened. Bob was the victim of a scam by a dishonest store clerk. That was bad enough, but he was also the victim of the OLG.

....

It started with one of our producers, Harvey Cashore. He had a friend who had covered a trial involving a man named Bob Edmonds and his complaint against the Ontario Lottery and Gaming Corporation. Edmonds said that he had somehow been ripped off and prevented from cashing in, even though he had bought a winning ticket. Harvey's friend had been shocked at what he heard at the trial. He had said something to Harvey like, "There's probably more here and it might be something for you guys to look at."

So Harvey went to see Bob Edmonds and his lawyer. Our original thinking was that there wasn't much of a story other than perhaps something about this charming elderly man who had gotten screwed by the OLG. Nothing bigger than that.

But the more we learned about the case, the more people we talked to, the more documentation we got, the more the suspicion grew that the problem wasn't just limited to Bob. We began to see that what had happened to him was first so easy to do, and second had received no scrutiny by the OLG. It seemed pretty clear that it was very likely that Bob Edmonds wasn't the first person who had been cheated. So we went ahead and started digging into the story.

Bob Edmonds was a regular player of the lottery. He lived in a small town north of Toronto. There were a couple of places where he would routinely buy lottery tickets and he'd always use the same numbers—a combination of birthdays from his family. So he would routinely go into the stores and check to see if he'd won anything.

One day he went in and when he checked his tickets at a lottery machine the bells started ringing. They rang twice. He was experienced enough as a lottery player to know that meant he had won twice. He walked over to the clerk at the store—a woman he had known for years and years, part of a small community—and she said he had indeed won. But just once. He'd won a free ticket and that was that.

At first Bob accepted that, and he went home. But he couldn't get over the fact that he had heard two rings of the bells. He knew he had won twice, not once. He was seventy-seven years old at the time, and though he thought there must be more to this, he was confused. So he called the OLG and he said, "There's something wrong here. I'm pretty sure I won something, but the clerk said I didn't."

And almost from the beginning the OLG made it clear that they didn't want to hear from him. He got no help. The attitude at the OLG was, "Just go away."

But he didn't go away because he wasn't that kind of a person. Bob Edmonds was the loveliest man in the world, he really was. Just the picture of integrity. He had worked at Ontario Hydro as a lineman for many years, lived a quiet life dedicated to his family. You couldn't have asked for a better protagonist for the story because there's no one who ever met Bob Edmonds who didn't come away in love with him. He was just as lovely and charming and honest as the day is long. He had a real sense that he had an obligation to force the OLG to do the right thing.

You often go into these investigative stories wondering what everybody's agenda is. How much do you believe people? I've done lots of stories where I went in hoping someone was telling the truth and then found out they weren't. And that's devastating. But I had this gut feeling with Bob from the very beginning that he wasn't hiding anything or telling me anything that wasn't 100 percent true.

Remember, by the time we entered the picture, Bob's case had been settled out of court. He had his money. He was now eighty-two years old, and he was just fighting for his good name. The OLG had essentially said, "Bob Edmonds is a liar." And he wasn't prepared to let them get away with that. By the time I met him, he had no money at stake. His motivation for wanting to be part of our story was that he wanted the world to know that what he'd said was true.

To get his settlement Bob had signed a confidentiality agreement. So he couldn't talk about how much money he had been given, or go into a lot of detail about the case publicly. If he violated the confidentiality agreement, the OLG could come after him for the money it had given him. But Bob wanted to talk about it publicly. He thought he had been poorly treated and he thought there might be other people like him out there. So we had a delicate dance with him. I wanted him to tell me everything he could, but I didn't want him to get into trouble by saying too much. His lawyer sat in during all our interviews.

Bob said that about three weeks after he had called the OLG, it became obvious what had happened. He read in his local newspaper that the clerk who had told him he had only one winning ticket had cashed in a ticket for herself worth $250,000.

Bob then went to the police. He called the Ontario Provincial Police and they started asking questions. *[The clerk and her husband were eventually charged with fraud. The charges were stayed and they paid Bob $150,000.]*

But still the OLG continued to deny there was any problem. So he hired a lawyer. The lawyer told me he expected the OLG to settle. He never thought the case would get to court, but it did. We found out the OLG spent more than $400,000 fighting Bob Edmonds before it finally agreed to settle.

Perhaps the OLG thought that would be the end of it. Unfortunately for them, we came along. We gave Bob an opportunity to tell the story he wanted to tell and through our efforts and good old-fashioned reporting we were able to show that the corporation had really behaved very badly.

Through access-to-information requests we got a bunch of documentation. Unwittingly, they had shared with us an internal document that showed that they were aware right from the beginning that Bob Edmonds was telling the truth. They had done some kind of internal review that led them to believe he probably had been scammed out of his winnings. But they weren't going to do anything about it. The implication was that he was an old guy who was going to die at some point and if they just managed to keep it all quiet, it would just eventually all go away.

I had that document when I sat down to interview a

spokeswoman from the OLG. It wasn't the first time where our reporting had given us information that the interview subject didn't know we had. I knew it was going to be a bit of a shock to her when she discovered what I knew.

We go through a process each time this circumstance arises. We ask ourselves if it's fair to surprise the person we're interviewing. You can always create cheap "gotcha" television by not revealing what you know in advance. But sometimes we decide to show our hand so they can perhaps provide a fuller explanation.

In this particular case the document was from their own files. It's not that someone had leaked something to us. It's not that we'd found a document lying on the street one day or while rummaging through their garbage cans. We had put in an access request and this document came back to us from their files. I would have presumed that when you're the person who's going to sit down and do the interview with a national television network, you would have refreshed your memory and gone through the files. I knew that she didn't know we had this document but I thought she might know of its existence. So that's why we handled it like we did.

I felt sorry for her in the sense she was the person put up by the OLG to defend the indefensible. I felt badly that she had been put in that position. When I showed her the document all she could do was say something about "putting things into perspective" and assure us that "our primary responsibility is to the taxpayers of Ontario," which had nothing to do with anything. When I asked her why the OLG had never told Bob directly that it believed him, she said, "I don't believe that opportunity ever came up." I almost jumped out of my chair at the absurdity of that. Imagine, in all those years the opportunity never came up! I don't think she came off well in the interview. But if that's where you choose to make your living, and you're prepared to sit down, knowing what the truth is, and you think you can say things in a way that people are going to believe, I guess you get what you get.

I truly don't understand how people can try to convince a journalist of something that they know is not true. I don't know how you do that. Maybe I'm just constitutionally or genetically missing something. When I encounter it, first of all it shocks me, and then frustrates me, and ultimately it makes me angry.

I do take some satisfaction from knowing that I have a way to combat that imperious attitude. I can piece together what the facts show. I can present the truth to an audience.

The OLG had already settled with Bob, but it was still refusing to concede he'd been swindled, or even admit to the possibility that he or anyone else had ever been victimized by a store clerk or other insider. [An "insider" is anyone who sells tickets or is a member of a ticket seller's family, or an OLG employee or supplier.]

I don't know what was in their heads when they took that position. I think it stems from an arrogance that they are this big corporation. That they have all this power behind them and Bob Edmonds has nothing. He was just a little guy. We finally got documents that showed that the OLG believed there were other cases where things had gone wrong, and they were wondering what they were going to do. The CEO said something to the effect that "sometimes you just have to hold your nose and keep going." This notion that the truth doesn't matter is astounding. How people get to that point, I don't know. I don't know what corruption of the process leads to that.

The OLG just kept ducking and weaving and hiding and threatening this old man that if he told anybody what had happened to him they would come after him to get back the money it had given him in the out-of-court settlement.

We looked at the number of insider wins at the OLG over a seven-year period and took our findings to a math professor at the University of Toronto. He said the chances of insiders winning at the rate they were winning was one in a trillion trillion trillion.

The OLG said, "Well, it's only because insiders play more often. You may play once a week, but these insiders—because they have access—they play a lot more so that explains why they win more." Then it became, "They are smart enough to play the games where they are more likely to win than others."

I understand that systems are flawed and things happen. I think managers are supposed to fix the flaws. The problem was that whenever the OLG started to understand they had a problem that had the potential to be quite large, they didn't fix it. They just kept denying it existed. That to me is the part that was most egregious.

The Ontario ombudsman began an investigation and finally the OLG was forced to change procedures. *[Any insider who wins more than $10,000 is now subject to an automatic investigation.]* The CEO and three other high-ranking people lost their jobs.

It doesn't feel good when that happens. They're people too, and they have families and it's going to impact their lives more than I'll probably ever know. I live with it because people have to be accountable for what they do, and it's our job to hold them accountable. I don't consider that I got them fired. They got fired themselves. They have only themselves to blame. I did my job. But that doesn't make it any easier to go home at night. When this happens no one in our office does a high-five and says, "Boy, we really kicked ass because that guy who made a bad decision is no longer there." Nobody takes that kind of personal satisfaction. I certainly don't.

Just six months after we broadcast Bob's story, he died. He was a cancer survivor and he wasn't in great health when I first met him. Over the course of talking with him I could see he was fading a bit, and eventually we got a phone call from one of his sons who said, "The cancer is back."

Bob was a talented watercolour painter. We had talked

about that, and I had seen some of his work. Just before he died he sent me a beautiful little watercolour of the lake where he lived. It was the nicest gesture.

He said several times to me, "I'm just glad it all ended the way it did. I'm really glad that I had this opportunity to set the record straight."

He was a bit of a public figure for a brief period of time. He was recognized as he walked down the street and I think he enjoyed that part of it. It was really important to him to have done what he did.

It was a lesson to me about journalism. I've covered wars, famine, scandals, politics, but you don't often see real acts of courage in everyday life. You see it on battlefields and you see people living through terrible hardships, but I had never really seen Bob's kind of quiet courage demonstrated in that way. So when he died I felt very bad, as did everybody. I was at least happy that we had given him his moment. I think it was important to him.

There are many kinds of journalism, and the kind of investigative journalism that I do is where I belong. It really matters to me that journalism be a way to make a difference. I remember working overseas. I was so privileged and so lucky to get the assignments I did, to be in places where history was being made. But the reality was that I was there to watch, and in most places I was one of many journalists doing exactly the same thing. No one journalist was going to make a difference.

But in this kind of story—where I had the time, the talents of others on the team and the resources to do good research and to be able to dig and to go where my instincts led me—you can actually come close to the truth. And when you tell the truth, you can actually make a difference. It doesn't happen very often. I can probably count on the fingers of one hand the number of times any reporting that I've done has actually made a big difference. But when it does, it's very satisfying.

Terence McKenna:

Son of al-Qaeda

TERENCE MCKENNA IS ONE
OF THE GREAT INVESTIGATIVE
DOCUMENTARY JOURNALISTS
of our time. He has produced some
of the most memorable TV series in
history, including *The Valour and the
Horror*, about Canadian bomber
pilots in World War II, and *Memoirs*,
covering the life of Pierre Trudeau.
He has written TV biographies of
Fidel Castro, Pope John Paul II and
Jean Chrétien. And he's won more
awards—important awards—than
many newsrooms put together.

Photo courtesy Ousama Farag

He started working at CBC in 1975, when he was twenty-one years old. And he's still there today.

It was with the instincts of a very smart journalist that Terence McKenna watched a 2003 news conference featuring Abdurahman Khadr.

After 9/11, reporters around the world were trying to break stories on a number of related topics: terrorism in general, al-Qaeda in particular, Osama bin Laden of course, the fight against terrorism. By the time the Khadr story came along, Terence McKenna had already produced several documentaries on the rise of Islamic extremism, including *Trail of a Terrorist*, about Ahmed Ressam's plan to cross the Canadian border into the United States and blow up the airport in Los Angeles.

Abdurahman Khadr was born in Bahrain and lived in Pakistan for a long while, but had come to Canada when he was just eleven years old. He was a Canadian citizen. He moved back to Pakistan with his family, and then to Afghanistan. American soldiers arrested him in Afghanistan in November 2001, and he ended up at the US prison camp in Guantánamo Bay, Cuba.

In 2003 he was back in Toronto, and at a news conference claimed the Americans had released him from custody in Cuba but set him free only after he'd been flown to Kabul. He said he travelled through Pakistan, Turkey and Bulgaria. Finally, he said, the Canadian Embassy in Bosnia had helped him return to Canada. He denied that his family had any connection to al-Qaeda.

....

The story sounded fishy to me, and so I asked Nazim Baksh, a longtime CBC producer who happens to be Muslim, to contact Abdurahman Khadr and try to get the real story and convince him to talk to us.

After a few days of trust-building meetings, Abdurahman told Naz what really happened, which was far more interesting. Now he claimed that after he was taken prisoner in Afghanistan, the American military turned him over to the US Central Intelligence Agency. He said he quickly offered to co-operate with the CIA, and told them everything he knew about al-Qaeda in Afghanistan, which was a lot because his family were friends and neighbours of Osama bin Laden.

He claimed that the CIA eventually convinced him to go under cover as a prisoner among suspected al-Qaeda terrorists, first at Bagram airbase in Afghanistan, and later in Guantánamo. He described in detail his prison experiences, and the intelligence training sessions he underwent. He claimed that the CIA eventually deployed him to Bosnia, where he decided things were getting much too dangerous for him, and so he fled.

He was kind of a big galoot—big hands, big feet. In many ways just a kid. Although he was adult size, he talked like a very young person. But when he told you stories he was pretty convincing. Before I met him I was very skeptical. I listened to him for a couple of hours. I have never had such a fantastical tale presented to me. But after I heard him out I said, "I believe this guy. I don't know how to prove any of it, but I believe him."

Naturally the CIA would never confirm the story, so how were we to find out if what he had told us was true?

Abdurahman mentioned that he'd been regularly polygraphed by the CIA. So I asked him to submit to a lie-detector test for us. I kind of took a breath before I asked him the question. I had discussed it beforehand with Nazim.

"Naz, how do you think he'll react to this?"

"I'm not sure. I'm not sure."

So I said, "You know, he talked about being polygraphed by the CIA, so we're just asking him to do something he's done before."

Well, Abdurahman agreed to it right away.

"Sure I'll do that. You put the pads on your chest and

the sensors on your head, and everything attaches to a little machine and they ask you questions. Sure, sure, sure. I've done that before. I can do it again."

His description made me think, "Okay, he seems to know what he's talking about. He has done it before."

And then on the day we did the polygraph, the tester walked into the room and Abdurahman opened his shirt and he said, "Yeah, you put that wire here and put one here, and another one here." So he certainly acted as if he had been through this before and that was more confirmation for me that his story was consistent.

And he passed the test. That wouldn't be good enough to put the story on air, but it was good enough to let us pursue the story further.

Abdurahman arranged for me to meet other members of his family in Pakistan. So Naz and I flew to Islamabad.

On the first morning, at breakfast at our hotel, a guy walked over to Naz and handed him a note and just walked away. It was an invitation to meet with someone we knew had close connections to al-Qaeda. In fact, it was the al-Qaeda operative that Daniel Pearl was going to meet the day he disappeared. *[Pearl was an American journalist, kidnapped and eventually murdered in Pakistan in 2002.]* And this just blew our minds. Kind of freaked us out. We wondered, "Is someone following us? How do they even know we're here?"

I should say that before I left Canada I was nervous about going. I walked into Tony Burman's office *[the head of CBC News at the time]* and I said, "What happens if I'm kidnapped? What happens next? What are you going to do? What is the CBC going to do? What is the government of Canada going to do? If I disappear I want things to be fired up very quickly." And Tony leaned over and pulled his passport out of his pocket and showed it to me. There was a visa inside for Pakistan. He said, "I'll come and get you."

In any case, we went off to our meeting with Abdurahman's mother, Maha, and his sister, Zaynab. When we got to the house they weren't there.

The people who were at the house said, "Just said sit down. We're not sure they're coming, but just sit here, have some tea and wait for them."

So we were sitting in this house and the mother and the sister finally walked in, and there was a man with them. He recognized Naz right away. On an earlier trip to the region, working on other terror-related stories, Naz had run into this guy and he'd denounced Naz as a traitor who worked with Western devils. When he saw Naz sitting there he almost blew a gasket, started pointing at him and said, "You. You."

I, of course, had no idea what was going on. Naz was thinking fast and he heard the call to prayer from outside. So he said, "Let's go pray."

They spent fifteen minutes praying while Naz tried to figure out what to do. In the end there was an elaborate negotiation, and finally we got to do the interview.

Both of the women were wearing niqabs. I tried to convince them to show us their faces. I knew that the mother at least had been photographed without a niqab in the past. But they insisted that they weren't coming off, particularly Zaynab, who was much more militant than her mother. So they did the interview with their niqabs covering their faces. And looking back, I'm sort of glad about that. They looked more striking on television, wearing their niqabs. I also think that because they weren't showing their faces, they felt freer to talk.

They were cautious at first. They didn't know how much Abdurahman had told us.

I said, "I understand you lived with Osama bin Laden."

And they looked at each other and Zaynab said, "Yes, that's true. We did. We did. He was a very interesting man. My father knew him. We didn't know him that well."

And I said, "Gee, I understand he attended your wedding."

And there was a pause and Zaynab said, "Yes that's true."

Eventually, they seemed to conclude that I knew a great deal, and there was no point in holding back.

They talked about how much they admired suicide bombers. And when I asked them about how they reacted to 9/11, Zaynab answered, "Well, they [Americans] deserved it. They've been doing it for such a long time, why shouldn't they feel it once in a while?"

And that put a chill through everyone who eventually saw the interview.

The mother and sister had confirmed many of the details of Abdurahman's story. But when we returned from Pakistan, we came up with one more confirmation technique, which provided one of my most rewarding experiences in journalism.

Abdurahman claimed that all the CIA and FBI intelligence agents gave him only their first names. They were very careful not to use surnames around him. But there was one agent who supposedly told him, "I like you. And if you ever get back to Canada or the United States you can look me up. You can find me at the FBI. My name is Steve Bongardt."

So now we had to find out if Abdurahman was just giving us the name of an FBI agent he'd seen in a news story, or if he really knew him.

We looked through all the online stories we could find from the time Abdurahman was involved with al-Qaeda and we couldn't find Steve Bongardt's name anywhere.

So then we went to a site that you can subscribe to where you can search American court documents. And that's where we found the arrest warrants for the people who were involved in the 1998 African embassy bombings. [On the same August day in 1998, bombs exploded at the US embassies in both Nairobi, Kenya, and Dar es Salaam, Tanzania; 234 people were killed.] And Steve Bongardt was a name that was listed as one of the

FBI agents. He was one of the agents who had arrested the suspects in Nairobi and brought them back to the United States.

Now that website was pretty obscure, but if we had found Bongardt's name it was theoretically possible that Abdurahman had found it too.

That's when CBC producer Alex Shprintsen came up with an ingenious plan. I never would've come up with this idea in a million years. We found out that Bongardt had graduated from the US Naval Academy. The academy would not provide us with a yearbook showing his graduating class, but we were able to obtain one on eBay. We prepared a photo-spread showing Bongardt along with other similar graduation pictures. We showed that photo-spread to Abdurahman, who immediately recognized Bongardt, even though he was much younger.

Now we were sure that Abdurahman really had had some contact with FBI agent Steve Bongardt. The next step was trying to get Bongardt to confirm everything. We discovered he was now back at FBI Headquarters in Washington, but he refused to talk with us.

I knew another FBI agent in Washington, so I asked him to be an intermediary. He said, "Yeah, I think I can do that for you. It will be totally off the record. But I'll see if I can get Steve Bongardt to talk to you."

He called back and he said, "I can't do anything for you."

I said, "Have you talked to Steve Bongardt?"

He said, "Yes, I have. He really doesn't want to talk to you."

"Well, can you tell me that the story is true?"

There was a long pause and then he said, "I have no reason to believe it is false."

Our documentary, *Son of al Qaeda*, ran in both Canada and the United States. The reaction was huge. There was just a wave of revulsion against the fact that this Canadian family was talking this way. It certainly woke people up to the fact that there were Canadians who thought that what Osama bin Laden had done on September 11, 2001, was just fine. The story was such a shocker that it went onto front pages around the world. I seldom had a story with such immediate impact.

I've never been more skeptical at the outset of a story, and never been more careful making sure that I felt totally comfortable with what we reporting on TV. It had been a fantastic team effort. Everybody just brought great devotion to the story and worked so hard to make all the elements come together. I really had never had that feeling before.

Wendy Mesley:
Scientific
Outcast

PEOPLE CALLING CHUM RADIO IN TORONTO IN THE MID-1970S may have been among the first to hear a voice that would one day become one of the most recognizable in the country. Wendy Mesley, still in high school, answered the phones at CHUM for a while. She has been in the media ever since. While at university she had part-time jobs at several Toronto radio stations.

Her first television job was at CFCF in Montreal. Because the first Quebec referendum was approaching, CFTO in Toronto decided it

Photo courtesy CBC

needed a reporter in Montreal and it hired Wendy. Then she joined CBC News in Montreal and over time became a major player. She was posted to Quebec City, then Halifax, before moving to Parliament Hill to track the Meech Lake Accord, and the Free Trade Agreement, among other stories. She became an anchor at CBC Newsworld in Toronto, then the host of her own program, *Undercurrents*. She moved to *Marketplace*, and then became a reporter and anchor at *The National*.

Wendy Mesley set out to investigate when an uproar erupted in 1999 over a study that a scientist had published on the long-term effects of Ritalin.

Attention Deficit Hyperactivity Disorder (ADHD) is diagnosed in 7 to 10 percent of Canadian children. The disorder is a major problem for school kids. They may have difficulty sitting still, paying attention, concentrating and controlling their impulses. In the 1960s researchers showed that the drug Methylphenidate increased a child's attentiveness and decreased his or her restlessness. The best-known brand name for that drug is Ritalin.

Today, there may not be a school in the country that doesn't have several of its students taking Ritalin every day. There seems to be little doubt that it works.

I've always been obsessed with stories about the abuse of power. Not so much stories on the bad contractor or the crooked insurance salesman, but systems that don't work or are abusive. There's a lot of great political reporting on Parliament Hill and in legislatures, but I really wanted that same kind of investigative rigour brought to the rest of the world.

In particular I love stories about science. I find that the media often laps up or can be easily swayed by any kind of scientific study because we don't think we have any real expertise to challenge it. Well, we don't have expertise on a lot of things.

But if it's a press release from the government we're pretty serious about seeing whether it all makes sense, if it holds up to scrutiny. We don't do that so much with science.

Which bring us to a woman named Nadine Lambert. She was the director of the School of Psychology at the University of California at Berkeley. I read a story about a new study she had done on Ritalin in 1999. She had actually been following the same kids for years—almost five hundred of them—and had written several studies. When she found that kids who were on Ritalin did better in school, she wrote a report on that. When she found that they did better in their personal relationships, that they were better husbands, boyfriends, wives, girlfriends, she wrote a report about that. When she found that as they started getting jobs they were adapting to the work environment better, she wrote a report on that too. Then when the kids were in their mid-twenties she noticed something else.

She noticed that these kids had about double the rate of cocaine abuse and addiction to cigarette smoking than kids who had never been on Ritalin. So she wrote a report on that. Overnight, she went from being a hero of many in the ADHD community to a villain. It was like she had thrown a grenade into the scientific research on Ritalin. A number of her peers who had been supportive of her methodology suddenly became extremely critical now that it showed negative side effects.

Two doctors in particular were very critical. Joseph Biederman was at Harvard Medical School, one of the most influential researchers into ADHD and a leading advocate of Ritalin. Russell Barkley was a professor of psychiatry and pediatrics at the Medical University of South Carolina in Charleston. They took aim at Lambert's new science.

There are lots of fights in the scientific world that are perfectly legitimate. But this fight was fascinating. These two other doctors published their own research, which showed that Ritalin had a protective effect, that kids on Ritalin were less likely to end up addicted to cocaine or cigarettes. They were both huge guns in the ADHD community and very, very influential. They were often on television and on the speech circuit talking about how amazing Ritalin can be.

Originally, some media reported Lambert's study, but as soon as the two well-known doctors came out with their studies the media went back to less critical coverage of Ritalin. To me, it showed just how easily the media can be swayed by experts. They interviewed Biederman and Barkley, who were saying that more people should be on Ritalin, that some adults should be on Ritalin too. It was like Nadine Lambert's study was made to disappear, even though her previous work had been so well respected and she had even won a distinguished service award from the American Psychological Association.

But the studies these two doctors had done were not as extensive as Lambert's. She had been watching 492 kids and she studied them for almost thirty years. I think the kids in the other studies were as young as eleven. You normally don't start doing coke at eleven, or smoking cigarettes at eleven.

I went to talk to Lambert at the University of California at Berkley. She was in her early seventies, very much a "just the facts ma'am" person. She was soft-spoken, very diplomatic. She said the studies that tried to disprove hers just weren't ready: "Come back and tell me what your studies say when those kids are at an age when they could have problems with an addiction to cocaine or tobacco. I've been studying them a lot longer."

She said, "My science isn't any different. It was the same science I applied to those kids when I was finding positive outcomes and everybody was happy. It's the same standard of research by the same scientist. Why don't you believe me now?"

She concluded that the reason they didn't believe her this time was that this time her study wasn't going to help sell a product.

She told me, "I'm not retiring. I'm not retiring until I have re-established my reputation." So she just kept working. She was a pistol. She wanted to do more studies, but after twenty-five or thirty years of being funded partly by the psychiatric establishment, she told me she couldn't get any more funding. And she was killed in a car accident on campus a few years later.

Lambert had been seen as a Ritalin booster for most of her career. But she published one study that upset the establishment. And really, the results weren't all that surprising. Cocaine and tobacco are both stimulants and are both addictive. Ritalin is thought to be too. So her findings didn't surprise her. She was surprised by the reaction. She thought she was there to do science, not sell pills. She said, "I don't think I'm particularly threatening."

I went to interview Dr. Barkley as well. His point was that nobody else's study was saying what Lambert's study was saying. I put it to him that comparing other studies to hers was like comparing apples and oranges. I said, "I've gone through most of the studies and a lot of them study kids that are as young as eleven years old—some may be seventeen. Her kids are much older. How can you talk about lifetime abuse or lifetime rates of addiction when the studies only go up to eleven or seventeen?"

Barkley said he wasn't out to get Lambert. "That makes for good TV, and a great movie, but it's fiction. Science doesn't operate that way. Scientists are totally independent and they don't gang up on one other individual just for the sake of ganging up on them or because they don't like their conclusion."

I said, "Why not warn people of a risk, even if it's a suspicion or a possibility?"

He said, "You want us to go out like Chicken Little every time a study gets published? Even though it's an outlier? We should be screaming to the world to change policy? Science would look foolish."

So that's what we called the story when we ran it on my old show *Undercurrents*, "The Outlier." What made this a story, without knowing who was right and who was wrong, was that it was curious that here was a woman who had been trusted by the Ritalin community for decades and was now being cast out. Why was a contrary voice treated with such disdain?

To me it was a really important piece of investigative journalism that would make a parent think twice when they're told that they should put their kid on drugs. I'm kind of tired of stories about how a pill will solve all your problems. I can see that on commercials on television. I would like to see more stories about people questioning the things we're being sold.

There are not a lot of media outlets that can afford to do complicated stories like this. It took us weeks to research this. To figure out that maybe Nadine Lambert had a strong argument. To believe a seventy-year-old lady who was mad that her peers were denigrating her science.

Journalists often get too swept up in scientific studies that are handed to them by people in the pharmaceutical and medical establishment. There are news releases and handouts that make it easy. "Here's your study. Here's your expert. Here are some illustrations. Here are some graphs. Here are some pictures of pills coming off a conveyor belt. We can provide you some kids to interview. We can even provide you a happy family."

You can do that story in a day.

But life is complicated. Science is sometimes grey. It's hard with newsrooms shrinking and PR and advertising budgets expanding. It's really hard to tell these kinds of stories. Sometimes the people who are the biggest experts are very close to the pharmaceutical industry.

In fact, the Harvard Medical School later disciplined

Dr. Joseph Biederman, not for his work on ADHD but another condition involving children. He was accused of receiving $2 million in consulting fees from pharmaceutical companies without disclosing that fact.

In that case it wasn't Ritalin but antipsychotics. He and two other Harvard scientists were recognized as trailblazers in the use of antipsychotic drugs in children. He said the money hadn't influenced him and he had never promoted a specific treatment.

Journalists are often reluctant to question these big guns. We should be questioning them, though. We're okay questioning cabinet ministers, prime ministers and CEOs. Why don't we question scientists or doctors or pill makers?

We like to think that journalistic success stories are the ones where the corrupt cabinet minister is fired or the faulty car is recalled. This was not one of those stories. This was just a story that I hope made people more aware, made them ask more questions and told them something they didn't know. Instead of just another news story about the great wonders of Ritalin, or another commercial about how a pill is going to solve all of your family's problems, I hope this was a story that made people say, "Maybe we should know more before popping a pill."

I thought that was a really important story to tell. To shine a light on part of the science world that I don't think is exposed nearly enough.

Saša Petricic: Inside Syria's War

Photo courtesy CBC

SAŠA PETRICIC IS A TV PIONEER. HE WAS THE FIRST NATIONAL VIDEOJOURNALIST FOR CBC News, which means he mastered the complexities of shooting and editing his own stories, combining technical know-how with artistic ability. At the same time he maintained a steady eye on editorial matters like getting the facts straight.

His first television work was in local news in London, Ontario, and in Ottawa, Montreal and Regina. Then he became a CBC national reporter in Winnipeg and on Parliament Hill. He became a one-man band in 2002, covering breaking news and doing documentaries, mostly abroad. He did stories from just about everywhere, including Thailand, Indonesia, Guatemala, Chile, Japan, Cuba and Antarctica. In 2011 he became the CBC's Middle East correspondent, based in Jerusalem. He moved to Beijing in 2015 to become the network's China correspondent.

In 2012, Saša Petricic was one of the few reporters who went to see the civil war in Syria up close.

The modern history of Syria is not a happy one. The country gained its independence in 1946, but until 1970 found little or no political stability. Then Hafez al-Assad took power in a coup. He provided stability, but only at the price of installing a grim dictatorship. When he died in 2000, his son Bashar was the heir apparent, but Syria's constitution said the president had to be at least forty years old. Bashar was just thirty-four. So the constitution was amended to lower the minimum age. That kind of manipulation was probably the first sign that Bashar was going to follow in the dictatorial footsteps of his father. And he did.

As part of the Arab Spring of 2011, demonstrations broke out across Syria demanding an end to the al-Assad years. But those demonstrations were met by an iron fist, and before long demonstrations became an uprising, and the uprising became civil war. The opposition was badly outgunned and the government showed the rebels, the Free Syrian Army (FSA), no mercy. The regime was even accused of using chemical weapons. Still, the FSA managed to take some territory and maintain shaky control over it.

The civil war was a human catastrophe: more than 100,000 dead, millions driven from their homes. The rest of the world watched. And it watched mostly from the outside.

....

We had been trying to cover the war from Jordan. We had been trying to cover it from Lebanon. We had been trying to cover it from Turkey. I had done stories from all those places. I went to the refugee camps. I talked to people who had fled Syria. But it was all on the periphery. When it came to what was actually happening inside Syria, it was a black hole.

We had been reduced to running amateur video on air. And we had to admit we didn't really know where the pictures were coming from or whether they showed what they purported to show. We saw things blowing up and they could conceivably have come from this area inside Syria, and they could have been shot recently, and those dead people could have been fighters or civilians. But we really didn't know. We decided it was time to go in to see for ourselves.

First I had to make a choice about which side we were going to report from—the government side or the rebel side. At that point the Syrians were not giving visas to journalists. And without a visa I couldn't hook myself up with the government side because I just wasn't allowed in. On the other hand, the whole northern part of Syria—with small exceptions—had been under the control of the FSA for months. So I decided to go into northern Syria through Turkey.

There were just six of us. Two of us were reporters. We had a fixer—someone who knew his way around Syria and could translate for us. There were two Canadian doctors who were coming in with us because they wanted to help victims of the war. And we had a security guy. He was British and he was unarmed, but he could act as a trained pair of eyes looking for trouble. At one point we were driving down a road and we weren't talking about anything in particular, and he said, "If someone started shooting at us right now we would stop the van. You would jump into that ditch over there and we would stay down there until we had an opportunity to get out." At different times he would come up with this kind of thing to remind us to stay alert.

The border we crossed was in the hands of the Free Syrian

Army. There were posters there in English that said, "The Free Syrian Army welcomes you to Syria." Despite that, northern Syria wasn't 100 percent safe. There were still several government military facilities along the road and checkpoints to avoid. If we got caught at one of those checkpoints we would have been arrested because we were in Syria illegally. Also, there were some villages in the north that were technically in FSA control but they had been friendlier to the government army and these were iffy areas. Before we arrived, and in fact after we left, we heard about other foreign journalists who had been kidnapped in these villages.

The civilian militias were essentially thugs for the government. So every once in a while they would set up a roadblock. Or perhaps they would just show up out of the shadows, and if they felt they could make some money or felt they could score some points with the government, they would arrest a journalist and the journalist would be shipped off to Damascus. So for us the area was as safe as Syria was at the time. It wasn't safe, but it was the safest option.

It was raining when we crossed the border. We started driving through small villages. None of them had stop signs; they had speed bumps. We were in an old Toyota van and every time the driver came to one of the speed bumps he'd hit the brakes to slow down. Well, there was some sort of short in the van's wiring, so every time he touched the brake pedal, the horn would go off. We were trying to be as inconspicuous as possible and suddenly we're making this loud noise every few minutes. It was one of those stupid things you just can't anticipate.

By nightfall we were just outside Aleppo. That's the biggest city in Syria. The war was very intense there. The FSA controlled about 50 percent of the city and the government controlled about 50 percent. We weren't going to go any farther in the dark. So we started thinking, "Where are we going to sleep?"

We found a four-storey cement house. We knew the government ordered air raids in the area from time to time. We could see large holes at the top of the house from bombs that had been dropped, but the bombs don't make it through four layers of concrete. So we slept on the bottom floor. We hoped there would be no planes sent to bomb that night. But if the house was attacked, then we hoped the bombs wouldn't make it down to where we were.

I should say we were connected to the outside world by a very thin string. We had satellite phones, but we never turned them on. This was in the wake of the killing of Marie Colvin. *[Colvin was an American journalist who worked for the* Sunday Times *of London. She had been killed, alongside a French journalist, in a rocket attack in the city of Homs.]* We knew that the Syrian military was able to zero in on satellite phones. And that was more than likely how they targeted her. Because who uses satellite phones? Only foreign journalists. We didn't want the government to find us that way.

So our communication came down to a device we had with us that was programmed to send a ping to a satellite at a predetermined time. That was safe enough because the ping lasted for about a second and there was no way the Syrians could lock in on that. We could also send programmed messages in short bursts. So we would send a message that said, "We've settled down for the night and we're safe." That signal was monitored both in Canada and by a producer on the Turkish side of the border.

In the morning we met the FSA commander. He had been a colonel in the Syrian army, but a couple of years before the revolution he decided he had had enough. So he left the country and was living in Belgium. But once the war started he decided that he was needed, so he moved back. He seemed honest and well informed about what was going on. We thought he was someone we could trust. He was one of the few well-trained soldiers that we ran into. Most of the rest of them were used-car salesmen, computer technicians, whatever. They had either lost their jobs or had left their jobs, and had picked up a gun and gone off to start fighting.

We rode with the commander toward the front line in Aleppo. We passed several FSA checkpoints. He was constantly on his cellphone with his people, checking to see what was going on. "Is there fighting? Where are the snipers today? Are there any land mines that have been set? Are roads blocked?" He was constantly checking, so we got a sense of how far we could go and still be reasonably safe.

We stopped at one of the hospitals. There were soldiers who had been shot. There were also people being treated for the usual sort of routine illnesses and accidents. There was no water, no oxygen, very little in the way of drugs, but there were a bunch of doctors working there. It was six or seven storeys high, but they were using only the ground floor for the same reasons that we had stayed on the ground floor where we slept. From time to time the government would try to hit the hospital with an air raid. Two weeks later it was hit and flattened. I looked at the pictures that came out and I recognized the very same lobby where we had been standing, the very same treatment rooms that we had seen. We stayed for half an hour, interviewing the doctors and the patients. Then we packed up and headed toward the front lines.

It didn't take long to get there. The wall of the old city divided the two sides that were fighting. We could tell in an instant that the biggest threat to us came from snipers. They were hidden in what had been government office buildings. Those were generally the tallest buildings around. The snipers perched there all day long and took potshots whenever they wanted to. We could look through the holes in the city wall and see the flashes from their guns and hear the shots that were going off. And we could hear people near us shooting back.

There was this constant back and forth. It wasn't a heavy-duty battle with things blowing up right, left and centre. But if you stuck your head up, there was a good chance you'd be shot. The snipers presumed that anybody on the wall was an FSA fighter.

People without guns were also in great danger. On one road there was a government checkpoint, and every once in a while the soldiers there just sprayed machine-gunfire down the street. Yet we could see people with shopping bags walking on that street because they had to get from A to B. That was part of their daily reality. Soldiers would shoot at people who lived in those areas who just had to move around to go to work or to buy food. Basically if it wasn't their day, they'd get hit. It wasn't like a Hollywood movie where people were ripping the pins from grenades with their teeth and throwing them over the embankment. It was a city that had settled into a wartime situation and people were living through it.

It was all so random for them. The government would fire in the general direction of the FSA's territory. But it usually wasn't very well targeted. They would just go out and hit whatever target of opportunity existed. They'd see a convoy of three or four cars, and they'd assume that that might be linked to the FSA, so they hit it. They'd see a bread line and in order to terrorize the area held by the FSA, they would strafe it and kill as many people as they could. I've been in other war zones—in Gaza for instance—where there was a constant pounding, where things were blowing up all over the place. There were missiles and mortars and all kinds of things that were coming in. But in Syria the danger seemed greater because you didn't know when the planes would come over the horizon.

This was a substantial population centre that was trying to live through a war without any city services, without any of the things we take for granted, and at the same time they were targets every single day. That was the kind of story I had come to tell—the kind of story I could not get unless I actually was there. I had taken a risk, of course, but I chose to take it. Here were people who had no choice. I wanted to put faces and names to people who were either fighting or surviving through the war. Then it wouldn't be an abstract thing that was happening in some generic far-off land. They could explain what the war was doing to their lives.

You could see how difficult it was for them. They answered my questions: Where do you get food? How do you live with no power, no telephone, no water? How do hospitals operate with no oxygen, no water, no generators? Or if they have generators, no guaranteed source of fuel—how does that work? It was a unique glimpse of what was going on every day.

At the time we were the only Canadian journalists in Syria. And as journalists we take some pride in telling a story that nobody else is telling. And this was important to tell. It was journalism in the true sense of collecting information firsthand from the people who knew it, saw it and lived it.

It was also journalism of discovery. I went into Syria not really knowing how far I could get, whether it would be safe to get there, who we would find there or what we would find there. So the stories really were what I discovered. And I think that's journalism at its best.

Terry Milewski: The Air India Bombing

Photo courtesy CBC

WHEN TERRY MILEWSKI CAME TO CANADA FROM ENGLAND he knew he wanted to be a journalist. But the first job he found was working in a lumber mill in British Columbia. When he saw a newspaper ad from a small radio station in Williams Lake that was looking for someone, he applied and got the job. Over time, he moved along to Nanaimo, then to Toronto for a short spell, before moving back to the West Coast for a job in Victoria.

He worked for ITV in Edmonton and then joined CBC News in Calgary. He has been at the corporation ever since—as science correspondent in Toronto; on Parliament Hill in Ottawa; as the first CBC correspondent based in Jerusalem; as a correspondent covering the Reagan, "Bush 41" (George H.W. Bush) and Clinton administrations in Washington; as a reporter in Vancouver, where his coverage of the Asia-Pacific Economic Cooperation (APEC) summit was singular; and as senior correspondent in Ottawa.

Terry Milewski has covered the story of the deadliest act of terror in Canadian history from the first moment possible.

One Saturday night in June 1985, two passengers managed to put luggage onto two separate flights in Vancouver without actually boarding the planes themselves. One plane headed west, over the Pacific Ocean to Tokyo. The unaccompanied bag from Vancouver was being transferred to an Air India flight to Bangkok when it exploded. Two baggage handlers were killed.

The other plane headed east to Toronto. The bag with no passenger was put on an Air India 747 that would stop in Montreal before taking off for London and eventually Bombay. When it left Canadian soil it was designated Air India Flight 182. As it approached the coast of Ireland six hours later, it was blown from the sky—329 people were killed. The dead included 280 Canadians; 86 of those on board were children.

The story of Flight 182 is profoundly sad. And it is maddening and frustrating. In the years since the bombing we have learned that Canadian security forces should have and could have prevented the crime. And though the men who plotted to bring down the airliner are widely known, they have not paid for their cold brutality. Just one man has ever been convicted, and then only for manslaughter and perjury.

The phone rang on that Sunday morning at my home in Ottawa. I was told to scramble out to Shannon Airport in Ireland. My competitors were out of the starting gate faster than me and got from Ottawa to New York and should have been at London Heathrow way before me. But because I was a little too late for that connection I had to fly to Shannon, which meant I'd have a long drive south, to the coast nearest the crash site. However, it turned out that all flights from Heathrow to Ireland were cancelled because of the crash, whereas Shannon Airport was still open. So I landed ahead of everyone.

We had to rent two cars because we had so much equipment. In those days we travelled with twenty-two cases of gear. My cameraman had never driven on the left side of the road in his life before, so it made for a nightmarish drive as he just kept going into the ditch. He just could not keep it on the left side of the road. And of course we had flown all night so he was also jet-lagged. But we made it to the scene.

The reason I mention this tale of our travels and how we felt is because of my astonishment then, which continues to this day, at the grace and dignity of the Indian families who arrived to retrieve the bodies of their loved ones. We were the unwashed horde of international media thrusting microphones in the faces of exhausted, grief-stricken families arriving from all over the world, many of them from India. Women in elegant saris patiently stopped to explain to us the Hindu philosophy of life and death. They were polite, and gracious, and decent, and unfailingly kind to us even though they were the ones under the most appalling stress. I remember thinking then, "Wow. These people could teach us all a lesson in grace under pressure."

It was just a bizarre and horrifying situation. Most of the bodies were never found. Most of these families never even had a body to take home. Most of the bodies went to the bottom of the sea still strapped into their seats. Only a minority of them ever floated to the surface. Some of the bodies were torn apart. It was an absolutely horrific scene. I remember the people who engaged in what was called a rescue operation, though no one was being rescued. They were overwhelmed at the time. They had post-traumatic stress disorders and are still burdened by the memories of fishing the bodies, soaked in aviation fuel, out of the Atlantic Ocean. One of the first bodies they grabbed, according to one seaman, was a Sikh man with very long hair. He had obviously lost his turban, and they had to grab the body by the hair and drag it into the boat. Absolutely awful, awful experiences for everyone involved.

There were heartbreaking stories about the families' experiences in southern Ireland and the bond they formed with the people who lived in the community closest to where the plane came down. There's the story, for example, of a twelve-year-old boy whose mother had been killed on the plane. He was walking with his father through the streets of Cork, looking for a hotel. He didn't know what the hell was happening. It was raining. He was jet-lagged. It was miserable. A local man popped out of his house and gave him a raincoat. Just gave him a raincoat. Said, "Here, take this." The boy eventually became a federal prosecutor and now he's in the private sector. He made a life for himself. But he remembers to this day—and many of them remember—the kindness of the people.

The whole experience was unforgettable and at the same time horrifying. There was no way after that that this story would ever let me go. But I confess I knew next to nothing about the background at first. Everybody knew that the previous year Indira Gandhi *[India's prime minister]* had been assassinated by her Sikh bodyguards. I was dimly aware that there was a problem between the Indian government and Sikh separatists. But beyond that I knew virtually nothing.

If you roll forward twenty years to 2005, there was another particularly striking moment. That was the news conference of the families who had come to hear the verdict at what came to be known as the Air India trial. *[Ripudaman Singh Malik*

*and Ajaib Singh Bagri were charged with 331 counts of murder,
attempted murder and conspiracy to commit murder. The trial,
in front of a judge alone, lasted more than a year and a half. In
March 2005 they were found not guilty and set free.]* The best
way I can describe it is that the families were weeping with
rage. If that's possible to do, they did it. Some of them had come
from the other side of the world—from India and from Austra-
lia. And they had come in the hope that after so very long, they
would get justice.

I remember Lata Pada, whose husband and two daughters
were on the plane. She's a very elegant woman, a classical
Indian dancer of some renown. She was completely shattered
by her loss, of course. She spoke at that news conference of her
dedication to the idea of Pierre Trudeau that Canada was a just
society. In her view it wasn't. And it had just proved that by
letting these guys off the hook.

The families still carried themselves with the grace and
dignity that they had shown twenty years earlier. I had come
to know many of these families. I still know many of them. I
have lifelong friendships with some of them. They still exhib-
ited this dignity, which was so lacking in the treatment they
received from the authorities.

The failure of the trial to produce convictions seemed like a
betrayal of the families, and it caused me to re-dedicate myself
to getting after this, to reporting how badly we had failed to
advocate for the families' interests in getting a judicial inquiry.
That's still allowed in journalism —advocacy. So I began doing
some more work on what had gone wrong and where accountability had not happened. And how the families' demands for
a judicial inquiry seemed justified.

Three weeks before the bombing there'd been a telex from
Air India headquarters, copied to the RCMP, saying that we've
got to have maximum security measures because there are
going to be attempts to bomb an Air India plane. The RCMP

claimed originally that they had transmitted this intelligence to CSIS *[the Canadian Security Intelligence Service]*. It turns out that they lied. CSIS never received it.

It turned out that CSIS also lied about their destruction of the wiretaps from Talwinder Singh Parmar *[a suspected terrorist whose phone had been tapped for three months before the bombing]*. They said there was nothing on those tapes and that's why they destroyed them. But then we found in the translator's notes that there was abundant evidence on those tapes—compelling evidence—of the plotting that was going on.

The CSIS officer in charge of that surveillance had been away on holiday when the bombing happened. He arrived home that night and his wife told him what had happened. And he recorded that his first thought was, "Parmar." He knew exactly who had done it the moment it happened.

There were police cars stationed on the tarmac as Flight 182 was loaded because of the clear danger to the plane. They all sat there, surrounding the plane, while an unaccompanied bag was loaded on.

That news conference after the verdict, carried live on television, had a powerful impact—and not just on me. People's sympathy with the families grew exponentially. The whole story had always been seen as foreign. A large part of the Canadian public thought, "Well, you know, they were a bunch of Indians who got blown up. It's not really our problem. It was an Indian problem." And of course there's some truth in that. The politics that gave rise to the terrorist group that bombed Air India was Indian politics. Brian Mulroney, the prime minister when the plane went down, famously called Rajiv Gandhi to express his condolences for the loss of so many Indians. But of course most of the people on the plane were Canadian citizens. It should have been Gandhi calling Mulroney. These were Canadian citizens who had been killed. And they were Canadian terrorists who planted the bombs.

A year after the trial, I went back to Ireland for a memorial service on yet another anniversary of the bombing. Prime Minister Paul Martin finally said what the families wanted to hear—"Make no mistake: The flight may have been Air India's, it may have taken place off the coast of Ireland, but this is a Canadian tragedy." I saw all the faces nodding in the cold Irish mist. He had said something neat and proper. This is what they wanted him to say. This is what they felt had been denied for way too long; this was not somebody else's problem but our Canadian problem.

Finally, Stephen Harper's government agreed to an inquiry. And almost twenty-five years to the day after the bombing, the former Supreme Court Justice John Major made some trenchant observations about the failure of the authorities to prevent the tragedy. There had been official claims such as "There was no way we could have known," "There was nothing we could have done," "This was not foreseeable," "We did the best we could." And he made it absolutely clear that all these claims were rubbish. And I don't put that too strongly. Warnings before the bombing had in fact been abundant and clear and repeated and specific.

But I'm completely unsatisfied that the lessons have been learned. Don't take it from me. Take it from Justice Major, who, having conducted a very thorough inquiry and having produced evidence-based recommendations directly addressing the many and different failures that were evident in the Air India file, sees that the government didn't act on anything. It rejected even his most important recommendation, for a national security "czar" to improve communication among all the police and security forces so that intelligence information doesn't fall between the cracks.

Still, from the first moment of the explosion and the phone call I got in my home in Ottawa, up to and including the trial and the verdict and the inquiry that eventually followed, I would have felt dirty had I let the story drop. I would have felt guilty. I would have felt that I was part of the problem if I had walked away without giving the families, the seamen who picked up the bodies, and the victims themselves a voice.

Susan Bonner:
Killing bin Laden

Photo courtesy CBC

A GLANCE AT SUSAN BON-
NER'S RÉSUMÉ GIVES YOU AN
APPRECIATION of how wacky and
wonderful a career in journalism can
be. She has covered grasshoppers
in Saskatchewan, the Olympics in
Calgary, patronage in Nova Scotia,
the Charlottetown Accord referendum from Quebec, economics in
Toronto, ten years of politics from
Parliament Hill and the superpower
goings-on in Washington, DC. She
has been a reporter, news writer,
producer and anchor. In 2014 she
became the host of CBC Radio's *The
World at Six*.

On the Sunday night when US President Barack Obama went on television to announce the killing of Osama bin Laden, Susan Bonner was one of CBC's Washington correspondents—and she almost didn't see the speech.

For 3,518 days, bin Laden was the most wanted man in the world. On day 3,519 they got him. It was May 1, 2011. Bin Laden, of course, was the mastermind behind the September 11 attacks in the United States. He was therefore directly responsible for murdering 2,977 people. He was also at least indirectly responsible for all the death that ensued in what the US called its war on terror.

The Americans were said to have been close to getting him several times, but bin Laden not only eluded the most intense manhunt in history, he also taunted his pursuers with videotaped messages that promised more attacks. Some took comfort in believing that bin Laden was hiding in caves, free, but unbearably miserable. That turned out to be fiction.

The CIA tracked him with near but not total certainty, to a compound in Abbottabad, Pakistan. President Obama then ordered US Special Forces to go get him. Two Black Hawk helicopters swooped in under cover of darkness and forty minutes later, bin Laden was dead. He had been shot in the head. The president set off a wave of patriotic euphoria across the United States when he went on TV to announce "the most significant achievement to date in our nation's effort to defeat al-Qaeda."

....

The first thing you have to know is that the next day was a federal election day in Canada. So for someone based in Washington it should have been very quiet. I had spent the night before—Saturday night—at the White House Correspondents' Dinner. That's an annual event where the president shows up to be comedian-in-chief. He got serious for a minute at the end of his performance and said something about having incredible young men and women serving in uniform overseas in extraordinary circumstances. But nobody thought much about that.

Since Monday should have been quiet for a Canadian in Washington, I had scheduled a little medical procedure for Monday morning. So I went to bed at about 9:45 on Sunday night. I had fallen asleep quickly, so when my cellphone started ringing I was disoriented. I answered it and I could hardly hear the person on the other end because she was outside the White House where a crowd had gathered and there was a lot of noise. She said, "Is there any way to get down here for eleven o'clock so you can do a report for the newscast?"

I said, "I don't think so. What's happening, anyway?" She told me to turn on the TV, so I did. And there was Brian Williams on NBC. I knew right away that if Brian Williams was on the air on a Sunday night, something big was in the works. But he was saying he didn't actually know why he was on the air. He said everyone had been called in because there was a major announcement coming from the White House.

A few minutes later we saw the president—that stark image of him walking down the corridor and then announcing that they had killed bin Laden. Neil Macdonald took care of the newscasts that night. But I was awake now, emailing back and forth with news editors in Toronto to plan our coverage for the morning, starting at 5 AM.

At about 3 AM I had to leave for the office. My husband was away, overseas in fact. I had somebody coming in to take care of my ten-year-old son and get him to school. But she wouldn't be arriving until seven o'clock. So I woke Sam up and told him, "I have to go to work and you'd better get ready to come with me." He said, "No. I don't want to go to work with you. I'll just go back to sleep and I'll wait for the babysitter in the morning." So I gave him the phone. I brought the dog into his room. And I went to work.

In the cab on the way in, the driver was listening to all-news radio and I just kept taking notes. We went by one of the universities and we saw some kids hanging around, cheering. It was actually a little bit chilling to see the blood lust in the air. And of course we'd see a lot of it across the country that day. People screaming and chanting and that sort of thing.

Almost as soon as I got to the office, my son was on the phone, sobbing: "I'm scared. I couldn't go back to sleep. I just want to be with you."

So as I was trying to get organized to start a day of live reporting, I started working the phones to put my son into a cab and get him to the CBC. It took two or three of us to make that happen. The cab companies said they couldn't pick up an unescorted minor. I finally managed to get hold of a manager at one of the companies and I said to him, "You've got to help me."

Once I told him I was a journalist and told him I was covering the bin Laden story, he said, "Fine." They put Sam in a cab and drove him down to me. So my son sat in the office watching way too much graphic television coverage of Osama bin Laden.

I had another experience with just how happy Americans were that Monday morning. In the middle of the night I had called the doctor's office to leave a message to cancel my procedure. They called back at about six o'clock and said, "No problem. We don't care. No charge. We got bin Laden. Isn't that great?"

I was on the air at the top of the clock and the bottom of the clock, starting at five in the morning.

Each time I was on for about five minutes, and it didn't stop all day long. My son was still there and I literally couldn't even buy him any food. I was at the mercy of anybody in the office who had a minute to go grab him a bagel or something because we were all just working like maniacs. Sam said to me at one point, "Is this what your day is always like?"

At about 2 PM, a producer in Toronto told me I was going to be anchoring a special from 5 PM to 8 PM. A three-hour live program. And this is where it's important to remember that it was election night in Canada. That meant almost all our news resources were tied up, getting ready for the election night broadcast. Our Toronto studio was busy. So our special would go through a studio in Ottawa. But there was no producer there. All the people I would normally have worked with on this kind of important story were doing the election. We were on our own.

We started to find experts. We had to decide what angles we could cover. I corralled Neil Macdonald and told him he couldn't go home. We set him up in another corner with a camera so I could talk with him when we didn't have another guest.

The story never stopped developing. I remember at one point we got word that there were pictures of bin Laden's body and government officials were trying to decide if they should be released. On Capitol Hill everyone in Congress had an opinion. There was an endless amount of material to talk about and sift through. I have never felt like I used more of my professional and personal self. You had to know a little bit about everything—about military equipment and about why it was important that one of the Black Hawk helicopters had been left on the ground; about national airspace and what it meant that the Pakistanis had not been consulted about the raid; about diplomacy; and all the 9/11 and al-Qaeda background.

There was no producer talking into my ear, guiding things. Instead, an editorial assistant sat on the floor with a big pad of paper, holding up scribbled names of who the next guest was and what that person's title was. And I would try to read that while giving it some heft and elegance. It was crazy. It was madness. But I've never had so much fun in my life.

At eight o'clock we got off the air and I crawled home and went to bed. I was exhausted. I couldn't even stay up to watch the Canadian election. That says a lot about how tired I was. I had spent so much of my life covering Canadian politics, but now I didn't have it in me to watch.

The story was obviously the biggest one in the world that day. It was something every Canadian could connect with because we had all lived through 9/11. Now we were closing an important chapter. Bin Laden was evil personified. That made a good story. The president, who was considered soft, was the one who got bin Laden—not the tough president, Bush. That made a good story. And the mission itself, an adventure story to rival any other. So on every level it was just one of the best stories I've ever covered.

The day that Osama bin Laden died is a really big day in our son's life too.

Reg Sherren:

Return to

Nagasaki

Photo courtesy Reg Sherren

FOR REG SHERREN, IT ALL STARTED IN A 250-WATT RADIO STATION IN WABUSH, Labrador. At the age of fifteen he was hired as the weekend deejay, also responsible for making sure all the garbage cans were clean and the wire service teletype had a full paper roll for Monday morning. While still in school, he worked for CBC TV in Labrador City. When he graduated he became the news anchor for a station in Thunder Bay, Ontario, that was really two stations—both the CBC and CTV affiliates were owned by the same person. The news would play for an hour on one channel, and then again on the other, both at suppertime and late at night. So Reg was on television three hours a day.

Then he confined his work to CBC. His career stops were Calgary, St. John's and Winnipeg. He did hard news, short features and documentaries, and he was the last anchor of one of CBC's longest-running programs, *Country Canada*.

Fifty-seven years after John Ford had been in Nagasaki during the atomic bomb explosion there in 1945, Reg Sherren documented the Canadian man's return to the Japanese city.

There is no shortage of horror stories emerging from World War II. Among them is the story of the fall of Singapore in February 1942. It was the first time the British Army had encountered an attack by the Japanese. They were not nearly well enough prepared. They underestimated the speed of the Japanese advance and, it must be said, they underestimated the savagery of the Japanese military. The Japanese took no prisoners during the battle. Captured soldiers were simply murdered. Patients at a hospital were murdered as well. After only a week of fighting, the British surrendered.

Altogether 100,000 men were then taken prisoner. One of them was John Ford of Newfoundland, which was then not part of Canada. Ford was taken to a forced-labour camp in Nagasaki, where he endured unspeakable brutality, and where he witnessed the atomic bomb explosion of August 9, 1945.

....

I met John Ford through my father, who knew him through the Canadian Legion. My father said, "You really need to meet this man."

John was from the Port aux Basques area and my mother's people are from the southwest coast of Newfoundland as well. It turned out that his wife, Margaret, had gone to school with my grandmother back in Grade 5. So we had that connection.

I went over to John's house with my father. He was a very gracious fellow—eighty years old, a lifelong employee of the Newfoundland Railway who had never missed a day of work. He told me the basics of his story. He brought out a very small rice can in which he had received his daily allotment of food at the prison camp. He also showed me his personal identification number from his internment, which had been hand-carved into a piece of wood.

There was nothing Japanese at his house—no piece of Japanese electronics, certainly no Japanese car. He told me he had no love for the Japanese, but he also said he had no hatred for them either.

I was living in Winnipeg, but I would get to Newfoundland two or three times a year either for personal reasons or on business. Every time I came back, I'd sit down with John. There were two things about him that stood out. First, he had an incredible memory. He could remember every single incident in his life in great detail, down to the exact time of day everything had happened. And second, he held nothing back.

Over the course of probably three conversations in a year and a half, each lasting an hour, he unfolded in great chronological detail what took place, and was very open with his emotions. He recalled the long marches that the prisoners suffered through. When somebody stumbled or fell, a bullet was put into his head and he was rolled into the ditch. John said he knew that if he didn't keep marching he was going to be in the ditch. The cruelty of the things that he witnessed!

Finally one day I said, "John, I think I'd like to take you back to Nagasaki. Would you be willing to go?"

He said, "Yes. I would go with you, if you want to take me."

I just knew that if I could take him on this journey, this was something that was going to be monumental. Not only as a piece of journalism, but also in John's life because there were things that he spoke about that seemed to me to be unresolved for him as a man. When he agreed to go I realized that I had taken on a tremendous responsibility. He was an eighty-two-year-old man enjoying fairly good health but who was also going to be heading out into the abyss emotionally. I realized the weight of what I was doing not only as a journalist but also as a man who was taking responsibility for somebody's grandfather, for somebody's father, for somebody else's psychological well-being.

I started to arrange things, and the first thing I did was contact the University of Nagasaki. I knew I would need an interpreter and I would also need someone who could help me through the cultural differences and the protocol of doing things in Japan. I came upon a fellow who responded to my queries and who was from Winnipeg. In fact, his father had once worked for CBC. In any case, this fellow was now teaching at the University of Nagasaki. So he became our liaison.

I tried to set up meetings before we left Canada, but I wasn't able to do much of anything because of the language barrier. So in many respects I was flying blind, and that was a little unnerving.

The day after we arrived in Nagasaki we were taking it a bit easy, trying to get over our jet lag. That evening we got on a little tour boat in Nagasaki harbour. I had chosen it just because it didn't cost very much. But all of a sudden John said, "That's it right there. That's where it happened, right in there." And he was pointing to the hypocentre of the atomic explosion, right at the head of the bay. He became quite emotional.

I asked him what he was feeling.

He said, "Difficult. Difficult. Difficult to see that it happened."

The next day we went to the atomic museum, an incredibly powerful place. You could see where people's bones fused together in the heat of the flash of the atomic explosion. Then we went out onto the plaza to meet someone else who had survived the Nagasaki bombing. We exchanged greetings and he invited us to his home. So off we went to this traditional Japanese home. We met his lovely wife and she invited us in. In a few minutes we were all kneeling and drinking tea. You could feel in the air that something was going to happen. Here were two men who went through the same experience from opposite sides.

Our host said that he had lied to avoid military service in the war. He told the military he was colour blind, which wasn't true. He said he hated what his country was doing. So he became a streetcar operator. He said the reason he was saved on the day the bomb dropped was because his streetcar happened to be behind a large concrete building when the explosion went off and he was protected to some degree. He was still burned and all he had to soothe the pain was axel grease from the streetcar. He described taking to the hills around the city where he saw a friend who had been burned. He saw something on his friend's face and he went to wipe it away and discovered it was his eyeball that had fallen out of its socket. The man died shortly after. I looked over at John and the tears were coming down his face. In fact, we all had tears. It was an incredibly powerful moment. We spent about an hour in the house and we were all just completely emotionally drained.

The next morning we decided we were going to try to find the prison camp where John had been interned. We had been given directions to a high school that sat on the grounds where the camp had been. We took a taxi, but the driver got lost and when we finally found it, it was exactly two minutes after 11 AM—the exact time the atomic bomb was dropped on Nagasaki. I looked up at a big clock on the side of the school and it was two minutes after eleven.

John recognized the area immediately. He started wandering around and the stories came pouring out of him. He remembered an Australian prisoner who had leprosy. The Japanese put him in a cage by the front gate and the men walked by him every day to go off to work as slave labour. The Australian used to whistle "There'll Always Be an England." The Japanese didn't know what he was whistling. John said that little act of defiance was a real morale booster.

The stories just kept coming. And the tears and the anger. John told us if a prisoner did something the Japanese didn't like, they would make him hold a bucket of water in each hand with his arms extended, and they'd make him kneel on a broomstick. Incredibly painful. If the prisoner dropped his arms the Japanese would beat him.

If somebody got sick, everybody in that barrack had their ration cut until that prisoner went back to work.

The demons were coming out of John. You could feel them in the air. I really didn't know what to do. I was so overwhelmed myself by what I was feeling. I had done quite a bit of research and knew about some of this, but here was a man who had lived through it and was now walking the grounds. As a journalist, as a Canadian, as a Newfoundlander, this was a moment I realized why I did what I did for a living.

The next day we went to the mayor's office. It became a media frenzy. By now the local media knew that John was in Nagasaki. He'd already given a couple of interviews and now there were fifteen or twenty cameras plus radio people in a room with the mayor of Nagasaki. We had little gifts from Canada—maple syrup and the like—and we received Japanese presents in exchange.

Then the mayor apologized to John, on behalf of the people of Nagasaki, for what had been done to him. Nobody had ever apologized to John before. Then the mayor offered John free medical care for the rest of his life. John had already had three melanomas in his life, probably related to the flash of the atomic bomb. When he got out of that prison camp he weighed less than 100 pounds. He was told he wouldn't live to see forty years of age.

John responded to the mayor's offer by saying, "No. I'm a

Canadian citizen and the Canadian government takes care of me very well, thank you very much."

And then he broke. He could barely get the words out. "There should never be another Hiroshima or Nagasaki."

I'm pretty sure it had taken him fifty-seven years to find the capacity to see those people—the seventy-five thousand people killed at Nagasaki—to see them as human beings. He was a religious man, a pious man. He went to church every Sunday. He knew about the concept of forgiveness, but it was not something that came easily. I think meeting the streetcar operator and the mayor gave him what he was looking for in terms of peace. He found it there.

When I brought him back home, his wife, Margaret, said, "You know Reg, he slept through the night. It's the first night he's slept through in fifty-seven years." A few years later he actually bought a Honda Accord.

I wound up accomplishing what I wanted to accomplish as a journalist. The documentary *Return to Nagasaki* became part of the curriculum at four Japanese universities, including the University of Nagasaki. And there is now a monument to the prisoners of war that were held in Nagasaki, an acknowledgment of what happened there, and a plaque on the side of the school where the camp was. So not only were we able to tell a story, but we were able to effect some change, and for me as a journalist it was one of the proudest things I've ever done.

John and I became good friends. I never went to Newfoundland again without showing up on his doorstep to have a conversation. He liked to talk about politics, and he liked to talk about baseball, which I know very little about but humoured him anyway. Then one day in 2013 I got a call that his health had taken a turn for the worse and in a matter of hours he passed away. He was ninety-four years old.

Acknowledgments

If you read the Introduction at the front of this book, then you know I loved my career in journalism. But I can't say it enough. It was the people I worked with who made it special. I was grateful to them every day, and I remain grateful now for the memories.

That this book exists is a credit to several people at Douglas & McIntyre, including Anna Comfort O'Keeffe and Nicola Goshulak who kept the enterprise on track.

Cheryl Cohen edited the manuscript with an eye that eagles must envy.

Everything I do is built on the strongest of foundations—my family. Rhonda, Melissa and Jessica often watched me run out the door to deal with breaking news, leaving them suddenly without a husband and father, and with carefully laid plans in millions of pieces. Reid knows only a less unpredictable man, a grandfather who asks a lot of questions about what she reads in the morning newspaper.

Those four? They're the best stories of my life.

Index

Page numbers in **bold** refer to photos